Otto Rank

Jessie Taft is the author of

THE DYNAMICS OF THERAPY IN A CONTROLLED RELATIONSHIP
published in 1933 by The Macmillan Co.

and has translated from the German

WILL THERAPY, An Analysis of the Therapeutic Relationship
by Otto Rank

TRUTH AND REALITY, A Life History of the Human Will
by Otto Rank

(both titles re-issued in one volume, 1945 by Alfred A. Knopf)

OTTO RANK

A BIOGRAPHICAL STUDY BASED ON
NOTEBOOKS, LETTERS, COLLECTED
WRITINGS, THERAPEUTIC ACHIEVEMENTS
AND PERSONAL ASSOCIATIONS.

BY *Jessie Taft*

THE JULIAN PRESS, INC.   NEW YORK   1958
Publishers

PUBLISHED BY THE JULIAN PRESS INC.

80 EAST 11TH STREET, NEW YORK 3

© COPYRIGHT 1958 BY JESSIE TAFT

LIBRARY OF CONGRESS CATALOG CARD NUMBER 58–9814

MANUFACTURED IN THE UNITED STATES OF AMERICA

BY H. WOLFF, NEW YORK

DESIGN: MARSHALL LEE

CONTENTS

ACKNOWLEDGMENTS

In the preparation of this book, I have depended upon the unfailing support and understanding of my lifelong friend and fellow-worker, Virginia P. Robinson, and upon the combination of secretarial and editorial help together with library research that only my friend, Anita J. Faatz, could have provided. I am indebted to Ira Fishman and Mrs. Herman Busch for help with the problems of translation. To Mrs. Beata Rank and her daughter, Dr. Helene Rank Veltfort, and to Madame Estelle Rank Simon, I am grateful for sustained interest and unfailing confidence in my use of the Rank papers.

Acknowledgment is made with thanks to the following publishers and individuals for permission to quote as follows:

To Basic Books, Inc., New York, for permission to quote from Dr. Ernest Jones, *The Life and Works of Sigmund Freud*, Vols. II and III, 1955 and 1957; and from Otto Rank, *The Trauma of Birth*, 1952.

To Alfred A. Knopf, New York, for permission to quote from Otto Rank, *Will Therapy* and *Truth and Reality*, 1945; and from Otto Rank, *Art and Artist*, 1932.

To Harvard University Press, Cambridge, Massachusetts, for permission to quote from Hanns Sachs, *Freud, Master and Friend*, 1944.

To George Allen and Unwin, Ltd., London, for permission to quote from *The Collected Papers of Sigmund Freud*.

To Routledge and Kegan Paul Ltd., London, for permission to quote from Otto Rank, *The Trauma of Birth*, 1929.

To Sigmund Freud Copyrights, Ltd., for permission to quote from the Freud-Rank-Ferenczi correspondence in my possession.

To Dr. Michael Balint, literary executor for Sandor Ferenczi's papers, for permission to quote from the Freud-Rank-Ferenczi correspondence and for helpful suggestions regarding translation.

To Dr. Ernest Jones for his co-operation and for permission to quote from the Freud-Rank letters to the Committee.

To Dr. Lovell Langstroth, San Francisco, California, for permission to quote from three personal letters, 1950–1952.

To Estelle B. Rank Simon, for permission to quote from Otto Rank, *Beyond Psychology*, 1941.

FOREWORD

M Y first contact with Otto Rank occurred on June 3, 1924, at a meeting of the American Psychoanalytic Association in Atlantic City where he was to give a paper in English on *The Trauma of Birth*, the title of his book recently published in German. As a clinical psychologist from Philadelphia working chiefly with children, I had no official right to participate in a psychoanalytic conference, but I was interested in psychoanalysis as a further training measure for myself in the future and I wanted to see who these analysts were and what they were like. An acquaintance who had worked in Vienna with both Freud and Rank had told me of something new and different in Rank's theory as well as in his therapeutic technique that had aroused immediate interest, although I had known nothing of Rank previously except his name and a title, *The Myth of the Birth of the Hero*.

I do not remember how I got to the meeting nor what was said there, but I still retain a vivid impression regarding the quality of the several speakers. With one exception all seemed to me unimpressive, if not actually dull, until the slight, boyish figure of Rank appeared beside the speaker's desk. He was the very image of my idea of the scholarly German student and he spoke so quietly, so directly and simply, without circumlocution or apology, that despite the strong German accent I was able to follow his argument and I thought to myself, "Here is a man one could trust."

It took two years, with letters and a single interview, before I finally pinned myself down to a definite date for analysis with Rank in New York in the fall of 1926. Meantime, I had been saved from myself and my attempt to escape by engaging a substitute analyst, through the latter's untimely death. Later I was able to appreciate what a fateful accident it had been for me, as I remembered the two application interviews with their portent for the future of the analysis. The first man, in spite of his frank doubts of my suitability in terms of age and my limited time allowance, had ended by accepting me, but only after I had remarked, with full awareness of its possible influence on a man who had himself been analyzed by Rank, that Dr. Rank had previously agreed to take me. I left that interview knowing in my heart that I was the stronger of the two and had conquered in the first round.

In contrast, my meeting with Rank had been quiet, brief, without controversy. No doubts were expressed by him, no fear of my age, no interest in my life history, nor was there any contest regarding my rigid time limit. He did not promise anything. He merely agreed to try, on the basis of the time at my disposal. I can recall only one remark from that interview in response to something I had presented about myself. "Perhaps the problem lies there." And that was all, but on that one sentence I began to make myself over before anyone else should have the chance.

Coming to the point of being willing to subject myself to anything as strange as was psychoanalysis in the United States at this time was not due to any conscious personal need nor to lack of professional success, but to the deep awareness of being stopped in professional development. I knew that I had not the basis for helping other people, however deep my desire. Psychological testing of children was useful but, as I knew only too well, it was not therapeutic. Failure with the few neurotic adults who had been referred to me had filled me with guilt and fear. Psychoanalysis seemed to be the only resource, however fearful.

When I finally came to my first hour with Rank, while consciously submissive, afraid, and fully aware of my ignorance of psychoanalysis, my underlying attitude was far from humble. I was, after all, a psychologist. I had some knowledge of myself and my problems. I had achieved a point of view, psychologically. If there was anything in my unconscious in terms of buried memories, I would have to be shown. And so the battle was joined; but I soon found that it was a battle with myself. I was deprived of a foe. It took only two weeks for me to yield to a new kind of relationship, in the experiencing of which the nature of my own therapeutic failures became suddenly clear. No verbal explanation was ever needed; my first experience of taking help for a need that had been denied was enough to give a basis for the years of learning to follow.

At this time I had no idea of Rank's growing difference from Freud or of his alienation from the Vienna group. In cheerful ignorance, I combined with my daily hour a weekly evening lecture given by Rank for the New York School of Social Work, another by Ferenczi for the New School of Social Research, a regular seminar for social work students with a Rankian analyst, and still a third evening lecture course, by whom I do not recall. To this extreme activity on my part Rank offered no objection, but turned my naïve daily reports to good account in terms of their meaning for me in the therapeutic process. Never did I sense on Rank's part the bitterness or resentment that he might well have been feeling at a time when Ferenczi, who had but recently been his friend and collaborator, was refusing to speak to him. I did not try to account for the look of pain and constraint that characterized his appearance at the evening lectures, except by recognizing the hardship of reading such difficult material in English to a group no better prepared than myself to understand, and by projecting upon him my own exquisite embarrassment at these revelations of the secrets of the analytic hour.

At the end of an eight or nine week period—the time altered just enough to undo my original intent to control it—I returned to Philadelphia overflowing with emotion engendered by a vital experience, at that point quite innocent of theory of any kind, but eager to give to others the kind of help that had been given to me. It was not long before I realized that emotion and intuition were not enough. I had to earn a point of view by my own efforts, had to face Freudian difference, painful as it was, not merely through Rank but in my own thinking, reading, and use of the therapeutic relationship.

Consequently I was grateful for the opportunity to join a Rankian group in New York and gain support for both theory and practice through their weekly evening seminar in the winter and early spring of 1927. This group of fifteen or twenty was made up chiefly of psychiatrists, both men and women, some with previous analytic experience and all with an original Freudian base, who had been in analysis with Rank either in Vienna or New York. They included most of the younger New York psychiatrists of that period, with a few from Boston and one or two other cities, plus an occasional Ph.D. like myself. There were none from the older established institutional group such as Hoch, Meyer, Campbell, White, and Southard, and none from the original Freudian analysts such as Brill. We were a hard-working group, using as our text Part

I of Rank's *Genetische Psychologie*[1] that he had given in the evening lecture course of 1926. Our problems in understanding the text, as well as our common difficulties in applying it therapeutically with no help from Rank, were only too obvious.

When Rank returned to this country in the fall of 1927, he established himself in Philadelphia, gave in lecture form Part II of *Genetische Psychologie,* and continued the New York seminar with what was now recognized generally as a Rankian group. I was among those who had individual help with practice during that period, as well as the benefit of the discussion of cases in the seminar. Although interrupted by Rank's sudden return to Paris, this seminar was finally completed by him (in the spring of 1928), still utilizing the material from Part I of *Genetische Psychologie,* with emphasis on the relation to the mother as fundamental in the analytic situation and in the difficult problems of end-setting. He was back in 1928–29, meeting with the seminar, and lecturing in New York and Philadelphia.

Thus far, although there must have been increasing awareness of Rank's estrangement from Freud and the Vienna group, heightened by growing opposition on the part of the established Freudian analysts in New York, seminar discussions were still carried on in the familiar Freudian terminology, while Rank's innate authority and rich experience provided the support and guidance needed by these younger analysts, who were far from assured in their own theory and practice.

It was into this uncertain, loosely organized group that, on their first meeting in the winter of 1929–30, Rank, newly returned from Paris and the completion of the second volume of his clearly anti-Freudian *Technik der Psychoanalyse,*

[1] The lengthy Introductory part, with its general discussion of the current problems in psychoanalysis, theoretical and practical, was not used as far as I can recall.

launched without previous warning or preparation a new psychology and therapeutic method. I can still recall the sudden shock created by his use of the word "will," so long taboo in academic circles as a remnant of faculty psychology and therapeutically akin to quackery. Only someone with the force and brilliance of a Rank could have carried this medically oriented group through a change so sudden and complete as to have felt like desertion.

The situation was not unlike what happened in the Freudian "Committee" when Rank, their youngest member, suddenly produced without previous consultation *The Trauma of Birth*, but in this case the process is reversed and Rank can use his leadership to hold the group together. The actual course of discussion through that 1930 seminar I have forgotten, and even the minutes that I have preserved do not recall it. There remains only the memory of the initial shock, followed for me by the revelation of the reality of will as a key to my own as well as to my patients' psychology. As I look back I believe that I was perhaps the only one for whom the transition came easily and naturally. I had no medical ties and no stake in Freudian psychology. I had been brought up on pragmatism and the thinking of George Herbert Mead and John Dewey. For me there was nothing to lose.

By external standards the 1930 seminar was a brilliant success, marked by full attendance and interesting material. Several members were benefiting from controlled analyses; there were even plans for a book on Rankian psychology to be made up of contributions from various members. Editorial leadership had been assigned to the Boston contingent, while financing remained with the New York group. The existence of an internal problem was not in evidence until the program of the International Mental Hygiene Association, to be held in the United States for the first time early in May of 1930, came up for discussion. As Rank was scheduled to deliver a paper there, the selection of discussants was important. It became suddenly clear to me that everyone withdrew from the assignment, largely, as I thought, because of the difficulty of commenting on Rank's material. Although at the time I was in a stage of resentful independence, I realized somewhat bitterly that I was the only person in the group who would undertake it; if I did not volunteer, nothing would happen, there would be no friendly discussant from the seminar. Thus I became involved in the first meeting of the International Mental Hygiene Association in Washington that gave Rank the welcome opportunity to declare himself publicly and to face the Freudian opposition openly. Although the majority of the New York seminar was present, no medical adherent stood up to be counted.

This occasion was important in that it marked the end of Rank's leadership with the psychoanalytic group in New York. It also marked the price that would have to be paid by any analyst who separated himself from the medical sanction that remained with Freud. There was no one in the seminar of the caliber to carry on such a fight, no one with sufficiently developed ideological conviction, no one with the requisite therapeutic skill. Thus it was only a matter of time for former adherents and students of Rank gradually to disappear under their protective medical coloring. The projected book was abandoned without explanation. I do not doubt that the many psychiatrists who had been analyzed by Rank between 1924 and 1930 were influenced away from strict Freudian theory and practice, but they failed to proclaim it and, to my knowledge, not a single one understood, much less affirmed, Rank's will psychology or the ultimate form of his dynamic therapy. For adherents of Freudian psychoanalysis, Rank's fate was sealed at this point; he was to be treated thereafter as nonexistent.

The fact that I was not medical and never dependent on medical support for my point of view or practice, together with an innate interest in theory and the conviction engendered by my own experience of Rankian therapy, may account for Rank's acceptance of me at this time as a friend and fellow worker. At all events, from that time until his death in 1939, I was usually in communication with him by letter or personal contact. It was owing to this friendship and to my understanding of his point of view that, at his death, there came into my possession the papers on which this biographical study has relied, particularly for material preceding 1926. These papers were not willed to me by Rank, for he made no will, but were sent to me by his second wife with the approval of his daughter and her mother, his first wife as the person to whom he would have entrusted them.

There has been little or no biographical material available on Rank from any source other than biographies of Freud, which is probably a result of his unusual reserve. Whatever he had to say came out freely in his books but always impersonally. In the thirteen years of my association with him he never discussed with me his relation to Freud or to others on the "Committee" except once in answer to something I had said about their attachment to Freud, when he replied, "and I was in the deepest of all"; and once painfully about Ferenczi, whom he had met in the railroad station in New York in 1926, "He was my best friend and he refused to speak to me." To his early youth, his parents, his older brother, there was no reference, except one to the fact that his mother had died recently.

Fortunately, however extreme his reticence about personal matters in daily conversation, in his papers one finds preserved with his customary care and organization an account of what he considered vital in his early experience. In addition to manuscripts, typescripts, and galley proofs of almost everything he had ever written, including numerous preliminary notes, there are four notebooks, *Tagebücher* as he entitles them, together with a fifth notebook of poems, written during the years 1903 and 1904 when he was nineteen and twenty.[2]

The first section of my book, therefore, is made up largely of quotations from the four *Daybooks,** selected by me for the purpose of following the development so clearly portrayed. I have omitted nothing that seemed to me essential for understanding the nature of this young man for whom the very fact of Freud's existence, as well as the friendly reception later to be accorded to him, was like an answer to prayer. In my translation, which can be trusted in its faithfulness to Rank, I have tried to leave the flavor of the German construction. It is therefore not polished, but it is like Rank as anyone who knew him will affirm.

For the years 1905–1925 there is now no lack of information about Rank from the Freudian standpoint, in view of the completion of Dr. Ernest Jones's definitive biography of Freud. However, Rank also has left his own record of this period in three carefully separated folders of letters organized by him both chronologically and logically.[3] The first group, which includes twenty-seven letters covering the period 1907–1922, is chiefly between Rank and Freud. The second group of thirty letters, 1924–1925, follows the controversy developing over *Entwicklungsziele der Psychoanalyse* (*Development of Psychoanalysis*), a joint work by Ferenczi and Rank, which reached a climax in Rank's *Das Trauma der Geburt* (*The Trauma of Birth*). The third group of fourteen letters is devoted to the problems of publication, particularly as they arose between the Press in London and the Publishing House

* The literal translation of "Tagebücher" has been used because it seems to fit the nature and organization of the material better than journal or diary.
[2] All the Rank letters, papers, and manuscripts in my possession, together with many of his books in German and in English, have been given to the Special Collections Division of the Columbia University Libraries headed by Dr. Roland Baughman.
[3] Copies of the originals of the Rund-briefe circulated among the Committee in this period are also preserved in this collection.

in Vienna; or in effect between Jones and Rank, including Freud's efforts to mediate in letters to the Committee.

For these letters, a professional translator who worked with me was employed. They form the core of the second section of my book. The quotations and summarizations from these letters are intended primarily to follow the developmental process therein revealed as Rank experienced it, for the sake of relationship rather than theory. Nothing factually important has been omitted except the argumentative details. My interest was focused on the fact and meaning of developing differences rather than on their rationalizations.

In the third section, which covers the period of my personal knowledge of Rank, there has been no problem of translation but where I have had no documents to rely on, there may be errors of memory, for time tends to become condensed and deceptive after so many years. The feeling memories, however, are reliable in themselves, even though they may be misplaced as to date and circumstance.

When I reread the many letters from Rank that I have preserved over the years, because I could not bear to destroy them, I realized that they gave a picture of his later personal development that could be conveyed in no other way. Since there was nothing in his relation to me that needed concealment, I have used them freely, with no major reservations, in order to follow the personal struggles and internal triumphs of his life in the United States.

The fourth and last section depends for its characterization of Rank on his own final summing up of a lifelong attempt to understand genius and its relation to culture as expressed in his book *Art and Artist.*

It has been my aim to present throughout something about Rank as a genius, an artist in his own right, not as a disciple of Freud but in terms of his own self-development; the inestimable value for him of his finding of Freud and the inner necessity (for his genius) as well as the personal tragedy of his separation from the Freudian group. For this presentation, I alone am responsible. It rests upon a deep identification as well as many years of taking back into myself projections that have been gradually withdrawn in the face of age and death.

JESSIE TAFT

Flourtown, Pa.

1 *The early years*

PIOUS SIGH OF A MODERN MAN ON HIS NINETEENTH BIRTHDAY

Only nineteen years young!
O good fortune! O bliss!
How much you can now create
In this long time!

Already nineteen years old!
As long as this you have carried the pain?
Your tough will to live—
It has not yet said, "No"?

TRANSLATED BY ANITA J. FAATZ

For information regarding Rank's early years I am entirely dependent upon his four *Daybooks* (covering 1903–1905), written in the finest German script almost without correction, as if copied from rough notes. The first is dated January 1, 1903, when he was nineteen years and nine months old and closes with the entry of February 22, 1904. It begins with a formal title page. His purpose is stated clearly and with his usual authority, for even at twenty he wrote, however secretly, with the introspective assurance and sense of universality that characterized his thinking from the beginning.

OPINIONS AND THOUGHTS

ABOUT MEN AND THINGS*

IN THE FORM OF A DAYBOOK

by

OTTO RANK (ROSENFELD)[1]

Begun on January 1, 1903, in Vienna

(*with the incorporation of the poems, there would be added "in verse and prose")

Vienna, January 1, 1903

I begin this book for my own enlightenment. Before everything, I want to make progress in psychology. By that I understand not the professional definition and explanation of certain technical terms established by a few professors, but the comprehensive knowledge of mankind that explains the riddles of our thinking, acting, and speaking, and leads back to certain basic characteristics. For an approach to this idealistic goal, which only a few souls have tried to reach, self-observation is a prime essential and to that end I am making these notes. I am attempting in them to fix passing moods, impressions, and feelings, to preserve the stripped-off layers that I have outgrown and in this way to keep a picture of my abandoned way of life, whereby if, in reading these notes later on I want to trace the inner connections and external incidents of my development, I shall have the material for it, namely, my overcome attitudes and viewpoints displayed in order before me.

[1] The name *Rank*, first used as a pen name in his early writings, was made legal on March 30, 1909.

4

This is my aim in this book and if it satisfies this aim, it will also have satisfied me. Whoever seeks something else, seeks well; he will find perhaps even more than he antici- pated.

In this bold statement one already discerns Rank's natural bent as a psychologist, but far more unusual is his acceptance of growth as an inevitable psychological process. For, strange as it may seem, nothing is rarer among psychiatrists and psychologists than an understanding of growth in relation to personality, which is as real and defined as physiological growth. Change, yes, that can be accepted or at least perceived but the fact of an irreversible process in the developing of personality as genuine as the growth of nerves, muscles, and bones is seldom acknowledged.

The first *Daybook* is filled with quotations from his current reading, criticisms of plays he is seeing and evaluation of music he is hearing, interspersed with sketches of a particular event, a poem, suggestions for a story or a play, little fables or parables of his own devising, and a few purely personal descriptions of moods, illness, and work.

His youth is betrayed not by the quality of his thinking but by his bitter cynicism regarding women, marriage, parents, religion, and even life itself. He does not hesitate to improve upon the Ten Commandments:

1. *Thou shalt have no God.*
2. *Thou shalt not suffer any other besides thyself.*
3. *Thou shalt not bear false witness against thyself.*
4. *Thou shalt create daily for thyself a day of joy (holy day).*
5. *Fathers and mothers: Honor your children and love them so that you do not beget them if you are not able to support and educate them.*
6. *Thou shalt not want to steal.*
7. *Thou shalt not contract marriage.*

5

8. *Thou shalt not give birth reluctantly.*
9. *Thou shalt not desire thy neighbor's wife, for there are plenty of others.*
10. *Thou shalt not venture to want to tell the truth.*

Aphorisms flow from him, universals are his meat:

Girls think about marriage, young women about breaking up marriage, widows about remarriage, and the old women think about their youth. Boys think about nothing, young men about young girls, mature men about making money and about women, and old men again think about nothing (but they still haven't forgotten women).

Again:

Poverty or inherited wealth is a privilege of the philosopher. Whoever will win riches for himself, to him no time remains for philosophizing. Every philosophy comes from the feeling of superiority to other men: it is therefore a scorning of men. The able man creates something in his philosophy equal to him, a community.

At birth, life is given to one; in suicide, for the first time, one takes it. Therefore a distinguished deed!

Despite his scorn for human nature, there is always warmth for animal life and even when the animal is used to carry a barb against humans, a certain sweetness creeps in as in the following characteristic description.

July 28, 10 o'clock in the evening
Today I saw two little wagons passing each other. The one was drawn by an ass, the other by a she-ass. The ass who by means of his sense of smell already perceived the lady from a distance, began to bray loudly and behaved wildly. He paid no attention either to the entreaties or to the threats and

blows of the driver, who up to that time had sat indifferently on the wagon. The lady seemed the whole time not to notice. She went peacefully, slowly on her way, her eyes toward the ground (just like a woman) and seemed quite content as if she had escaped a danger. Whence comes this difference in perception? Are asses really not so stupid as one usually assumes? The mating instinct is just as strongly developed in women. The woman is passive and—shy. It has been divided up, so that the man is always the stumbling block; he must begin, the ass must make the "declaration of love." To this arrangement, many a woman who would not propose to the man has to thank her so-called "bad fate." (For the fate of woman is a man, whom she loves, that is, who maintains her according to her rank and situation.)

But to the truly great, as he conceives them, he gives a profound respect that with him never means total acceptance:

I seek to comprehend distinguished individuals always completely and at once. I strive to become acquainted with their collected works, but above all with their lives, their correspondence, and their diaries and first of all to comprehend completely the artist through the man. I then transfer myself so vividly into their thought world that I am not only inspired to create something similar in their form but often quite independently, before I know all their ideas, I pick up a theme that they have treated already.

He reads widely: the novels of Stendhal and Dostoevsky, the plays of Wedekind and Ibsen, Hebbel's daybooks (obviously a model), Darwin's *Origin of Species*; but above all Nietzsche and Schopenhauer, who are his great source of inspiration and insight.

His attitude toward himself fluctuates between despair and profound belief. In reply to his own question, "What do I value in myself?" he answers "Nothing! I shall live in vain. As I am not able to live a full life and also can create nothing whole, so my pride decides to pass away wholly and completely without value. Only no middle ground, no cattle life." But toward the end of the first *Daybook* one finds him asserting,

I am an artist, even if I never succeed in bringing forth a single work of art. . . . There are moments in which I believe firmly in my high endowment and therein that I belong to those who, even if they are not immortal, still live on for several centuries in their works. In such moments I have an indescribable feeling of happiness, although I know that it is empty. If I have erred, then will come a disillusionment so frightful that I shall never overcome it. If I am not mistaken, then I know that I have a hard battle before me in which only joy of creating and the consciousness of my ability can protect me from disgust. And one demands of the artist, modesty. . . .

Self-confidence, not modesty, is the first condition for greatness. To test every word under the microscope and under the hammer, before one writes it down. And then still to doubt its origin and meaning.

Fortunately, one does not have to depend on gossip or inference regarding Rank's beginnings. Dr. Jones's careful inclusion[2] of the fact that "Rank came from a distinctly lower stratum than the others" is borne out by the *Autobiography* that forms part of the first *Daybook*, a bitter document indeed. Although Jones's conclusion that this accounted for Rank's "timid and even deferential air" might be disputed by those who knew Rank in his maturity, certainly there is neither deference nor timidity in the thinking and feeling of this

[2] Ernest Jones, M.D., *Life and Work of Sigmund Freud*, New York: Basic Books Inc., 1955, Vol. 2, p. 160.

nineteen-year-old as he faces the facts of his personal life and turns to poetry, music, and philosophy for sustenance.

There follows his own account of his life up to October 26, 1903 when *Autobiography* was written.

AUTOBIOGRAPHY

It is astonishing with what similarity the life of most humans runs its course; how empty and worthless it appears. Even the genius, sit venia verbo, is no exception, at least as concerns his youth. The apparently unusual in it was usually put into it by interpretation afterward either by him or by his friends.

Still, there is in the life of many men occasionally an event that has a determining and directing influence on their development and to put up and point out these milestones in the life-course is the concern of biography. The biographer, therefore, has to lift out whatever seems characteristic, unique, and influential in the life that he will picture, all else he leaves for enlargement to the experience of the reader.

As parents usually do not keep notes on the lives of their children, do not even retain long in memory the most important facts about them and otherwise no one devotes his life to this task, as interesting and instructive as it is hard, therefore every man is himself best qualified to write down his own life story, not his stupid, sensation-hungry compatriots or even his successors. However, it has apparently been difficult for important men of fine feeling, the very ones whose life history and development are of greater value, to give a correct presentation of what they have seen and experienced as each one, in a survey and closer consideration of his life up to the present, finds enough ground and opportunity to be ashamed of his past; but on the writing to spin it out or to falsify is forbidden by his integrity and creative sincerity. Less gifted, weaker men without any such scruples

9

will deliver a distorted false life picture because they are not in a position to displace themselves back into earlier conditions. The simplest means to avoid the temptation and to sketch as faithful a picture as possible appears to me to be the supposition that the autobiography will be prepared only for self-reading and that after my death—But then I would already be at the end before I had even made a beginning.

I was born on April 22, 1884, in Vienna, with hair complete, as the third child of weak but apparently healthy parents. I followed the usual course from the first bath to teething, and the usual children's diseases and unpleasantnesses, as measles, diphtheria, school, and so forth, in quick succession, only to fall back broken with the first milestone of my dangerous path. Joint rheumatism was there. One may not underestimate its influence on my life, for when I was nineteen, it caused a heart ailment.

As the second important occurrence, even today after thirteen years, stands my introduction to erotic experience in my seventh year through one of my friends, for which I still curse him even today, vividly remembering. With my extraordinary curiosity and desire for knowledge and my deep-rooted propensity for experimenting, the foundation stone of my later sufferings was laid at that time; it was at the same time the gravestone of my joy. My father, who is a quiet drinker, wherewith it is not to be said that he is also quiet after the drinking, bothered himself little about me and my brother (my sister had died when a few months old) and my mother found her satisfaction in the fact that at least we lived, that is, had something to eat and went decently clothed. So I grew up, left to myself, without education, without friends, without books. I must here note that all that I had read up to my fifteenth year was pure senseless stuff that had worth only insofar as I, with its help, acquired a certain skill in reading. I did not even have a religion, to which I might have been able to appeal, for my parents lived, as Jews now live even in the towns, holding fast to one or two holy days, customs, usages, prejudices, and leaving the rest to the dear God.

Death, the mysterious phenomenon that many thinking people have attempted to explain, became a problem to me above all. I still remember that I did not sleep for many nights and thought only about dying with terror and chattering teeth. Especially that never-never-never coming again, and the impossibility of thinking it through to the end, filled me with terrible fear.

As I was also by nature somewhat rachitic, held by no one to a prudent way of living, and in my free hours was not watched over, I sickened early with joint rheumatism; which anyway seems to be at home in our family.

Up to this time my only diversion was school. My brother, who is about three years older than I, had his own comrades, with whom he naturally associated more gladly than with me, and also I felt myself drawn to "big men" more than to my colleagues. One of these gentlemen gave me his special favor and thought to show it by enlightening me on some already mentioned phenomena. Now truly I had satisfying material, besides the school, but, as I feared, too little strength for other diversion.

So the years passed. As my brother already attended the Gymnasium and as one must get returns from his sons as soon as possible, I was put in the middle-class school, on whose advice I still do not know today, but certainly not by my own desire. Once more I had then to become aware, from a distance, of my first milestone. After that, the severe rheumatism kept away, although I still will often be plagued by it after great exertion or in damp weather. The middle-class school I completed, without improving in knowledge, and indifferently in skills, with the good result that they considered in what way I could obtain a somewhat better education and also a more lucrative position.

11

Of a better use and development of my abilities, they certainly never thought. Going over into the secondary school was not to be considered because of the long period of study, and so there offered itself the technical school as the only possibility of getting a higher education and at the same time the expectation of a higher income. From that time on, my uncle, a perfect Philistine and slave of work, to whom I am still in debt, put something into my career and forced it by "higher morality" into the Procrustian bed of machine-making, which role is just as unrelated to me today after six years of application as at my birth. As I was still too young for acceptance in the said establishment, the director advised me, as a good preparation, to complete a workshop course, into which I was again stretched by help of my uncle. With my weak constitution, my irrational upbringing and way of life, the quite heavy work so affected me both in winter and in holidays that I had to let myself be transferred to the office. There it was somewhat better, but I must note that already I had the dull dark feeling of the aimlessness of my work.

About this time, I was once taken by my brother, who frequently received so-called student tickets to the school performances, to the Royal Theatre. The first performance, the "Jungfrau von Orleans," made an impression on me and after a few more sporadic visits to the theater, I became a steady patron for four years (1899–1902). Since I also attended other theaters besides the Royal, I was hardly ever at home in the evening. Meantime I had entered the technical school, which altered nothing in my life and interests. I have much to thank the four theater years for, besides many a lost evening, as the evening illusion of the theater cast a veil over the raw reality of the day. The holidays (fortunately school and theater holidays came together) I apparently spent regularly in the country with relatives in Mähren, where I and my brother were suffered every year for a few weeks and, just as at home, were left to ourselves or, what was worse, to the men and maids.

At home the old life continued again, interrupted by a few attempts to throw off the oppressive fetters that limited me. I had for a long time the most earnest thoughts of suicide which, as Nietzsche says, have helped me through many a night and also many a day. Then as reaction there came an intense desire for life and joy in creativity that pressed me violently into activity. I decided firmly at that time to become an actor and this thought took such a hold on me that I at once began to study a few roles. I still recall vividly how I memorized "Faust" and declaimed it with relatively little comprehension but with instinctive correctness. As I myself was too shy to display my talents before my colleagues, I never came to the practical exercise of the actor's art and so at last lost the interest in it. I have noticed in general and especially in this instance that projects that seem to satisfy me completely, conditions into which I throw myself wholly, very soon lose their influence on me. At first I thought that was progress, development, a striving after higher things; now, however, I no longer trust my moods and wanderings, for I recognize their instability and unreliability.

As we brothers very early, actually since our birth, were left to ourselves, a certain selfdependence was soon formed in each; incidentally, the only advantage of this method of rearing. We had our own opinions and views on all kinds of beliefs and superstitions, judgments, and prejudices that we concealed from no one. Especially my brother, one of those men whose uprightness never harmed but profited, went ahead of me in that regard with a good example. Under such circumstances my father, whose more intimate portrait I will spare myself with the reference to "Hjalmar Ekdal" [3] whom he resembles feature for feature, attempted to exert his paternal authority, certainly a little late. Thereby how-

[3] Ibsen, *The Wild Duck.*

ever he struck a hard resistance, so that we finally fell out with him completely and did not even greet him any more.

From then on began an idyllic family life. Almost no word was spoken in the house, but if a voice ever became loud, it became very loud, i.e., it screamed. For every one of us had a deep rage inside, to which he tried to give vent, as often as it started. The chief antagonists were my father and my brother; my mother and I (from whom above all I have inherited this peculiarity, besides many others) could not bear a row and we fled accordingly, as often as we could. Almost every evening I was in the theater or begged for quiet to study when I was at home; that was respected. I possess especially an iron industry that many of my colleagues envied me; and what I begin I carry to the end with zeal and efficiency.

About this time I found the lack of friends very painful. Now I find this loss no longer deep, for I have learned that friends are mostly a prop or a burden and in both cases are bad. Anyway, up to now I have learned to know no one whom I would have wanted for a friend, really and truly. Only to one person I felt myself somewhat drawn at first. He was my classmate, sharer of studies and therefore fellow sufferer, a gifted fellow for whom I prophesy a great future, if his talents are not stifled by hard unbearable conditions or stuck in the self-satisfying contentment of the most essential life needs.

In the last year of my study, the theater craze let up a little, and a zeal for reading took over, which finally mounted to a drive for knowledge. I now read whatever came under my hands and eyes; among them a few important authors and good novels. The high point of this period and perhaps its unconscious goal was my acquaintance with the philosophy of Schopenhauer. What I have him to thank for, I will express in another place. Here I will only note that I looked at the world with other eyes.

But I hurried by this milestone also with painful farewell and vowed never to forget the man Schopenhauer. I entered now a barren stony road. I felt like the wanderer who looks out from the oasis into the wide open wastes. Again I read a lot of bad stuff, with the exception of some average works until, on this devilish path, I ruined my feet, my stomach, and my eyes. At the right moment I found Hendrik Ibsen. To him also in a later writing I will give special thanks. I only note here that I honor him as above all the one who understands and can describe human beings, and that the Wild Duck especially caught me as I again discovered well-known persons in the married pair "Ekdal."

So with this milestone I caught a little breath and went forward somewhat cheered.

It seems, however, that my getting acquainted with the works of illustrious men took place as it had in the case of these men in their development. Just as whole races of average men prepare unconsciously for the possibility of the coming of the one superior being, so must I slowly and unconscious of the goal go through a lot of average works in order to reach the worthwhile ones.

After saying this in advance, I note a third similar period, whose goal and climax was Friedrich Nietzsche. To him also I will set up a special memorial, for he was to me at once ideal leader and guide. At the same time, through his works, actually guided by them, I learned to know the music of Richard Wagner. It was hard for me to press into his "work in itself," i.e., to "Tristan," since to this end his other works must be completely grasped and conquered, no light task for a modern man, as Wagner, who is an essentially modern composer, lets his characters feel and experience as entirely modern. That best becomes clear in his instrumentation, which indeed is only a symbol of the rich, complex, spiritual life in which, despite the seeming variety of the motifs, the work considered as a whole carries the imprint of unity in

15

which one gently sounded tone releases a whole series of related emotions and moods. Now let us descend from the
cloudy height, from the Valhalla of great souls to the depths
and bogs of everyday.

Meantime I had finished my studies; besides, had taken
my examinations and received a "leaving certificate" (for a
one-year voluntary service). Four years sacrificed for two. The
example is in accord with the civil regulation.

In the last days before the exam, in which I had to work
six hours, partly sitting, partly standing, I felt an oppressive
exhaustion in my limbs and severe head pains, which I had
experienced before but not to this degree and duration. As
my condition improved only a little, in spite of a regulated
and rational living, and I discovered in my letters and other
writings errors of inflections, articles, particles, pronouns, pre-
fixes, I became an ever more attentive observer of my illness,
until at one stroke the situation cleared and out of the immediate as well as from the earlier not well-observed experiences I had in a trice the diagnosis complete.

My father, an apparently sensible man, easily excitable,
who is in addition a drinker, complained often of head pains,
and just at this time he had an attack; I believe it was a
drunken frenzy. I was alone with him in the house and still
remember clearly how he bellowed hoarsely and struck his
hands against the table till they bled, while I sat motionless
in a corner as if turned to stone and followed him with my
eyes.

I myself have been weak and no good (wurmstichig) from
birth, and have perhaps no single bodily part that is completely right. With my senseless way of living, I had added
my own share—shortly there remained for me no doubt: it
was the first signs of the beginning of brain paralysis. Although from that, even from that most disagreeable experience, I tried to get the best for myself or at least to hope for
it, it grew hard for me in this instance, in view of this decided

certainty, just to maintain my sanity. And yet a few weeks later I drew from it an untroubled indifference so light that from then on, I derided all the little human needs.

Since I had at last finished with my study period, they pressed me to take a position as soon as possible. Fortunately up to then I could not find one and so it drove me again to Nietzsche, to whose entire works I had not yet been able to return. So I left gladly my dark cold milestone and since in the distance before me, far away, no new goal was to be seen, while cold gray mist covered everything, I willingly turned round again; I bathed, as it were, in Nietzsche's spirit and got a charmed, weatherproof, bulletproof skin, that should protect me in the meantime against external attacks. However, in order to get a correct judgment about something and no one-sided, exaggerated, short-sighted picture of it, to maintain it for life, it is necessary first to experience it fully and then to look at it from a proper distance, from a standpoint that lies outside its province. Therefore I had not to go forward but to fly upward:

> Und wird mir leicht, so geht es rasch bergauf.
> Ich gratuliere Dir, zum neuen Lebenslauf.

Out of the barren cultural background supplied by a home entirely lacking in books, pictures, and music, not desperately poor, but too poor to provide higher education or special advantage, we find emerging a youth of nineteen who is able to evaluate without apology everything great he reads, sees, or hears. An entry on August 26, 1903, reads:

Charles Darwin, "On the Origin of Species through Natural Selection or the Survival of the Most Favored Breeds in the Struggle for Existence"—the title is so long with good reason, for it gives the content of the work. True, it indicates great understanding when the author can comprehend a whole theory in so few words; on the other hand it shows little taste

17

to abstract this so condensed title from a thick book. For the strengthening of the assertion presented in the title, Darwin offers a lot of experiments, observations, and authorities, many of which are of interest only to the expert. Admirable are Darwin's wide reading, his scholarly modesty, and his pure English collector's patience. This sentence is characteristic: "Everyone knows the difference between the middle and the outside petals of the daisy (Bellis)." Everyone! In my opinion, a theory like Darwin's must be built on a philosophical system or rise to the peak in one. But Darwin keeps anxiously away from everything. that is not tangible and visible. On the somewhat more interesting heading "Instinct" he says at once, "I will assert at once, that I have nothing to do with the origin of spiritual strengths nor with that of life itself." In another place it says, "The same (namely, many natural scientists) are of the opinion, that very many organic forms occur only for the sake of beauty, to delight the eyes of men or the creator (but the latter assumption lies beyond the boundaries of scientific discussions)."

Although, up to now, I knew as little as nothing about Darwin's theories, their fundamental principles do not seem strange and are almost self-explanatory and I can only ascribe to the envy of the scientists and the deeply rooted prejudices of the people that his theory was fought so long and so obstinately. The envy of his colleagues was lost with Darwin's death; the prejudices of a people usually are lost only with their own death.

Again, with regard to music, in which he seemingly had had no training or instruction, he expresses himself with complete assurance:

Leoncavallo's "Bajazzo" is a little masterpiece. A jewel of music drama. From the Bajazzo-Columbine-Harlequin subject used to the limit in and with all the arts, a new, effective

18

side is extracted. The music is interesting. It has that mixture of sweet, insinuating Italian melody with the Wagnerian nature and feeling motifs that is an indication of the gradual disappearance of Italian opera music. We see composers of all nations creating in the Wagnerian manner. The great result of this tendency is to be ascribed to the admirable union of "tone and word" on the one hand, on the other to the dominance of the dramatic action. One often hears the complaint that our great musicians, Beethoven, Mozart, had no dramatic material for their compositions. And thus they could therewith have created nothing other or finer. Beethoven with his powerful themes might have blotted out the action, might have concealed it with his manifold ornamental musical inventions and only worked out certain features as vines cover the walls of houses and leave only windows exposed.

Earlier, people were content to hear only music in the opera. An overture, a couple of arias, duets, chorus, a ballet and they were satisfied. Meyerbeer's school. Today they still want all that, plus a beautiful setting, but they demand action, action above all. And here is the source of Wagner's influence. With his music dramas he in part met a need, in part he created it. In his dramas music retreated to the background in favor of the action: although it is true one speaks now only of Wagner's music—assuming that one can speak of music at all. For music above all must operate through itself.*** In the symphony, the ultimate that the musician can produce, it is even true for each single movement. One cannot explain Wagner's music without knowledge of the corresponding libretto and in general it is not effective in and of itself. I know only two compositions that can measure up to Wagner in unity of "tone and word" and dramatic power, whose music is effective as such and for which I could not even think of supplying other texts: "Carmen" and "Der Bajazzo."

Again, his midnight entry of January 21:

I just heard Beethoven's IX Symphony. I staggered home and wrote this down. Beethoven is . . . Beethoven has . . . Hebbel's thought, which I wrote down here six days ago, occurs to me again, "There are names—Beethoven."

And the evening entry of February 16, 1904:

I have just heard Hugo Wolf's "Corregidor." Too bad that Nietzsche could not hear opera any more. It is the prototype of European music as he conceived it. Its style lies between Bizet and Wagner and for this reason would have impressed Nietzsche (who had freed himself from Wagner) all the less, the more passionately he maintained it. By and large Wagner's music was too brutal, too penetrating for him, and Bizet on the other hand too un-Wagnerian, pathetic, too light. Wolf unites the merits of both in his music. It is light Wagner, bright, gay, gifted. No tedious struggle.

The scorn this young man feels for others but never expresses openly is revealed without restraint in this first *Daybook*: "If anything could drive me to suicide, it would be the stupidity and commonness of mankind." His contempt for the average extends even to the readers of books. "It is a comfort that every book seeks its reader and also finds him. Many books have at certain periods no readers at all; they are as rare as the writers. The fewer readers a book has, the better it is for the book and the higher it goes in my regard." Thus he prepares himself for future rejection and obscurity. With his usual frankness and considerable insight he admits, "The most stupid of my acquaintances was the most use to me. With everything that I wanted to comprehend, I always thought about it as if I had to make it clear to him. Thus I came upon very simple things that earlier, because of their

20

simplicity, I had not thought about at all. That should be no self-compliment, but also not the opposite. Without skepticism, an intelligent man falls into self-admiration (many times also with me). I rejoice that I am exactly as I am. Others do the same, however, as I believe, with less justification. *That* others also believe about me." He questions—while he wonders at his own writing.

And yet, arrogant as he was regarding others, he faced himself always with introspective accuracy:

October 3, 1903

Many times I read my thoughts as though they were those of another: it doesn't occur to me at all that I could have written it, and I would like to meet the man who has composed it. Is it that I am in another state when I write? Is it a higher one? I see in myself no steadily growing development but one by leaps and bounds. I generally have periods for certain states. It will happen that for months I do not work, and then suddenly I go into a feverish activity. I'm like that in many other things.

And what is this work of which he speaks? Early in the new year, January 19, 1904, now fully twenty, he outlines his program:

I am occupied with the following plans, of which I have already outlined some:
  I. *A Novella:*
  II. *A Novel: The Life of a Girl*
  III. *Four dramas,* 1. *Don Juan, the man who seeks for his ideal of woman and cannot find her.*
  2. *Tragedy of Gambling Rooms.*
  3. *The life of the child, the girl, the wife, the mother, in one individual.*
  4. *Three days out of the future life.*

21

IV. *Eight poems,* 1. *In the country—Cycle of four poems*
  a. *Spring morning*
  b. *Summer noon* (*Sunday*)
  c. *Autumn evening*
  d. *Winter night*
  2. *To the old year*
  3. *To the new year*
  4. *Day and night*
  5. *After the rain*
V. *A discussion; On the three seasons*
VI. *Three essays*
  1. *On Religion*
  2. *On Education*
  3. *The World*
VII. *My Will*

Of these ambitious plans, the poems were completed and are extant; the first act of a play, *Goetzen,* has also been preserved among his papers, as well as thirteen pages of a novel, *Der Freund,* but it is evident that none of these held his interest or satisfied his creativity. Of *Goetzen* he says, "I would like to improve every sentence. Nothing is good enough for me. This work disgusts me. What is not successful for me at the first attempt, has already failed." His interest in Don Juan was to continue into maturity and eventuate in the *Don Juan Gestalt* of 1922.

The "Will," however, he entered in his *Daybook* and a painfully adolescent document it is, with its overassertion of the deep sense of difference that his genius had already established. This difference he expresses many times, as in the following comment: "I feel for most people no sympathy, only for animals, a phenomenon which I have not yet traced to its cause." And again, "I have an aversion to every contact with people, I mean even to every physical contact. It costs me an effort to extend my hand to anyone, and if I must do it, I first put on gloves. I couldn't kiss anyone." This isolation and withdrawal was even more marked in relation to his writing, and seems to be something other than timidity, or fear of the judgment of others:

I cannot bring myself to share my manuscripts with anyone. Also I have no one. No person knows that I write. I could not bear a confidant. Only the greatest ambition, which however I might be able to down, or the most extreme need, which I perhaps could not prevent, could move me to make something public.

The "Will" tries to anticipate and prevent every kind of publicity or formal recognition of his demise. His brother is to be entrusted with all details:

Finally, I wish as I have already noted incidentally not to be buried but to be burned. Should the necessary money not be found in my estate, then I ask my brother to sell my goods until the necessary sum is reached.

If the obtaining of the money is not possible in this way either, then will my brother have the goodness to obtain the money somehow. If in spite of his greatest effort he is not successful, so must I let myself be buried for good or evil. In this case I wish to be wrapped completely in a white cloth, to be laid in a simple, unadorned coffin of planed boards, which should be buried without ceremony neither in a general grave nor in a sectarian burying ground. I wish to lie alone outside of all cemetery walls and boundaries, in a quiet place if possible on the edge of the forest, and beg my brother in the enforcement of the fulfilment relative to this my wish to refer expressly to my so-called "absence of confession." As a grave marker, I would like a rough, unpolished block of stone of medium height.

Since, according to my reckoning, a conventional burial

would not cost less than cremation, I hope still to be de-
stroyed by my fiery ideal. If that happens, my brother is to
receive the ashes for free disposal. Perhaps he may let them
fly to the winds on a stormy April day!

DAYBOOK II

With the second *Daybook* dated February 22, 1904, to December 30, 1904, the center of conflict is altered and made
acutely real by the necessity of taking the kind of job that
naturally followed upon his technical training. The entry of
March 19 states: "Today I took a position in a Vienna machine shop. I suffered horribly. I receive 31¼ Heller—15⅝
Kreuzer paid by the hour."

March 30—When I wake up now in the morning, the first
thought that enters my consciousness is the hollowness, emp-
tiness, and aimlessness of my present life. The feeling is aw-
ful. I would like to go to sleep again at once and forever.
April 11—I feel my present occupation so painfully because
it goes directly against my character and my talents. I find
myself constantly in a dream state and the kind of reality to
which I am forced hurts me.

The tension mounts to the point where some solution must
be found. On April 24, driven almost to the point of suicide,
he is brought to the possibility of making an appeal for help
and actually inserts in his *Daybook* what he calls the "Sketch
for a Letter," a letter that I feel sure was never sent, although
he may have had a real person in mind as recipient. Here one
sees the desperate nature of his conflict, both internal and
external:

You will probably wonder at getting a letter from me once
more and such a long one. I am one of the few men who

write only when they have something to say, and as it is impossible for me to write a conventional letter except partially, I write only when absolutely necessary and preferably even then to those with whom I can permit certain liberties in form and content. I take for granted that this is the case with you as some time since you were willing to receive a few verses of mine. Still, what one is accustomed to allow the poet (pardon the bold word) as a concession, that one usually allows with difficulty to everyday, unimportant-seeming prose, and so I must probably wait to see how you will receive my letter.

Before I share with you briefly its object, which will doubtless surprise you, I must introduce the immediate circumstances that pressed me to the writing of it, in part not to let my request seem to be the outgrowth of a deep conceit and in part in order to give it foundation and support.

First I beg of you to accept the seriousness of my revelations, for I give you no momentary moods and ideas, but the results of long and mature consideration.

One thing more: there is nothing more painful for a person than to have to reveal to a stranger, as I am now compelled to do, his innermost thoughts and feelings, like the retina of his soul, in which his whole being is reflected. However, it is just as tormenting and terrible, when this innermost part is imparted to third persons without his knowledge or against his will. I beg you, therefore, for the greatest secrecy toward everyone in regard to all my revelations, for the thought that there would be several persons who know of my situation would be unbearable to me.

So, I have won the firm conviction that I am a poet, not yesterday or today but for a long time, little by little. The most striking proof of my assertion I am sorry to say I cannot give you; it rests on my unbreakable faith in my talents. I hope, however, to convince you of it with other, less striking but easier-to-share proofs, namely, with a few poems, a drama, a completely developed essay, a number of aphorisms, thoughts, plans, sketches, and attempts.

As soon as I began school, I had frequently the firm intention to get out of it, as the calling into which I had fallen, the devil knows how, was inimical to my spirit. Only the thought of the early ending of my studies and the winning of the right to a year's voluntary service thereby kept me from it. Later I learned that even that had been for nothing.

When I had completed school, fortune seemed to be favorable to me. I fell into feverish activity, I worked from eight to ten hours a day, and collected an immense amount of material. Suddenly in one day, as if in an ecstacy, I wrote down a four-act drama; in addition to and apart from all thought activity, this takes a real writer's hand. Then my genius broke through with elemental force. I became, to use a figure of speech, like a lightning conductor of God; like a tool, without my own will. When the inspiration was over, I myself was often astonished at my work and found that I had put in it and anticipated things that knowledge and experience confirmed only much later. Upon these periods of restless tireless activity there followed a time of inactivity and exhaustion that then seemed very serious and made me doubt my abilities. Later I found this periodic activity common with all poets and now I saw it as essential to their way of working. A poet is like a sponge. He absorbs himself in an experience, an adventure, a pain and then puts out all the accumulated material in a concentrated form. There follows of necessity a time of thinness, dryness, and emptiness until a new life experience stirs him up again. The more the poet, unlike the average man, knows the higher condition of creativity, the more extreme is the reaction that follows it.

But these apparently hopeless periods passed and my works began slowly to crystallize, when I obtained a position in a Vienna machine shop. With mixed feelings I began. Although from my earliest youth I had been a dreamer and maker of fantasies, still it became clear beyond dispute that I must earn enough money to feed and clothe myself. My striving had never been directed toward money-making and high positions. I wanted only to succeed to that extent. Obvious and to the highest degree ridiculous seemed to me the situation that to be able to live, I had to sacrifice exactly that which I called living. I hoped, however, that my occupation would afford enough time for the cultivation of my talents that lay entirely outside the scope of this activity, but I was bitterly disillusioned in that regard.

I belong to the kind of man who can do nothing superficial but must follow up everything to the last ground and corner. Every work that has been started occupies me completely until it is finished. So the tasks that were given me in the shop went round and round in my head; many a time, if I attempted in my free time to follow my own thoughts, they would be gone before I had got rid of the shop business and entered into my own work. Realization of the aimlessness and nothingness of my shop activity together with its aridity and mindlessness created in me a terrible mood. The road to the shop I traversed like one condemned, who is led into slavery and not once for all executed. Although I worked through every problem with the greatest concentration of all my energy, I was many times obliged to do violence to myself in order to keep my attention directed only moderately. Myriads of thoughts would go through my head, so fast that they could keep pace with my breathing, so that I never once had time even to write them all down. I am of the opinion that in the last five years I have experienced and learned more than formerly the whole race during its existence; but the almost sick brain activity that took place with me on a few days of the last month exceeded all that had gone before. I felt as if the questions struck my brain as the thoughts from a small center made ever wider circles, in order finally to break on the borders of the unthinkable, just as a little stone that has been thrown into the water causes ever larger rings that finally dissolve on the shore without trace. My head hurt me terribly, I had fever, and was close to madness. You can have no approximate idea of what I suffered. And besides, I could not even give free rein to my pain. The external wearing of a—if not satisfied, at least indifferent—mask was the most terrible part. The whole misery turned itself inside and smoldered there until a wind from I know not where kindled it to a bright flame that lit up my heart and brain.

I know well that you have never read a letter like this. Its words would have to work like whiplashes if they were to give the reader even the smallest intimation of the pain they cost the writer. It is really not to be called a letter; it is the image of a quivering human soul under the microscope, an interesting case for experimental psychologists. I propose now to make an end of the whole thing. I must do it, if I do not want to risk a violent conclusion. I shall give up my position as soon as possible, leave my parents, in whose neighborhood it is no longer possible for me to live, and begin on my own course as writer.

I would now like to ask whether you are willing to support me in the beginning of my new activity. I am far from desiring a present from you, but I would beg you for a loan that I would repay with thanks just as soon as I am able to do it. I must be prepared for a learning year, even if perhaps I may earn something in a few months. In this year I should need, with the greatest frugality, as is right, since I intend to provide only the essential needs, about 1,000 Kroner. On the whole it would apparently be the same wherever I lived. I would therefore first of all go to Paris where, with a little industry, I could learn the French language in half a year. Meanwhile it might be possible to earn something as a teacher of German. Once in control of the language I could undertake translations, some of which promise important results as the most important French psychologists—Montaigne,

LaBruyère, Fontenelle, Vauvenargues—are still not translated into German, except in part, very lacking and incomplete.

When I once have firm ground under my feet, then you shall see how fast I progress.

However your answer may turn out, which I beg of you at once, I will owe you thanks in any case, for you were still the only human being to whom I could turn and that itself will mean much in my condition, namely, a hope.

If I should not have given you from the beginning of our acquaintance the attention and honor you have perhaps expected, this is to be considered and therewith pardoned purely as the expression of need for independence and my peculiar, strange disposition cultivated by an early self-reliance. In conclusion I beg you once more for the greatest discretion toward everyone for nothing could rectify a slip, and in case this request should be superfluous I ask pardon for it.

This desperate cry for help, although probably never uttered aloud, seems to have eased him somewhat; it may have helped just to have glimpsed a possible way out, to have admitted his need for another. At any rate it marked a crisis out of which he emerged with affirmation of himself and renewed urge to create.

May 14—Today I bought a weapon to kill myself. Afterward the keenest lust for life and the greatest courage toward death grew up in me. What do I know!

Everything that I think, do, or read seems to bring me closer to a goal. In all things I recognize and wonder at the manifold connections that unite me with them, the thousand fine and still so tough threads, by which my fate is directed. It is, however, also possible that things have no affinity to me at all but that I, like every other man, project upon the things, reflect into them, mirror myself in them. . . .

Up to now I have known no living man whom I would

have considered more complete in every respect than myself, although I experienced a deep need for association with such a man. The people with whom I became acquainted were usually so confined, little, narrow, and suffering that I was glad to come away from them. I have noticed, however, that among them I feel myself creative and very easily become productive. I believe that is because, in relation to their nullity, I learn to prize my worth all the more and in view of their incapacity, much that had fermented in me for a long time, which I would not release but through stern self-discipline and implacable criticism, now escapes from me laughing. . . .

May 25

> Die I would, but swiftly
> Before the thoughts harden;
> For I love them formless, as they are,
> And so I might keep them forever.

June 9

This evening on a walk, I recited to myself, when I had been quite hopeless all day, my sonnet on Hebbel; it is fine and I believe that the judgment is entirely objective. I felt therewith a foolish joy.

The lack of a superior individual in the environment against whom to measure himself is painfully apparent here. His deep uncertainty, together with an equally deep conviction about his own ability, will have to continue until he gains some social evidence or affirmation of his quality. Thus far he has only the negative, subjective assurance of his own sense of superiority in relation to the group he knows. But that is far from satisfactory as a criterion for testing his kinship to the great men on whose creations he is nourished and to whom alone he feels himself to be related. Thus it is inevitable that he will pursue greatness and attempt to analyze its elements and its function.

Accordingly in this second *Daybook* he is already intent upon a theme that will never be abandoned, the nature and significance of the artist, the genius, the hero. He begins to characterize great men with boldness, to examine their relation to sex, to productivity, to the life of the average man. He has been reading Otto Weiniger's *Sex and Character* and finds himself in surprising agreement with his ideas, although he adds a keen observation. "Weiniger was very sensitively endowed and consequently as a thinker, antifeminine. The longing for the feminine components whose natural satisfaction his antifeminine thinking forbade, he satisfied through the very feministic Wagnerian music." In pursuit of heroic greatness he enters into an elaborate outline for a biography of Napoleon, *his* kind of biography.

The piece must be written in prose and indeed in German prose. Every word with the impact of a deed. The French language is too light and fine. German words—blows of a club. Napoleon fell because he wanted to direct and possess everything alone. And still he achieved only the greatness that he alone accomplished. At last however the burden became colossal. He utilized men as means.

All former plays about Napoleon have handled episodes from his life. I, however, treat his life as an episode of that strenuous time in which he lived. Napoleon: representative of the general history of all men of action. One act of the gigantic drama of humanity. Napoleon's empire psychologically based. He did not stride over corpses but he pushed out of his way everything, living or dead.

Napoleon, the opposite of Hamlet! He enters the circle of actual life with no theoretical, preconceived world view, so that astonishment, wonder, and discouragement over the fact that all was not as he had thought did not discourage him. Napoleon acts and looks to the effects, as to whether his acts were wise and good or bad.

. . . *Napoleon also considers the world bad (in his mean-ing) but he considers himself capable of setting it right accord-ing to his conception.*

His effort to understand Nietzsche, whom he compares with Jesus, ends in the painful discovery described in his entry of November 28:

The case of Christ is repeated in every man of genius. He is only the symbolic expression of an eternally recurring process. And if Jesus had never lived? Belief awakes not only the dead, it gives birth also to a man.

Today I learned that Nietzsche died of syphilis and al-though I am not narrow-minded in the comprehension of such things the information shattered me. I had hitherto taken him for a man who, brought into the world by a suffer-ing nervous father addicted to drink, in the beginning too sensitive and instinctively shy, was diverted to masturbation by his disgust for the woman, which he also maintained later, and was brought to grief on the one hand partly by in-heritance from the father, on the other through continued self-abuse; finally however in conjunction with this, the un-wholesome, grinding, enervating mental activity, which how-ever only because of the above mentioned conditions was so feverish, irregular, and exhausting. But syphilis! I could not grasp it. Probably because it shattered my pretty theories in which I had considered all points as correct.

That it also shattered an identification, on which he had depended is obvious. While there is no indication from the *Daybook* thus far that Rank has discovered Freud, he seems always to be aware of the significance of his own dreams and never ceases to examine sex in terms of the characteristic dif-ferences between men and women, especially in relation to the artist, the gifted man, through whom his innermost self is objectified.

Great men are usually woman-haters because the sensuality, which is only a momentary stimulus with them, does not fill their lives as with the average man (also with all women), but hems it in, limits and degrades. But after its fulfilment they realize the whole ridiculousness, aimlessness, and shamefulness of these desires and now rage against the woman instead of against their own senses, against themselves. Ascetics were never enemies of women. Illustrious men project their rejection of their own lust upon the woman who actually allays it, only, however, to make it flare up all the more violently.

The most illustrious men are therefore usually childless and if they have children, they resemble them little, because a child is the embodiment of the will to completion, however unconscious. As now with these men a climax is impossible, so there is also present no longing for a child, for a woman, for coitus. This explains the often noticeable anti-sexuality of genius. The superfluous strength derived from this sexual sterility is devoted in part to the conquering of sex desire, in great part, however, to their works.

Highly gifted masters are always fine students of men, deep psychologists because they unite in themselves the whole content of human nature; they have the tendencies of all the possibilities of mankind in themselves and can develop them in idea.

Here we find in Rank's approach to psychology through his understanding of the creative man, the artist, the germ of his final conception of sex and its relation to will, to which he will inevitably return after the long excursion initiated by his discovery of Freud.

By August, 1904, he is occupied with the concept of time and association of ideas and suddenly in October a quotation from Freud appears without comment, as if what he reads in *Traumdeutung* comes naturally and is instantly put to use.

To represent time as a serpent is a contribution of genius, for first through it came the idea of time, together with that of end and death in the world. Serpent—paradise—Nietzsche.

Association of ideas is the foundation of all thinking. Without the concept of time, no thinking, no philosophy.

. . . In addition to memory, association of ideas is the foundation of all thinking, all speech, all mental activity. Idleness is the mainspring of action.

October 17

Meistersinger—(Freud: Interpretation of Dreams) Dream Song.

October 28

"Our perceptions as also in memory occur in connection with one another and especially in reference to their future concurrence, simultaneously. We call this the phenomenon of association." Freud.

Insofar as dreams are connected with the unconscious, in which "nothing is brought to an end, in which nothing is left behind and forgotten" (Freud), the time concept is lacking in them as it is in external objects insofar as they are connected with infinity. But the intellect cannot comprehend anything otherwise than as limited, namely in time, space, and causality, which are its forms; while in itself, it is unconscious and endless.

November 10

I am working now on a novel and repeat the already many times repeated remark that in everything I create, always the scene with all its details stands before me as in a dream. (Not that I had first to assemble it from the parts necessary to accompany the action, to base it or continue it; I have only to describe it out of my head.) And as often as I think of the subject, it again stands before me exactly.

Composing (writing poetry) is nothing other than dreaming awake (artistic dreams, willed dreams). The dream

34

"composes," also it creates the events, lifts out the essential, comprises the experiences.

If poetry and dream are identical, then dream play is the summit of the poetic art.

Association in poetry and in dream.

In poetic creation, the poet as in the dream says many a thing that he would otherwise not say and also veils and displaces as in dreams: he lets it be said by other persons. (Dream and drama—identical).

November 21

Youth appears to men like a dream, in which he remembers himself. Always a basic affect accompanies this recollection, mostly joys (of the living wish), which are comparable to the affect that marks the own person in dreams. This affect is related to experience as the dream to the period of youth.

At this point Rank, usually so quick to give quotations, to acknowledge sources, plunges into the analysis of dreams or rather the phenomenon of dreaming, in relation to art and life, with his characteristic turning to the universal application of an idea, but with no further reference to Freud's *Traumdeutung*, which is obviously his inspiration. It is as though in Freud he found a psychology so apparently akin to his own that it supplied just the impetus he needed to develop his nearly formulated thinking on dreams. While he is interested in his own dreams and frequently records them, he seems not to dwell on their personal interpretation in Freudian terms but always to turn to the fact of dreaming as such and its place in art and the creative necessity of the artist. Now he creates on the Freudian base his own understanding of what the dreamer experiences, in vivid, dramatic terms:

The dream begins when the dream thoughts become unpleasant (when thoughts become oppressive internally, then

35

art begins also). *Dream thoughts:* in waking, those wishes in the way of whose fulfilment lie obvious difficulties are always repressed, suppressed, postponed. If the man has fallen asleep, the conventional dress stripped off, then these denied elements (reality) can stir and force the man to look at the impossibility of his wish. If they now press him so strongly that he cannot avoid it, then the dream sets in; torn at the same time by the persistent opposition of these voices, which try to overcome his ego, his abilities, his success, his hopes, which attack his honor, will he wake up to defend his personality (which sometimes happens when one, without having dreamed, suddenly starts wildly from sleep)? Generally, however, sleep is stronger and does not wholly release him. Then he brews for himself a middle way. He opposes to these negations not only his real deeds, qualifications, abilities, but to make the effect more certain, he exaggerates (convention is again awakened), in order to take the field against convention, he enhances, he falsifies, he sets up his wishes as facts, as if he would say: see there! But in any position the dreamer is ensnared, goaded by the hostile voices, into the web of lies at the point where the connection between dream and reality splits open most clearly; he still tries with a new web of lies to close the holes; but the more he entangles himself, the more clearly the opponents point at the deception. When the man now knows no more to do, he might, in order to spare himself the disgrace of being blamed, (convention) wake up. Although the forces pressing toward waking are already stronger than they were earlier, still usually sleep is stronger; the scene of the dream is transposed and the game begins anew.

The first hint of any therapeutic interest is found in the entry of November 30:

How a physician can even interpret the dream of a patient. In order to be able to unravel all the fine implications, hints, connecting threads, he must know not only the life of the patient as it is in his memory, as he can perhaps tell it to him, but as it has actually happened. For the dream has its source probably in the memories of youth, but they are first awakened through interpretation as the dream itself does not let them come over the threshold of consciousness.

At the close of the second *Daybook*, where he is recreating Freud's dream theories freely with no apparent thought of differing, he actually gives utterance to what will return to him after twenty years of discipleship as fundamental difference, although at this point he does not appreciate its significance:

December 1
The dream can only be directed to the fulfilment of wishes in the truest scene of the word and cannot fulfil the deepest striving of man, nor the core of his highest life; for generally a dream of one short night is sufficient to bring out the desired result, as if the wish were really fulfilled; to the fulfilment of this highest willing, however, a whole life is always demanded. (Wish: something that could have been left undone; lustful—sensuous.)

And again: "Wishes are phenomena of will. The dream splits the will into wishes. In a dream the wishes are the driving element, in life the will itself."

DAYBOOK III

The third *Daybook*, dated January, 1905—April, 1905, begins with a quotation from Kierkegaard that foreshadows the trend of Rank's development:

And this is the marvelous thing about life, that every man, who takes cognizance of himself, knows what no science

*knows, for he knows how he himself is: and this is the deep
insight of the Greek. . . .*

Kierkegaard, 1813

The rapidly growing maturity is evidenced by the shift
from the recording of purely personal pain to psychological
interest in his own inner processes, which runs parallel to his
deepening grasp on the lives and works of the great men with
whom his every moment seems to be occupied. The extent of
his reading, the scope of his writing, increase by such bounds
that one might well believe he was without a job, as he no
longer complains of its encroachment on the intellectual life.
While he is obviously utilizing the Freudian psychology at
every step, he keeps his relation to Schopenhauer's will and
to Nietzsche's insights. One might expect him to give thanks
to Freud, as he has repeatedly to Schopenhauer and Nietzsche,
but never a word is recorded. He seems to take Freud for
granted, to be used as a tool already familiar and actually
only a sharpening of something inherently his own. With the
help of this tool, he will analyze the great artists, and art itself,
as well as his own development; but always in his own unique
terms.

January 23

*I have now completed three novels.[5] I can't believe that
they are entirely without some importance, for in each inheres
so much life, seen, experienced, written; dreams, so much
heart's blood, one might say. I would not be able to sit down
now and without ado write such an outline although I lack
neither material nor thoughts for it. These novels had to be
written (just as dreams must be dreamed), had to be written
just as they are. I will perhaps sometime describe how they
have arisen; that would make a very interesting study. And
these three little works are inwardly organically related, at least*

[5] Fragments of these novels are found among his manuscripts.

for me; each a preserved bit of my life and in each the previous overcoming, but still with gentle, dreamy, sad echoes in them, like a lost youth. And to think that perhaps sometime the first fellow can smear them with his dirty fingers, his bleary eyes, his filthy soul.

The three novels are the different settings of a dream. The end comes every time, when something is about to happen against my will.

Another entry refers casually to an uncompleted essay on Wagner and thoughts that then went into *Der Künstler*. There is no further reference in the *Daybooks* to what is to be his first book and the basis for his introduction to Freud, although he was evidently absorbed in extracting the essence of his wide reading and extensive writing for use in the major effort of these early years.

There follows as entries of *Daybook III* what must be the result of months of previous work, detailed analyses of every opera of Wagner as to plot, characterization, development, and symbolic meaning; a tremendous task. The ultimate published result of all this thought and labor is to be found in his doctoral dissertation for the University of Vienna on "The Lohengrin Saga."

The following comments give some indication of the nature of his thinking about one artist, Wagner. He is giving a kind of outline or plan for the contemplated essay but concludes as he inevitably does, with generalizations on art and artist:

The man of genius perceives sex impulse as sin and through his purity the woman becomes useless, aimless, she is released from the slavery of sensuality; but as she cannot know the metaphysical, the divine, so she dies.
Wagner: Evolution of all art into the drama.
  Form: Drama—Dream
  The same results with poet and dreamer

The displacement of the dream: dream work, means, end analagous.

The displacement of the drama: work—means—end

The agreement—unity

Particularly Wagner: Transition: in addition to the music, the unconscious

Effect—Methods (Dream within dream, Hero)

The several works (analyses)

General consideration.

Dutchman—masturbation

Tannhäuser—prostitutes

Lohengrin—impotence

Tristan—adultery (sorrow of love)

Ring—for the power of degenerate sex drive

Meistersinger—art

Parsifal—Purity of man (sexual abstinence) and thereby conditioned purity of the woman

Wolfram and Sachs sublimate their love: they are artists. Elizabeth saves Tannhäuser. II Act—Eva "saves" Stolzing. Entrance March: Entrance of Meistersinger. The fact is that just in the Meistersinger the thematic fugue and counterpoint are carried out with such art and skill, are connected with the material internally; it expresses very well the conventional, inherited, customary, the form in which still in spite of all the pedantic rules and commands the new can evolve, even if it were through the disrupting of these forms.

Stolzing's figure remains thus, even from the first conception where Wagner identifies himself only with him; later he identified himself also with Sachs; he contrasts in the Meistersinger at once his youth and his ripe age.

Wagner's works are therefore the highest art, because they not only give back the being of man, increased, concentrated, made poetry, but the essence of the gifted (Lohengrin); in Wagner there is already much that is conscious.

One of the critical moments in Wagner's art is the personification of the emotions of his hero. (Dream) Motifs are then only the essential moments, the formed appearances of the unconscious, not the unconscious itself.

Myth harmonizes with Wagner's own demands for the ideal form of a work of art; besides it was the feeling content immanent in the myth, the powerful perceptivity, which drew the musician.

Wagner as artist, the highest form of this species. The always clearly and fully recognizable personal influence on the creating. (Through the detailed Biography.) The constant dissatisfaction in the life of the present, even under favorable outer conditions; all in the highest measure: the suffering of genius.

Just as the dreamer opposes to the denying voices (the repressed) not only his affirming promises, hopes, but handles his wishes as facts, so the artist opposes to the oppressive threatening life not only his power of resistance, his abilities, his individuality, his genius, but he incorporates all simultaneously in the deed, in creative work. Great artists always had to struggle and to suffer. In the dream the wishes through the burning point of the will are guided through and made into the universal. In art that is the work of genius, to lift out from the individual wishes the universal and pure human.

While in *Daybook III* he never tires of his efforts to understand Jesus of Nazareth, whom he is forever analyzing in comparison with Nietzsche, and works ceaselessly on his comprehension of the artist through his intensive study of Wagner, his deepest concern lies inevitably in the realization of his developing self, with only a single reference to physical pain or illness.

January 14, 1905

If the world is my projection, so is becoming conscious of this projection my birth. The will expresses itself through the act of becoming born; from there on it is no longer present as such. Life is a constant struggle between will and intellect.

January 15

My soul seems to have in it something of the sting of the donkey-whip. The more I struggle against it, the deeper it cuts into my flesh. A modern sword of Damocles hung within the man, by which he pricks himself with every movement, like Demosthenes. Illness can scourge a man! Oh! (Written about half past eight o'clock at night with terrible head and foot pains. The acute pain in the legs.)

January 17

I can now picture the growth of the child in the mother's body approximately; also the emotions and sensations of the mother. I trace a work of mine in its growth; not somewhat slowly and gradually, so that I constantly at every moment noticed something about it, but I often do not know at all for a long time that I am carrying something around with me; but then, all at once I perceive that it has grown; not just in the sense of becoming larger; many a time it has fallen through and become replaced by something more complete, or has been put together for clearer form, as with the embryo. This backward growing seems accordingly to come at long intervals, so that I must always first lie low for a time, before the work can draw out the essence necessary to its growth (like nourishment).

Already he is going beyond the *work* of the artist to the value of the personality as itself a creation, perhaps with a reproach to himself for his many exhaustive and exhausting hours of study and his withdrawal from the social.

January 24

The most beautiful in an artist's life is that which he can not work out. An artist, whose work would be his life! the

42

ultimate! If the whole man, the whole life is not contained in every moment of life, as the sea in its drops, then life has no sense! What is nature doing with the many lost days, hours, lives? How much the least of living men has the advantage over even the greatest of the dead.

and again:

March 27

What another has said never has validity for me until I have experienced it myself; then, however, it has validity only for me.

Living is the only point. How can one do nothing but write as long as one still has the expectation of living? Art has hitherto been entirely falsely directed. Life itself must be formed creatively and indeed in and of itself, not confused with an artificial artist life. The actual life must be so created that it needs no art of any other life, lying beyond itself.

There is a new realization, as well as a new despair, in his entry of January 28:

I know very surely that I have not been made to write mere novels or romances or poems or essays. For that I already know much too much of such things; for that, I have already looked too deeply into the inner world mechanism. Also dramas, in the sense in which they are understood, I can not write. But still no goal, no prospect; the struggle between science and fantasy in me. I stand outside, an unrelated spectator.

Even the following brief comment seems to anticipate Rank the analyst, who would one day refuse to annihilate the individual with theory:

February 15

A medically constituted artist!

Often I grasp a whole man in one glance: what he is and

thinks, his past and his future. I make his whole life thereby superfluous, I kill him because I think him through to an end: for what then does he live? May he not be able to live his life more beautifully than I think!

The following entry I have included because it typifies Rank's intense feeling for animals, particularly dogs, but also shows his use of every experience to deepen psychological insight. However, it is noteworthy that the insight never prevents the immediacy and reality of the emotion.

February 18

Today I saw a dog, trembling and with tail between legs, sitting on the street. From his sad eyes shone all the suffering that ever was endured in the world. The sight brought a lump to my throat and tears to my eyes. I had to turn away and go on quickly. But I could not forget it, so unspeakably sad was the picture. The dog certainly felt nothing in particular, perhaps hunger and cold; but I identified myself probably quite unconsciously and unintentionally with him, that is, I felt what I would have felt in his position; however, in order to be able to feel it, I must have perceived myself already partially in this condition or better said (inwardly, that is), humanized and exaggerated (to that corresponds also the exaggerated pity) which again more than partially is, as it were, concentrated, symbolized, and created; the outer picture was the symbol of my inner one. As sadly as his eyes appeared, my mood looked into the world on all the passers-by. How quickly, without any thought, sympathy accomplishes this comparison—the man knows nothing of it: he must first interpret the act.

There follows a keen analysis of Schopenhauer's will in relation to the function of the intellect. Schopenhauer exerts a profound influence on Rank's thinking but never seems to come into the picture in terms of his personality as does Nietzsche.

The closing entry of *Daybook III*, made in March, 1905, shows us what Rank himself has not yet grasped, the clear indication of the direction his genius is taking, however obscured by his aloneness and isolation:

Self-observation is not only one of the most wonderful but also one of the most rewarding capacities of man. Thus I know nothing more interesting than me myself, than my development. I grow steadily always forward in a certain direction. I do not know whether my activity, thinking, reading, writing, observing, is the cause of this growth or whether I only do everything from the outside, in order to pass the time and thereby only seek not to hinder the inner ripening. I almost believe it is that way: for in the first place nothing that comes to me from the outside does me any good before I am inwardly ready for it, before I myself have experienced it. Secondly, however, my activity satisfies me not at all; what I read has not the height and depth that dazzle the hours in which I doubt myself; what I write has not the form and the content that would give me the courage, to create self-consciously (overconsciously would be the right word) and undisturbed by all else; what I think—yes, that is really my best part—that I cannot put into form without thereby losing its character and what I see is so horribly superficial that it is not worth the trouble of going to the bottom of it. The most exciting is introspection and the feeling of joy that streams through me in such moments. However, I cannot entice these moments at will, but they come over me from time to time, as it were to strengthen me, so that I may hold out. And at every such moment I feel myself tremendously grown, as contrasted with the earlier stages; in the interval, all has ripened silently and unconsciously, as in an embryo.

Then my plans of yesterday and the day before seem to me childish and immature and I seize from this experience only the briefest moment, in order to see it emerge again next time even more deepened and refined. That is also the reason why I cannot bring any work to completion now: for to do that I would have to break into my development violently. Also it has to do with an unconquerable, firm, inner resistance that keeps me from creating something amid the intricacy of thinking. I would have to confine the growing, the going forward and upward into one point, and let the development go into breadth, like a wanderer who, arriving at a river, does not know how to get across, and who now runs back and forth anxiously on the bank. If he had only jumped when he was still in motion; now he must go back and take a run. However, were the strongest resistance overcome, had I made the stoppage, therewith would also have been connected a monstrous advantage. I could free myself from all ballast, from all overflowingness. Ripening could free me of my burden, which I already drag painfully, for it grows like an avalanche. I could then be free and go forward easily—and more quickly—If the growing would only stop! Woe!

How much limitation still lies in the word "Freedom." The goal of humankind lies neither in their end nor in the highest specimens but in strife, struggle, excelling, overcoming. Among the many people I know are three with whom I could perhaps associate for a long time, that is, with them the perception has not yet penetrated that I would not be able to associate with them. And now these sacred three!! With the one I come in contact almost daily; accordingly for the most part there is between us only the habitual interchange. This one possesses much that I lack: skill, unshatterable courage for living, blind optimism, iron will, desire for power, and much courage. Therefore I am satisfied by the mere being together with him.

With the second I am less often in contact. Our intercourse extends now and then to higher fields; but the age difference between us is still so important that nothing useful happens for me. He is so apparently finished; married, children, vocation, money, established views, character already congealed, completely my opposite. But on that account he is very useful to me. I learn from him tranquillity in thinking and speaking in the way of regular living. With the third I do not come in contact at all; I long for him the most; same age, like me in much, in much superior; flexible mind, keen judgment, iron industry, admirable ability to comprehend.

What I lack, that I love in the three. I am alone, quite alone. (That, no man can think through who has not previously felt it through.) I have no one with whom I can speak, no one to whom I can write. The most and the best remains inside me, as nourishment (in good and evil sense), the rest is Daybook.

All art is representation of a whole for the power of imagination. A new whole, as said, or an old one to bring the new in the truest and most vital way to the souls of men, is art.

Night before last at daybreak there came to me, I know not whether in dream or half waking (I think it was that) the thought that Schopenhauer's will were better called the primary intellect, in contrast to the actual intellect (the secondary). Evidently I would deduce that the intellect is better called the secondary will.

Whence would I have had my practical psychological knowledge if I had not been guided to it by J.F.N. (Nietzsche). The mixture in me is above all the most wonderful that I know.

DAYBOOK IV

Prophetic of the approaching end to the daybooks is the beginning paragraph of *Daybook IV*:

Vienna, April 10—July 1, 1905
It is actually quite unnecessary to carry on a daybook. Great thoughts, as often as they have any kind of associative connection, emerge into consciousness throughout our whole life. These thoughts are few in number with an individual and unforgettable but only such thoughts would deserve to be noted.

There is little of the purely personal in this period but that little contains the only reference to the possibility of a future love relation for himself.

"Love at first sight?" Yes, but it must have the chance to deepen. Two people who love at first sight and then never meet again will soon forget each other. Mostly opportunity (habit) counts in regard to love.
When I think that "the woman" who is "created for me" is yet to be found! I cannot believe that nature can produce something, where my boldest fantasy limps.

That he is only just twenty-one can still be discerned despite the increasing depth of his psychological theories.
I am reading "Goethe's sayings." I find a whole series of thoughts that I have thought independently and expressed often in almost the same words. How I rejoiced over it!!
I have been alone for the longest time. Entirely concentrated on myself. I associate only with me myself, with forms that I create. That might be not the least of the factors that have made me a poet, for that I am: the only question is whether I shall remain one?

Living and thinking are not to be combined. One must decide for one of the two, together they are impossible. But alternately! That is the highest! (Goethe?)

He to her: First I will tell you which of your faults disturb me, then I will tell you which I love. Your virtues do not interest me: they are for everyone!

Again, his entries go into universals:

April 15
An artist must be convinced blindly and immovably of his ability if he wants to create. Yes, I might maintain that the creators of great works of art must consider themselves as the greatest artists of mankind.
April 16
When a man has learned the compass and extent of his capacity for development, he ought really to die. The masters never learn to know themselves completely: with them, therefore, death always comes too early. The more seasonably one dies, the earlier was he mature, completed.

What then has he to expect, who has understood himself wholly? Of what then should his life consist? (This day, July 19, 1905, I should answer, "in living"; at that time I believed the highest life consisted in artistic creativity.[6] Instead of "know thyself" I would write over the doors of the temple of modern artists: "Seek to know thyself." The chief thing is the seeking.

Every great thinker holds himself to be the apex of evolution. That faith is the noblest kind of egoism.

The source of the change in his belief can be understood from the entry of April 20 and the succeeding development, as well as the dramatic alteration in his outlook for the future.

[6] Apparently he was copying into the *Daybook* notes written on April 16 but copied on July 19.

April 20

I have just begun, after a three-month pause, to work farther on my theory of artistic creativity. I read from the first notes (2-20-05) always only a key word and then write down freely anything further I have to add to it. Only when I have indicated everything that belongs to a thought complex do I look in the first ms. to see whether I have omitted a point, and then I notice in the repeated material that I have written much with exactly the same words as three months before although in the interval I have consciously not thought of it.

From this point on, Rank is obviously concentrating on the two chapters that constitute *Der Künstler*, the first fruit of his genius, the little manuscript that will prove to be the open sesame to a future of which he has never dared to dream. Now he is using Freud's writings freely, accepting them as psychological fact and learning from them the meaning of hysteria, neurosis, psychosis with such complete inner comprehension that he can utilize these categories in his attempt to characterize the function of the artist in cultural evolution. It is hard to remember, in his complete taking possession of all the psychoanalytic terms, that he has never had any firsthand experience in psychotherapeutic relationships. However, regardless of his dependence on Freud's writings, Rank's unique approach to art and artist is unmistakable.

April 29

There must be lacking in the dream some element of watchfulness. I believe it is reason: this is a function, a synthesis of the impressions of the sense organs. But in the dream the reversed process takes place and the inner cause here is the unconscious, which objectified itself out of the stored sense impressions, so the reason is absent therein.

Above all, the connection between memory and the unconscious!

One can't "bring up" an artist. For if one could do away with all that could inhibit the development of a man, then he could never come into that terrible conflict with the world that is necessary to make an artist of him. If, however, one wanted to introduce the conflicts intentionally this experiment would be very risky, as one could never observe the limits as finely as do the real relationships.

The greatest works come from the deeps.

The artist in the act of their creation fluctuates for the most part between life and death; he "chooses" between suicide and creating, between art and hysteria; if there is a grain too much of resistance, if the delivery does not occur at the right time, then the artist falls. But even if all that were possible, who would unburden on his son so many severe hardships, suffering that goes psychically as well as physically to the uttermost limits of life, which are, however, necessary to make a great artist. Living means then nothing other than to find resistances. The process of clarification, over which the entire development of the human race is spread out, is a resolving of the unconscious into consciousness: that is culture.

As the days go on, Rank's absorption in the unconscious, the affects, the instincts, especially the sexual instinct, would indicate that his final attempt at a complete organization of his views in *Der Künstler* is approaching a successful conclusion, for he declares on May 10:

It comes only to this, that one has the courage to universalize his experience; whoever has this courage, his generalizations are correct.

51

That courage Rank never lacked.

May 13 brings the triumphant outburst of youth that has found the answer, but with characteristic awareness of the penalty attached to absolutes:

Now I see everything clearly: the world process is no longer a riddle; I can explain the whole culture, yes, I can explain everything. What shall I be able to do with the remainder of my life?

DER KÜNSTLER

His answer, intellectually speaking, is to be found among his papers, in what would seem to be a carbon copy of the original, entitled *Der Künstler, Ansätze zu einer Sexual Psychologie*. (*The Artist, Approach to a Sexual Psychology*.) It consists of two chapters, of forty-eight pages typed double-space, entitled, I. *Die Sexuelle Grundlage* (*The Sexual Foundation*), and II. *Die Künstlerische Subliemierung* (*Artistic Sublimation*). He has rapidly assimilated and utilized for his own purpose everything of Freud's available in 1905: *Traumdeutung, Drei Abhandlungen zur Sexual Theorie, Der Witz und seine Beziehung zum Unbewussten, Zur Psychopathologie des Alltagslebens, Studien über Hysterie*.

One might expect him to be embarrassed by these riches but so complete is his possession of his own thinking, with its philosophic basis in Schopenhauer and Nietzsche, that Freudian theory merely provides affirmation and further material for its development. Not that he fails to acknowledge the source, as always, but it never hampers his freedom or his capacity for universalizing.

I will not attempt to indicate the content of *Der Künstler*, which I find extremely difficult to understand and to characterize; but I include two paragraphs from my rough translation of Chapter II that reveal the youth and daring of the author.

The external God with his praise of the Creation—and behold it was good—was a grave mistake, an expression of that "monstrous displacement of the affects" with which all human knowledge begins. Only philosophy after many thousand years of work finally brought it through in Schopenhauer to a revaluation of everything psychic; roughly, the human will is the long-sought God who directs and guides everything and now man dares to presume to bring down judgment on the world—and behold it was bad.

In the final paragraph, his youthful enthusiasm, sustained by Freudian doctrine, breaks forth in affirmation of faith for the future, an expression of the positive, constructive attitude, which, despite ill health, ill fortune, and alternation of mood, characterized his relation to life to the end.

And now as the conditions for the cure of neurosis have been given, there is opened up a broader outlook on the future of the human race. Humanity may face hysteria, the inevitable end of every cultural development, with hope, for now, if it can surmount this ending, it may be able to construct a way out, and if formerly the peoples came to grief in the neurosis, now they will go clear through it and thereby become enlightened. But only if a complete change of attitude toward everything psychic has come to pass, the whole unconscious become conscious, then will the "unartist" asexual man stand in the midst of life, light and strong like a God, and direct and rule his instincts with a sure hand.

At this juncture, the *Daybook* ends abruptly with no recording of how this proud, reticent young man ever reached

Freud with his manuscript. A single reference to Adler, in a footnote of *Der Künstler*, where he acknowledges as the source of an idea a lecture given by Adler to a teacher's association in April, 1905, indicates the way in which he probably got to Freud's lecture room, introduced and evidently encouraged by Adler himself, as Jones has noted.[7] The date is uncertain but Freud makes a brief reference to Rank's coming in his early account of the beginnings of psychoanalysis published in *Collected Papers*.

One day a young man who had passed through the technical training school introduced himself with a manuscript which showed very unusual comprehension. We induced him to go through the Gymnasium and the University and to devote himself to the nonmedical side of psychoanalytic investigation. The little society acquired in him a zealous and dependable secretary and I gained in Otto Rank a faithful helper and co-worker.[8]

What this must have opened up to the solitary youth who had seen no way out of his enslavement to mechanical work, who had found no friend or equal in his intellectual pursuits, and who alternated between despair of his fate and ecstatic realization of his gifts, is hardly to be imagined. But for Rank to take real help, as he certainly did, for he had neither backing of others nor resources of his own beyond the weekly wage, must have been a deeply moving experience. And to be encouraged thus by a generous appreciative Freud who made this miracle possible!

I could wish that there had been a *Daybook* V to give us the picture, but for him no daybook was needed—now he had a group of equals or even superiors to whom he could relate. Only one who understands what it could mean to a young man isolated by his own superiority to find in human acces-

[7] Jones, *op. cit.*, Vol. II, p. 8.
[8] Freud, *Collected Papers*, London: Hogarth Press, Ltd., Vol. I, p. 307.

sible form the ideal figure, denied to him in childhood, can estimate the depth of Rank's relation to Freud. It released him to what must have been a frenzy of work that he wanted for its own sake, but that he must have felt also that he owed to Freud, whose generosity had opened to him not only the higher education he could never have obtained unaided, but whose backing meant the opportunity to publish his own writings. At any rate he gave himself and his labor without stint to every new obligation.[9]

The first fruit of the new life was the publication of *Der Künstler* in 1907. The manuscript had been thoroughly discussed with Freud and rewritten on the basis of his criticism. Freud was always disturbed by Rank's impetuous way of breaking into the middle of a problem, taking the historical or scientific underpinning for granted, never hesitating to apply any conclusion in universal terms.

The immediate effect of Freud's teaching appears in Rank's introduction to the first edition. In this he gives a logical and chronological account of the development of Freudian psychoanalysis up to this point in a brief review of every one of the texts to which he had referred in the original version, for the most part in footnotes, and with assumption of the point of view as brought out in his own account. Freud, a scientist, insisted always on a systematic presentation of new material and deplored premature generalization or philosophic speculation. Freud was laboratory trained. Rank had no concrete experience with the data on which Freudian theory rested, aside from introspective observation and extensive reading. The astonishing fact, which no one seems to have noted, is that Freud saw in this slight work of an untutored youth of twenty-one something that had sufficient originality and value for psychoanalysis to warrant his careful criticism and help

[9] The struggle to finance his higher education during this period is indicated in a formal application to a state-controlled foundation, Die Leopold Trebisch'sche Stiftung, for a stipend in November, 1909, which was not granted.

toward its publication. That his judgment was correct is evidenced by the immediate success of the little book, which required a second edition in 1918, and a third and fourth, in 1925, when additional material from his literary studies was included as indicated in a new title, *Der Künstler und Andere Beiträge zur Psychoanalyse der Dichterischen Schaffens*.[10] It has never been translated into English although I find among Rank's papers a letter from a Mr. Adam Empie in New York, dated April 3, 1928, enclosing a translation of the first and second introduction as well as of Chapter I, showing that Rank was thinking of an English publication. I am using Mr. Empie's translation of the introduction to the second edition to show Rank's attitude toward his first work from the perspective of twelve years in time, the distance of many miles in space, and the separating experience of a military station in Poland at the time of the first world war.

There is always something awkward in observing oneself in the mirror of one's own past, particularly when no inner necessity but some outer impulse drives one to such a review and to meditation of this sort. Certainly it is not pleasant to be reminded that one has grown older; but it may be still more painful to observe how young one once was. . . . The single consolation in this fact, perhaps, is that just this involuntary pause in my own work makes possible a more objective judgment of this first step upon ticklish analytic ground, insofar as so generally subjective a way of observation and presentation as I employed at that time allows an objective appraisement. But it is just this that makes such a revision all the more worthwhile, as the final success of this little book shows that others were also able to find in it something allied to themselves. So it may be that the only solu-

---

[10] *The Artist and Other Contributions to the Psychoanalysis of Literary Creativity.*

tion is to test the earlier subjective theories at their present subjective value, which is nothing else than to explain the present attitude of the author to this product of his earlier period.

What, a priori, gives this work general foundation and scientific support is the fact that it rests upon the solid basis of Freud's psychology, and, moreover, has those immediate philosophical forerunners of psychoanalysis, Schopenhauer and Nietzsche, to thank for suggestions of many sorts. At the same time, the proneness to speculation, too much exaggeration, and a desire for a perception of the whole, is to be excused by the youthfulness of the author. . . .

The word "artist" is used here in a sense as comprehensive as Freud's use of the term "sexuality" and ultimately for the bounds that enclose the entire cultural development within which the artist is produced ontogenetically. . . . The viewpoint of individual psychology (which is the real psychoanalytic one) was neglected in favor of the genetic point of view. . . . To show the psychological factor by which the artist became possible, as well as inevitable in a cultural development, which progresses from the outward, inwardly and rises constantly, is the real, even though unconfessed purpose of this book. . . . For the artist represents the highest stage of development on the way from real (objective) civilization to inner culture, upon which mankind through inner enrichment seeks to replace these fragments of reality that were abandoned on account of outer need. According to a thought of Freud, the artist is able to restore by a peculiar roundabout way this originally pleasurable relationship to the outer world that mankind lost in attaining civilization. Thus, within the bounds of the highest culture, the artist resolves again in harmony the discord between the inner and the outer world, which had finally become unbearable.

. . . The time between has indeed enriched the author in

years and in experience but also has led mankind to the edge of a prodigious cultural catastrophe in the face of which all the deductions and prospects to be gotten from the possibilities of a straightforward development of civilization must seem to us transient and futile.

(Luhatschowitz, September, 1917)

11 *The years of association with Freud*

IN VIENNA, 1906-1925

For an immediate, vivid picture of the total change in Rank's environment in the first years of his association with Freud I have turned to Hanns Sachs's loving account of his own relation to Freud, which of necessity included mention of Rank, his close friend of this period. While Sachs makes no claim to objectivity, his honest acknowledgment of Rank's superior position in the inner circle carries conviction, the more that he can hardly bear the memory, much less the fact of Rank's later defection:

This is my confession: I have reason to think that Freud did not find in me some of those qualities which he valued most highly. In the bond between us something was missing —the something that leads to spontaneous intimacy between characters of similar type and tone. I am not speaking here

61

of the difference in our intellectual level, nor of the gulf that separates the genius from ordinary minds. I was aware of that all the time, but I took it for granted, as a necessary part of the relation between master and the eternal disciple. But these special qualifications which I did not possess, he found in others who were cast like me in the role of disciples; in Ferenczi and Abraham and certainly in Rank (until the time when a total change in Rank's character severed all former ties.)[1]

It was inevitable that Rank and Sachs should have combined, as of similar age and devotion to literature, together with the lack of medical training. They were constantly thrown together by their residence in Vienna and their common devotion to Freud. As Sachs records it:

In the meantime my friendship with Otto Rank had come as near to mutual intimacy as it is possible with a person of such extreme reticence in all personal matters as he was. Freud probably thought that it would be a good thing to have at least two men near him who were willing to team together without jealousies and animosities. Our friendship lasted until Rank turned his back on Freud and psychoanalysis, and during all these years our good relations were of great help to Freud in his task of building up the Psychoanalytic Association and in the editing of Zeitschrift and Imago.[2]

The intimacy of their contacts with Freud is revealed in the following account of the organizing of the first "Vorstand" (committee or board), a small intimate group that gathered around Freud in the lecture room once a week:

[1] Hanns Sachs, *Freud, Master and Friend*, Cambridge, Massachusetts: Harvard University Press, 1944, pp. 14–15.
[2] *Ibid.*, p. 60.

I think I was first appointed Librarian. The library consisted then of two or three shelves of books and the little work which was connected with it was performed by Rank, the secretary, who was "Lord Everything Else" with the exception of presiding at the meetings and keeping the accounts.

The actual change in my position was marked by my sitting from then on at the upper end of the table ("above the salt" so to speak) at Rank's side who, as secretary, had his place at Freud's left, and—this was of real importance— by the fact that Rank and I habitually accompanied Freud on his way home. In spite of his sedentary life, Freud was an indefatigable walker and the way home was extended to long promenades through the silent streets.[3]

During these delightful walks, the young men were privileged to hear about any new idea or theories that Freud was working on and even helped him to clarify his thoughts in discussion. They also shared in the rich store of anecdotes with which Freud often illustrated a point. Then came Sachs's suggestion for a new periodical to be devoted to applied psychoanalysis. This resulted in the founding of *Imago*, which was to be edited by himself and Rank, but for Sachs the most important part was the fact that with *Imago* and "the beginnings of my constant collaboration I became a regular guest (of Freud) on certain evenings—nearly always together with Otto Rank—and a permanent fixture of the 'inner circle.' "[4]

If one goes beyond this picture of the rare opportunity afforded these two for continuous contact with their idol, to inquire what else Rank was doing in this early period from the date of the publication of *Der Künstler* to his departure for Poland on army service in 1916, one is staggered by the

[3] *Ibid.*, p. 62.
[4] *Ibid.*, p. 66.

record of his labors indicated not only in the early letters from Freud [5] but in his own detailed listing and evaluation of his published work made for the benefit of the New York circle in 1930. How he managed to complete the Gymnasium and achieve a Ph.D. from the University of Vienna in 1912, while during the same period he published his second book, *Der Mythus von der Geburt des Helden*,[6] to which Freud himself contributed paragraphs on the family romance, is hard to understand unless one recalls the earlier reference to his "iron industry" and adds to that capacity an already fabulous background in literature and philosophy. If I did not have Rank's own accurate word for it, I could not credit the fact that he was also engaged in 1905 and 1906 on the writing of his first long detailed work entitled *Das Inzest-Motiv in Dichtung und Sage*.[7] For this monumental accomplishment he received much acclaim and on it probably established his reputation as a scholar.

Even Dr. Ernest Jones, who could never be accused of overestimating Rank's importance to Freud or to the psychoanalytic movement, confirms this picture in the following peculiarly conflicted statement:

Rank would have made an ideal private secretary and indeed he functioned in this way to Freud in many respects. He was always willing, never complained of any burden put upon him, was a man of all work for turning himself to any task and he was extraordinarily resourceful. He was highly intelligent and quick-witted. He had a special analytic flair for interpreting dreams, myths and legends. His great work on

[5] Although Rank seems to have saved every letter or note from Freud, there are only eight preceding the war in the collection. In view of their almost daily contact, letters were required chiefly when Freud was away from Vienna.

[6] *The Myth of the Birth of the Hero* together with *The Trauma of Birth* published by Robert Brunner, New York, 1952 (now Basic Books). Original English Translation 1914, *Nervous and Mental Disease Monograph Series*. Italian Translation, 1921.

[7] Published first in 1912, revised in 1926, translated into French in 1934, but never into English for publication.

incest myths which is not read enough nowadays is a tribute to his truly vast erudition; it was quite mysterious how he found time to read all that he did.[8]

The only reference I find to his work at the University, beyond the fact of his doctoral thesis, *Die Lohengrin Sage*,[9] which he records as "accepted by Professor Hans Much and probably the first one on psychoanalysis," is contained in an early letter from Freud on vacation that shows Freud's consideration for Rank's student labors and his wish to lighten them with an invitation to join him and Ferenczi in a visit to Dr. Jones in London as his guest if his work for the coming examinations will permit.[10] Evidently Rank accepted with pleasure, for Freud's warm letter of August 18, 1912[11] expresses gratification and also refers to "your book," which Ferenczi has praised, and hopes that Rank's decision in favor of the "pleasure principle" will not cause him to flunk his examinations in the fall. What the book in question may have been unless it was *Das Inzest-Motiv* I cannot determine. In any case the beautiful invitation came to nothing because of family trouble that kept Freud at home, and prevented the carrying out of a secondary objective, which, he says, was to bring Rank and Ferenczi into more intimate association.

As if these activities were not enough to occupy whatever time remained from his secretarial duties, I note that a long paper, "Ein Traum der Selbst Deutet" ("A Dream that Interprets Itself") appeared in the *Jahrbuch für Psychoanalyse*, II, 1910,[12] and received the following remarkable endorsement from Freud:

[8] Ernest Jones, *The Life and Work of Sigmund Freud*, New York: Basic Books, 1955, II, p. 160.
[9] Published 1911.
[10] Letter Freud to Rank, Karlsbad, August 11, 1912.
[11] Letter Freud to Rank, Karensee, August 18, 1912.
[12] An abstract of this article appeared in the *Psychoanalytic Review*, V, pp. 220–234.

Perhaps the best example of a dream interpretation is that published by Otto Rank, consisting of the analysis of two mutually related dreams of a young girl. These cover about two pages of print, while the analysis of them runs into seventy-six pages. It would need almost a whole term's lecture in order to give you a work of this magnitude.[13]

In the 1930 account of his works Rank adds:

There I modified Freud's formula for the dream in emphasizing the sexual material but also the actual wish fulfilment. Freud incorporated this formula in his third edition of Traumdeutung (1911) and carried it through to the last edition (the 7th, 1922). But when he prepared the volume of his collected papers in German published in 1925 he added a critical remark,[14] stating that he had only mentioned my formula but never accepted it. He adds that the quoting of my modification has led people to the repeated criticism that Psychoanalysis maintains that all dreams have a sexual content.

Although Freud ultimately took back, with this criticism, what had seemed to be complete approval, the fact remains that in 1910, only four years after his advent, Rank had dared to enter Freud's preserve in the analysis and interpretation of a young girl's dreams and had been applauded in print by the master.

In collaboration with Hanns Sachs he also published in 1913 a book entitled *Die Bedeutung der Psychoanalyse für die Geisteswissenschaften.*[15] To this add two substantial papers, *Die Nacktheit in Sage und Dictung*[16] (*Nakedness in Myth and Poetry*) read at the third International Conference

[13] Freud, *Introductory Lectures on Psycho-analysis,* London: G. Allen & Unwin, Ltd., 1922, p. 156.
[14] Freud, *Gesammelte Schriften* Bd. III, p. 31.
[15] *The Significance of Psychoanalysis for the Mental Sciences, Nervous and Mental Disease Monograph Series,* No. 23, 1915.
[16] *Imago,* II, 1913.

on Psychoanalysis, and *Der Doppelgänger*[17] (*The Double*), and it would seem that Rank's leisure time from 1906 to the war years and his period of service in Poland has been accounted for.

The call to service in 1914, when Austria began World War I with her declaration of war on Serbia, took both Rank and Sachs into a training camp, apparently not far from Vienna, but Sachs was soon released as his health was impaired. Rank, from his own account of his poor physical endowment, might well have anticipated a like outcome but apparently his editorial gifts were recognized and he was sent to Poland in January, 1916. There he became the energetic editor of the *Krakauer Zeitung*, which served as the official organ of the armed services. I find in the papers in my possession only a few fragments from that determining experience.[18] On the back of a masterly advertisement for the paper[19] (which is interesting in itself as well as a revela-

[17] *Imago*, III, 1914.
[18] In correspondence with Dr. Ernest Jones, I have learned of the existence of letters between Rank and Freud during this war interval that could have been made available to me had I been in England.
[19] KRAKAUER ZEITUNG

zugleich amtliches Organ des k.u.k. Festungs-Kommandos Krakau.

Krakau, Datum des Poststemples.

P.T.
Wir erlauben uns hiermit, ihre Augmerksamkeit auf die

"KRAKAUER ZEITUNG"

zu lenken, die die einzige deutsche Tageszeitung in Galizien (weit über 8 Millionen Einwohner) ist und von dem gebildeten, kaufkräftigen Publikum gelesen wird. Die "Krakauer Zeitung" ist gleichzeitig amtliches Organ des k.u.k. Festungs-Kommandos und geht nicht nur ins Hinterland, sondern auch an die Fronten, Sie verfügt über einen vorzüglichen Nachrichtendienst und pflegt auch den literarischen, künstlerischen und wissenschaftlichen Teil. Sie verzeichnet die einlaufenden Neuerscheinungen des Buchandels und bespricht die bedeutenderen Werke.

Bücheranzeigen haben in der "Krakauer Zeitung" den besten Erfolg und wir bitten um rechtzeitige unverlangte Einsendung von Rezensions-Exemplaren.

Gleichzeitig machen wir Sie auf unseren inseratentarif aufmerksam.

[*translation of above appears on page 68*]

tion of the responsibility assumed by Rank, now a man of thirty-two but without any direct experience in newspaper work) there is a typed poem to a child, written in a gay rhythm that contrasts strangely with its underlying acceptance of man's ultimate fate. There are also rather detailed notes and clippings on a woman writer of the period, Grete V. Urbanitzcke, which indicate a new interest in the psychological problem of woman as artist.

In the second volume of Dr. Jones's biography of Freud, he mentions as fact without verification that Rank had two spells of depression during his service in Poland. In Volume III the number of depressions is increased to three, now interpreted as the beginning symptoms of what was later to be accepted by the inner circle as the underlying cause of his deviation from psychoanalysis. The fact of three depressions within the three years of his exile, lightened only by a "month's holiday in Constantinople and a couple of fleeting visits to Vienna" [20] is not recognized by Jones as even partially related to the effect of a war that depressed many less sensitive souls than Rank and at a greater distance from its horrors. A few poems remaining from this period reveal the depth of melancholy to which he must often have been reduced but they also reveal the artist's ability to utilize every experience creatively. As one discerns from the *Daybooks*, Rank was always in possession of his inner experiences, however terrifying. Whatever was known of these wartime depressions was certainly revealed, if at all, by Rank

---

Roughly, footnote 19 reads: We beg to direct your attention to the Krakauer Times, which is the only German daily in Galicia (with over 8 million inhabitants) and is read by the educated, well-to-do public. The K.Z. is at the same time the official organ of the K.U.K. command-fortress and goes not only into the hinterland but also to the fronts. It provides a superior news service and also stresses the literary, artistic, and scientific interests. It notes the new publications of the booksellers and reviews the more important works. Ads for books give the best results in the K.Z. and we ask you to send in review copies without request. At the same time let us call your attention to our rates for advertising.
[20] Jones, *op. cit.*, Vol. II, p. 187.

himself, unless they may have been perceived by his wife or Freud in the brief visits to Vienna, but hardly in such definite numerical terms.

Whatever his moods, doubtless increased by the obligation to devote his best energies to an alien task, Rank managed to continue to the point of completion some literary investigations, probably already begun in Vienna, as indicated in his 1930 list of publications: "Homer, Psychologische Beiträge zur Entstehungsgeschichte des Volksepos," a first preliminary chapter in a study of the epics, and a second chapter, "Die Dichterische Phantasie-bildung."[21] He also brought out a second edition of *Der Künstler* and continued to work on *Psychologische Beiträge zur Mythenforschung* toward its publication in 1919. It is noteworthy that this marks the end of Rank's concentration on the application of psychoanalysis to literature and myth.

The literary studies and editorial duties that had occupied Rank so completely before the war years, as well as his swift rise to prominence in psychoanalytic circles, would have given him little opportunity to feel the need for a new role. Now with the war a new role has been forced upon him just at the point where his first driving interest in psychoanalysis, as the magic key to everything in literature, had been fulfilled and his craving for friends satisfied. Here for the first time he is standing alone with a responsible job, acquired because of his own qualifications. He is in a position of some power and community importance, which brings him in touch with many people and tests his ability for organization and adaptation in a new situation. Whatever Rank might be feeling, he had from childhood the ability to conceal the inner self and to carry on whatever was demanded of him with all his terrific energy concentrated on the task at hand. Here for the first time, it seems, Rank gets the ego reward of independence, of

---

[21] *Psychological Contributions to the Origin of the Folk Epic;* "Phantasy Formation in Poetry," *Imago,* V, 1917.

being his own man, responsible for others. He will never be "timid" or "deferential" [22] again, if he ever was inwardly, which is doubtful.

A marked change in the Rank who returned to Vienna in 1919 is emphasized by both Sachs and Jones. For the former friend, in the light of later events, it was an ethical change, a change in character; for the psychiatrist in looking back, it becomes primarily the manic state that would inevitably follow a depression. The astonishing fact, for Dr. Jones, is that Rank has lost his overpolite, deferential manner and has become, as he puts it, "tough," a man "with a masterful air."[23] That the new Rank could have been the end-result of a developmental growth process seems not to have occurred to anyone. Nor is there even an attempt to consider the emotional factors in the situation; the breaking up of the only effective group relationships Rank had ever known, the sudden release from the depths of his obligation to Freud, as well as the loss of the daily support on which he had come to depend with all the love and reverence he felt for this man, his first ego-ideal in the flesh.

The greatest change of all, however, goes with little attention to its importance, for in Cracow Rank met his fate, "the woman who is created for me,"[24] and married her on November 7, 1918, shortly before his return to Vienna. For a man with the make-up of the artist as Rank has understood it, this was indeed a tremendous event and if there were no fear or doubt associated with it one might well be surprised. To have come home to Vienna after three years' absence with a beautiful young wife, whose intellectual attainments rivaled her charm, must have done much to establish Rank on a new footing of equality as a man of family.

The return also coincides with the renewed functioning of

[22] Jones, *op. cit.*, Vol. II, p. 160.
[23] Jones, *op. cit.*, Vol. III, p. 12.
[24] Beata Tola Mincer.

the famous "Committee" originally suggested to Freud and Ferenczi by Jones at the time when defections from the group were disturbing to the movement, as early as 1912.[25] The intention was to form a small reliable group of psychoanalysts around Freud. Rank and Sachs were of course included and later Dr. Karl Abraham was induced to join them. The circle was completed by the addition of Dr. Max Eitingon in 1919. Sachs described the final plan given to this group by Freud following the disruption of the war years:

At the Hague in September, 1920, Freud called the six of us together and unfolded a plan to us which he had elaborated in detail. Henceforward we would form a co-ordinated, but strictly anonymous, group. The future of psychoanalysis should not be left to chance nor exposed to partisanship or personal ambition. It would be our duty to direct the ever widening movement by joining together and acting according to preconcerted plans. We ought to use for these ends our personal influence and our solidarity, but not rely on the authority given by office and title. To enable us to do our work unmolested the fact of our organization had to be kept secret. Our circle was to be considered as completed, once for all, without further co-operation by other members.

Since we lived in four different places (Freud and Rank in Vienna, Abraham, Eitingon, and myself in Berlin, Ferenczi in Budapest, Jones in London), we were to correspond at stated, not too long, intervals by circulating letters so that every member of the group would write and have the opportunity to read what had been written by all others. The letters were to include everything pertaining to our common interest: . . . At each convention we would meet and remain together a few days after the end of the meeting. When necessary a meeting of all or some of the group should be

25 Jones, *op. cit.*, Vol. II, p. 152.

arranged between conventions (which took place every second year).[26]

At the very center of this innermost circle was Rank, as the secretary by whom every communication was received and against whom every complaint could easily be lodged, especially as no one ever wished to blame Freud—who often tried to point out the misplaced affects but with little result.

That Rank, regardless of the lack of medical degree, should begin to practice psychoanalysis at this time was inevitable. Enveloped as he was in the continuous discussion of analytic problems, in intimate contact with Freud and every new development in his thinking, thrown into growing friendship with Ferenczi, who had keener interest in therapy than Freud, Rank's application of psychoanalytic insight could hardly be confined to myth and legend. Moreover, as a family man he must have been in need of more income than was available from his publications and his secretaryship. Freud, who never wanted more patients than were necessary to earn a living and provide him with material for research, certainly needed someone in Vienna to whom he could safely refer the applicants he was unwilling to accept, someone whom he trusted enough to recommend without reservation. Moreover, he would have been the first to see Rank's growing necessity for income and to try to meet it. While I find no reference to the exact date or occasion, it is evident from a letter of Freud to Ferenczi (March 20, 1924), relayed to Rank, in which he notes that Rank is only in his fourth year of practice, that Rank must have been taking patients by 1920.

To one who knows the incredible swiftness of Rank's intellectual processes and the immediacy of his awareness of a patient's emotional response, there would be every expectation that he would take possession of the therapeutic relationship with all the intensity of his interest in a new type of ex-

[26] Sachs, *op. cit.*, pp. 158–159.

perience and in the revelations bound to arise from his first direct contact with the original data of psychoanalysis. The turning of his energy to therapy, combined with the development of family concerns, now increased by the birth of a daughter (1920, August 23), and by the death of his elder brother Paul [27] (1921, January), must have influenced strongly his need for companionship with a fellow therapist, not as far above him as Freud, with whom to share the exciting new insights and whose family ties resembled his own. Ferenczi, although ten years Rank's senior and related to Freud on a more personal basis than Rank, seems to have had a similar need for the companionship Rank could offer. At any rate, this is the period, 1920–23, when their intimacy developed to the point of a joint undertaking resulting in 1923 in the little book entitled *Entwicklungsziele der Psychoanalyse*[28] upon which Freud looked somewhat askance from the first, for he always questioned Ferenczi's impulsive excursions from the beaten path.

In Rank's 1930 account of his works I find the following comment on *Entwicklungsziele*: "The first view of the analytic situation later incorporated in Volume I of *Technik der Psychoanalyse* . . . The main parts were written in the summer of 1922 and presented to Freud in September of 1922 before the International Conference of Psychoanalysis in Berlin. Whereupon he made our theme—the relation of theory and therapy and their mutual influence—a subject of competition.[29] In a letter, Freud appreciated the work as a correction of his understanding of the patient's repeating or acting out in the course of the analysis. Admitting that he

---

[27] A letter from an old friend, who was the lawyer for the Vienna Psychoanalytic Society, states that Paul had been working actively with Rank on the development of the society and the journals.

[28] *The Development of Psychoanalysis*. Nervous and Mental Disease Publishing Co., 1925. Translated by Caroline Newton.

[29] This is Rank's word, but its meaning is not clear. It may mean discussion or a topic for future papers.

73

had considered such occurrences as undesirable failures of technique, although he says that it is perfectly justifiable to try other ways, he himself is inclined to stick to his former technique."

This comment by Freud seems to me to be typical of his reactions to new findings by the disciples. He always asserts their right to experiment, but chiefly in matters of technique and usually ends with affirmation of his own former way, even though there might seem to be a contradiction involved. It is with Freud as with all human beings; no result is valid until one has been through the experience oneself. The actual analytic experiences of Rank and Ferenczi could never have been possible to Freud. But unless he could feel that basic psychoanalytic theory was threatened by them, there would be no indication of alienation on his side. These two were his hope for the future and such hope is not lightly abandoned.

For Ferenczi, the actual helping of patients was always a major concern. The so-called "active therapy" of this period was his contribution. What more natural than that he should have followed Rank's lead with enthusiasm at first? It was only much later, after Freud's final rejection of *The Trauma of Birth*, that he saw the threat to his relation to Freud and withdrew his name and contribution from their joint work.

Meantime, from the ten letters of this collection that Freud wrote to Rank during the vacation period July 8, 1922 through August 24, 1922, it becomes apparent that the problems arising through the Press, an English establishment directed by Jones, and the Publishing House in Vienna, directed by Rank, are increasing to an unpleasant degree.[30] Freud's sympathies and opinion are with Rank but he is anxious to smooth over the jealousies and antagonisms that he believes are being displaced upon Rank unfairly, and he is worried about their

[30] Dr. Jones's version of this situation, which naturally brings out his side, and attributes Freud's attitude to Rank's undue influence, is given in Vol. III, Chap. II, in detail.

effect upon the future of the movement in which he expects
Rank to fill an important role which, as he now sees, may be
hampered by the lack of a medical degree. He writes with his
usual honesty in the second letter of this period, July 8, 1922,
from Bad Gastein:

*I am never quite sure whether, at the crucial time, I did
right in keeping you from the study of medicine. I believe
upon the whole I was right; when I reflect upon my own
tedium during my medical studies I become more certain,
but when I see you move fully and rightly into the saddle of
the analyst, then the necessity to justify my own action
drops away.*

The tone of these letters, always friendly and full of consideration for Rank, would indicate to me a relationship of trust
and mutual liking on purely human grounds. There are always kind messages to Beata Rank and to "little Helen" with
concern for the interruption of their holidays by the delega-
tion of fresh tasks to Rank. There are painful references to
his own health and to a family tragedy but he is not too un-
well to continue his own writing or to give Rank the benefit
of his careful criticism of a proposed paper for the Congress.
In a second letter from Bad Gastein, dated July 10, 1922, he
writes:

Dear Doctor,
    *Yesterday I read your work through. As you know, I do not
like to judge the production of my close friends and colleagues because I have the fear that through my criticism I
will hamper their independence and because I myself am so
slow to take on anything new and I work away in my own
province. With your paper I am making an exception because you directly desire it and because it is your first pure-
analytic work.*

I believe it is not suitable for presentation before the Congress. Little new, and that very clear, is the stipulation for an effective Congress lecture. Your work is rich in content and lucid enough and omits the didactic advances that are already certain. It does not take into account the disinterested, ignorant, extremely limited listener in the audience. It will impress forcibly but confuse.

Moreover, apart from these considerations, I would throw out to you the thought that too much of prime importance is introduced and touched upon in passing that deserves more thoughtful and more penetrating treatment. For instance, there is the new idea regarding the mechanism of healing through identification, one that is very right, but in connection with which you do not dwell upon the limits of desirable identification. There is the excellent comprehension of the affect's satisfaction upon the wrong object, also the discussion of the manifold identifications in formal acts which is not very clear; the analysis of the masculine protest, etc. With such valuable content, the work lacks the inner structure through which the reader would be enabled to grasp the whole.

I therefore suggest that you rewrite the paper with much more breadth and ease and didactic and that you throw an easier fragment to the Congress. I do not need to say that such a work written by anyone else I would simply have judged to be very good and valuable.

With regret, I prove it as well-founded that today Bad Gastein is over. At least the article on "Meaning" will be finished before the day is over.

Cordially, your
Freud

Never was a young man's paper handled with greater warmth or with more direct criticism, praise following blame, in quick alternation. This letter, I believe, contains the es-

sence of Freud's reservation about Rank's writing and thinking: too unsystematic, too free, too universalized, too one-
sided. The paper that Freud has referred to as Rank's first
purely analytic work is further identified in the letter of July
17, 1922.

You have not said what I should do with your manuscript
on Potency.[31] *It gratified me very much that you received my*
criticism so well, but I am in favor of your appearing through-
out as the one who presents it and that with a pure analytic
assertion, so that people will become familiar with this side
of your activity.

Later, while still on vacation, he writes in a letter dated
August 4, 1922:

It will not have escaped you that for some time now I have
not felt sure of my health. I speak of it to no one else be-
cause one gets to hear nothing but the usual insincerities.
You are still the youngest and freshest among us while one
knows that age so near seventy is quite a serious matter.

Yet at this very moment Freud is working on a new book,
Das Ich und das Es.

  After an account of the wealthy patients he has not permitted to encroach on his holiday, he adds:

I sent by registered mail from Gastein the manuscript in-
tended for your paper. I am very glad to hear that you have
now decided upon writing on another more limited subject.
I think perhaps you did not value completely in their motiva-
tion, my recently expressed regrets that I had not permitted
you to study medicine. I thought that under these circum-
stances I would not now be in doubt as to whom I would

[31] *Psychische Potenz*, 1921, now a chapter in *Sexualität und Schuldgefühl.*
(Given in a footnote, p. 100, Vol. 1, *Technik.*)

leave the leading role in the Psychoanalytic movement. As it now stands I cannot help but wish that Abraham's clarity and accuracy could be merged with Ferenczi's endowments and to it be given Jones's untiring pen.

At this bitter moment of realization of his own failing health, he expresses with his usual frankness his sense of what he probably conceives as Rank's educational lack, the absence of the scientific basis that medicine might have given, as well as his awareness of the temperamental qualities that he deplored and that Ferenczi's fundamental sweetness of disposition could have mitigated. As for Jones's pen, one hardly sees how Rank's could have been busier.

The basis of mutual intimacy and trust that usually prevailed between Freud and Rank is revealed in two remarkable letters, written while both are in Vienna. Rank's letter begins, "Dear Professor, This evening an interpretation of the witty dream you told me today has occurred to me, which is too apt to be withheld from you and which, I hope, will amuse you." [32] Since the dream in question is not given, it is useless to quote Rank's analysis. The remarkable fact is that Freud could respond a few days later (November 26, 1923).

Dear Dr. Rank,

It is a long time since you have tried to interpret one of my dreams in such a powerful analytical way. Since then much has changed. You have grown enormously and you know so much more about me and the result too is different. . . . I cannot confirm everything you write like a Sadger with his patients after enlightenment, but I do not need to contradict you anywhere.

He continues with his own additions to Rank's interpretation at some length, ending with this astounding conclusion to his associative process:

[32] Letter November 20, 1923.

The super-ego merely says to this process: "All right you old jester and boaster. This is not true at all! . . . attention here, the old one and the young one are interchanged, you (the dreamer) are not David, you are the boasting giant Goliath, whom another one, the young David will slay." And now everything falls into place around this point that you (Rank) are the dreaded David who with his Trauma of Birth succeeds in depreciating my work. . . . Thus I can continue your interpretation. I hope to see you soon. I was not operated on again; I am free of pain and of medicines.

Cordially, your

Freud

This is perhaps Freud's only admission that he himself could experience the feeling of rivalry, even fear, of the younger man who at this point would be his choice as successor if only all the factors were within his control.

In the letters that follow, Rank's increasing concern about Freud's health becomes apparent and must have made it all the more difficult for him to have to transmit to Freud the mounting bitterness of the quarrels arising between the Press in London and the Publishing House in Vienna, combined with the constant complaints of Rank's management issuing from Abraham in Berlin. Freud, who was always deeply distressed by quarreling and would avoid it whenever possible, was finally forced to come to Rank's assistance in a letter to the Committee of November 26, 1922, in which he reminds them that, while Rank alone is the director of the Publishing House, every official communication goes through Freud's hands[33] and that blame must fall upon him too as equally responsible. He also expresses his dissatisfaction with some of Jones's activities as director of the Press and suggests that a completion of his short analysis with Ferenczi is in order.

[33] Dr. Jones is convinced that Rank did not show to Freud his frequent dictatorial letters to Jones (Vol. III, Chap. 2, p. 52).

He continues with a clear analysis of the problems arising from the present set-up and gives alternate possibilities for a solution. He closes with this paragraph:

That is the way I see the situation and again I find no reason to reproach Rank in anything, he who now, as always, has given his best. I think none of you would have had this idea if strange affects had not disturbed your friendly feelings toward each other. But you should not press me into the part of the old Attinghaus whose last words—as is well known— were "Be united—united." I am still alive and I hope to see you united by common work and above such hypersensitive reactions.

In a following letter from Rank to the Committee (November 20, 1922) that Freud had insisted upon his writing, although Rank acknowledges that Freud's letter has eased the problems for him, nevertheless the bitter feelings well up and have to be expressed before he can get to business matters:

For years I have been devoting myself to fighting against enormous external difficulties in the interest of the Psychoanalytic movement. I may say I have been fighting successfully, though often, it is true, with despair, in realization of the magnitude of the task and my own feeble powers and not without paralyzing lassitude and fatigue. I had wished at these moments that you might have helped me with your friendship instead of looking at each of my remarks through a magnifying glass to tell me that it was my fault when everything did not go smoothly.

A vivid description of the environmental factors affecting all members of the inner circle at this period is found in the third volume of Jones's biography:

In our joint plan of founding the English Press in 1919, which was to sustain the Verlag, we had made fatal miscalculations. . . . Then no one living had had the experience of a national currency not merely falling in value, but dissolving into nothingness as the Austrian, and soon afterward the German, currency did. Our joint work soon became a race against time. We were also, for different reasons, both working under strains and against obstacles that were hardly to be borne.

The general machinery of life had so run down in Austria after the war that there were indescribable difficulties in getting anything done. Papers and type had to be scrounged from odd corners, labor disputes were frequent, and communications exasperatingly slow. Rank struggled heroically with the endless problems and accomplished superhuman feats in coping with them almost single-handed; as a single example, he had to buy his own string, make up the parcels of books to be dispatched and carry them himself to the post office. But the strain told on his sensitive nature.[34]

It is a pity that Jones could not have left the matter without recourse to psychoanalytic interpretation of Rank's childhood experiences, of which he had no firsthand knowledge, and to a psychiatric diagnosis of the anticipated onset of a future condition, with which he could have had no direct contact after Rank's departure from Vienna in 1926. Nevertheless for him it is vitally important to account for Freud's siding with Rank against him, however temporarily, and to prepare for the only acceptable explanation of Rank's coming desertion of Freud, which at this point in the past was anticipated by no one, least of all by Rank himself. It is natural that Jones is unable to find any fault on his side beyond the admission of a "rather obsessive insistence on doing things in what I conceive to be the best way, with an impatience for

[34] Jones, *Life of Freud*, Vol. III, Ch. II, p. 46.

sloppiness, at the risk of provoking the sensibilities of the people concerned." [35] He could hardly have characterized one aspect of Rank's nature more accurately.

Regardless of who or what should be blamed for the conflicts, it seems clear that Rank's position in Vienna was becoming intolerable to him as well as to the disgruntled, distant members of the Committee, always excluding Ferenczi whose old friendship with Freud and new friendship with Rank still permitted of no ill feeling. The elements in this situation are so fraught with potentiality for disunity, one wonders how even the strength of a Freud was able to hold them together as long as it did. There is, first of all, the unsound business arrangement between Press and Publishing House, which included many financial obligations not met and competition for the translation rights to Freud's books. To this situation add the postwar hostility of the English to the Germans, the sensitivity of the Jewish members to any hint of anti-Semitism, the language difference (Jones always wrote in English, the others in German), the geographical as well as professional rivalries, and real differences in the culture and postwar hardships of three large cities, London, Berlin, and Vienna, and there would seem to be sufficient basis for trouble. But the heart of the disagreements could always be traced to the natural unity and geographical closeness of the two nearest to Freud, Ferenczi and Rank, however valiantly Freud struggled to maintain a just and consistent neutrality as well as an equally friendly concern for every member of the Committee. It is hardly necessary even to point out that to the distant medical members, the privileges of a young, non-medical, relatively inexperienced upstart like Rank, in almost daily contact with the Master and of necessity in his confidence, must have been a continuous source of unconscious envy and justifiable irritation, if not actual jealousy.

It was into the midst of this emotional powder keg that

[35] *Ibid.*, p. 46.

Rank threw, without previous warning, his *Trauma of Birth*. It was written in the spring of 1923, the year following the appearance of *Entwichlungsziele*, inspired by the insight gained from comparing the similar ending phenomena of a group of patients whose analyses he had been forced to close arbitrarily. However, unlike the book he had written with Ferenczi, it was not primarily concerned with analytic technique or even with psychoanalytic theory. The very secrecy for which the Committee and his friend Sachs reproached him was due to the fundamental difference for him in the writing of this book which, for the first time, permits his original creativity spontaneous expression. This is not the Rank of the technical papers so freely discussed in advance, nor of the literary applications of psychoanalysis. This is the Rank of the *Daybooks* for the first time giving full vent to his philosophic insight in the universal application of a tremendous realization of the meaning of birth. One does not tear inspiration to tatters in discussion with friends. Without apology, and with no awareness of deviation from the Freudian base, his opening sentence from the Preface reads, "The following arguments indicate a first attempt to apply the psychoanalytic way of thinking as such, to the comprehension of the whole development of mankind, even of the actual fact of becoming human." Later in the Preface he continues:

We have come up against the final origin of the psychical unconscious in the psycho-physical, which we can now make biologically comprehensible as well. In attempting to reconstruct for the first time from analytic experiences the to-all-appearances purely physical birth trauma with its prodigious psychical consequences for the whole development of mankind, we are led to recognize in the birth trauma the ultimate biological basis of the psychical.[36]

36 Otto Rank, *The Trauma of Birth*, International Library of Psychology, Philosophy, and Scientific Method, London: Kegan Paul, Trench, Trubner

There follows in the eleven succeeding chapters his account of the "continually recurring attempts" by mankind
to overcome the birth trauma, in neurosis, in religion, in
heroism, in art, and in philosophy.

It would be hard to imagine any greater assertion of omnis-
cience or any greater insult to the Committee, who had not
been informed in advance, much less consulted. There is
Sachs's expression of amazement and hurt: "All this (i.e.,
their exchange of all plans and ideas) came to a full stop with
Rank's book on the birth trauma. He did not say a word
about his new ideas to me until he presented me with a
printed copy, although we had stayed at the same summer-
resort and had seen each other daily while he was writing the
book." [37]

That Rank had never related to Sachs on the same level of
intimate friendship that existed with Ferenczi is clear from
Sachs's revelation that Freud was not surprised and much
later, "when he heard me deplore the loss of my best friend
and noticed how strongly I felt about it, he said musingly,
'Yes, I know that your friendship has always been somewhat
one-sided.' " [38] However mutual had been their literary interests, it seems clear that Rank's growing creativity would find
little in common with Sachs' somewhat limited ability and
complete subservience to Freud as Master.

For Ferenczi, there was no such violent separating experience in regard to Rank, at least for a long time. It is probable
that he did know that Rank was writing something about the
birth trauma as the result of his experience with certain patients at the forced conclusion of their analyses, for they exchanged letters constantly and shared their views on current
analytic phenomena; moreover, Ferenczi was occupied with

and Co., Ltd., 1929. New York: Harcourt, Brace and Company, 1929.
Preface, xi, xiii, xiv. Recently published with *Myth of Birth of Hero* by Robt.
Brunner, New York, 1952 (now taken over by Basic Books).
[37] Sachs, *op. cit.*, pp. 60–61.
[38] *Ibid.*, p. 61.

writing his own book on *Versuch einer Genitaltheorie* in which, Rank states, he referred with enthusiasm to Rank's findings in the *Trauma* as confirmation of his genital theory.

The possibility of a genuine rift in the relationship binding Ferenczi and Rank to Freud never occurred to either at this point, as far as one can tell, while Freud himself seemed to be oblivious to the danger, in his determination to permit independence to his followers, while himself differing vigorously, or at least failing to understand their conclusions. Moreover, Freud was absorbed with his health problems and his own writing. There is no doubt that he tended to put off the reading of difficult, already published material, in which he had had no part, while his daily reliance on Rank carried the personal connection for both, apparently undisturbed. Otherwise one could not account for Freud's brief but cordial note of December 1, 1923:

Vienna IX, Bergasse 19
12-1-23.

Dear Dr. Rank,

I gladly accept your dedication with the assurance of my most cordial thanks. If you could put it more modestly it would be all right with me. Handicapped as I am, I enjoy enormously your admirable productivity. That means for me, too: "Non omnis Moriar."

Your
Freud

P.S. *I am free Sunday morning, would like to see you Tuesday at the latest.*

Nor is it possible to conceive that a man with Rank's intense awareness of self, together with his attachment and obligation to Freud, could have dedicated to him his first independent work unless he believed it to be a contribution to psychoanalytic thought, and a partial return to the Master of his investment in an unknown youth.

However, there was no such blindness in the distant members of the Committee and their reactions to the *Trauma*, especially to the fact that they had not been informed or consulted, were immediate and hostile. Berlin was the most vocal and Abraham soon became the particular enemy for Ferenczi and Rank, who had to deal with him in connection with his ambition for advancement in the Psychoanalytic Congress. Within a month, Freud is forced to write a long letter to the Committee, in an effort to reduce the hostile feelings against *Entwicklungsziele* as well as the *Trauma* and to meet their accusations of a beginning split from orthodox psychoanalysis. The fact that Ferenczi is included in this onslaught probably accounts for the prolonged period of his adherence to Rank, and perhaps for Freud's continued trust in their relationship to him and to each other, since he can more easily allow the innovations by Ferenczi and Rank in practice even when he cannot himself confirm them, than he can contemplate any alteration of the theory as he has developed it.

In this fascinating letter[39] to the Committee, Freud expresses again his desire to leave them free to make their own judgment, and refers to the possibility that a conversation he had held with Sachs on the *Trauma* might have led them to think that he (Freud) was "completely out of sympathy with its content." He adds, "But I think the fact that I have accepted the dedication of the book should make such a conclusion impossible." There follows a characteristically open-minded assertion:

Complete agreement in all detailed questions of science and its newly opened problems is not possible among half a dozen men of different personality and is not even desirable. Only one condition is necessary for our fruitful cooperation, that nobody should desert the common ground of psycho-

[39] January 9, 1924.

analytical presuppositions and we may be sure of that with every member of the Committee.

The astonishing fact here is that he overlooks the one-mind determination of psychoanalytic presuppositions, in his assumption that they were the work of many and assumes for them a proved scientific validity. That any member of the Committee, above all Rank and Ferenczi, should be found wanting in adherence to them is not yet credible to Freud. With a charming acknowledgment of his own frailty, he continues:

There is, furthermore, a circumstance not unknown to you, which makes me especially unfit to function as a despotic, ever-wakeful censor. It is not easy for me to feel my way into another person's thinking; as a rule I have to wait until I have found a connection with it in my own devious ways. So if you want to hold back a new idea every time until I can agree with it, it runs the risk of aging considerably in the meantime.

He goes on to indicate his comparative approval of *Entwicklungsziele* as "a refreshing and upsetting attack on our analytic habits," but does not refrain from pointing out its incompleteness, the dangers of deviating from the classical technique, and his doubt about shortened analyses. Then he turns "to the second and incomparably more interesting book, *The Trauma of Birth* by Rank." "I do not deny," he writes, "that I think the book to be very important, that it gave me much to think about and that I have not arrived as yet at a definitive judgment." Nevertheless he proceeds to indicate in considerable detail the basis for future criticism and his inability to see its value in practice. Despite his many obvious objections, Freud is able to conclude with these words:

There is still much more to say, naturally, and I hope that this upsetting idea introduced by Rank will be the subject of many fertile discussions. What we have before us is no revolution, no contradiction of our established insights, but only an interesting enlargement whose value should be recognized by ourselves and by outsiders.

He cannot refrain, however, from one last expression of doubt:

If I add, furthermore, that it is not clear to me how the premature making-conscious of the therapeutic transference as tie to the mother can contribute to shortening the analysis, I have given you a true picture of my position in respect to both works under discussion. I value them, therefore, very much, I already acknowledge them partially, I have some doubts and scruples concerning parts of their content, I await clarification from continued consideration and experience and would recommend to all analysts not to form a judgment too quickly on these questions, least of all to form an adverse judgment.

It is difficult to understand that Freud could ignore or fail to anticipate the effect of his slightest criticism of Rank and Ferenczi upon the other members of the Committee. All the rivalry and antagonism already generated was released to unrestrained attack that was paralleled by the increasing conflict between the Press in London and the Publishing House in Vienna. Yet Freud, although he deplored Abraham's behavior toward Ferenczi and Rank, could never bring himself to act against him and refused to back the two in their desire to see a neutral candidate elected to the presidency of the Psychoanalytic Congress. Similarly, he tried to maintain his relation to Jones and the Press, in the matter of contracts for his works, however handicapping it seemed to Rank and the

Publishing House, while at the same time affirming Rank's authority and judgment. However, by March 20, 1924, as revealed in a letter from Rank to Ferenczi, even Freud had conceded the necessity for the final break-up of the Committee with a promise to declare his decision at the meeting of the Committee before the next Congress.

If the absent Committee members had taken comfort and courage from Freud's expression of doubt regarding the two books, one may imagine that for Rank it could have been the implication of a coming severance too painful to be faced, not merely as a matter of theoretical difference, but as the beginning realization of a flaw in his ego-ideal. He has offered his best in the uncritical belief that Freud would understand, would accept the gift, and even utilize it for the further development of psychoanalytic theory. Deep as the wound must have been, even at this date, when cordial acceptance of the dedication is followed so quickly with the ambiguous letter to the Committee, Rank, with his usual stoicism, confines his reactions to a formal letter to Freud (February 15, 1924) in which he admits merely to disappointment concerning "your real position toward my work."

Not that I had thought for a moment that you should have defended me and my work to the Committee; you should and could give only your own judgment, but it is just that that has disappointed me, as I had the impression that it was not quite objective and free of misunderstandings. As I have it deeply at heart that you do not misunderstand me —much more than recognition by the psychoanalytic colleagues, from the majority of whom I have never expected much understanding of my work—allow me to express candidly wherein I believe I was misunderstood.

The core of the situation is really in this last sentence—the desire that Freud should understand, should see what Rank has seen with all the conviction of his first analytic experiences and the insights gained thereby. With his usual fearless approach to theory, he goes on to meet Freud's misunderstandings point by point, but, as he will soon be forced to realize, with little effect. Not to be understood by the person who means everything is the most immediately painful, intolerable experience that life can provide for pushing the individual away from his so-called fixations, or for blinding him to the necessity of giving them up.

The immediate effect upon the complex relationships around Freud is to throw Rank and Ferenczi into a protective alliance in order to defend themselves against the Berlin attacks and to try to influence the "Professor" both practically and theoretically. Simultaneously, Freud turns to Ferenczi, as one who is on a more nearly equal footing of age and friendship with Rank. Among the letters in my possession are copies of letters from Ferenczi to Freud and from Freud to Ferenczi, relayed to Rank, as well as the Ferenczi-Rank correspondence. In these letters one sees Ferenczi as the natural mediator, whose loyalty to Freud is never in doubt, but who is also identified strongly with Rank through their common work, their close relation to Freud, and their mutual distrust of Abraham. Thus Freud feels free to write frankly about Rank, knowing that the content of his letter will be transmitted and evidently hoping to influence Rank indirectly. His genuine concern for Rank and his warm appreciation conflict with his irritation over the faults that he deems unnecessary handicaps. One can but be touched by the introductory paragraphs of a long letter to Ferenczi dated March 20, 1924:

Dear Friend,

I know that you correspond intensively with Rank and for a long time I have missed your direct letters, and hasten therefore to answer your letter of today.

My confidence in you and Rank is unconditional. It would be sad if one could find oneself deceived after a fifteen to seventeen years' relationship. But you stress too much that I should agree with you in every detail and Rank is terribly blunt, he stirs people up against him, does not make use of the assured superiority which would be due him as the person nearest to me in many respects. His achievements have been invaluable, his person irreplaceable. Now when he is preparing to go to America for half a year—certainly no secret to you—I am afraid that his health will not be up to the strains awaiting him there. On the other hand, I am not sure of seeing him again when he returns in the fall.

I do not doubt that also the other members of the former committee feel respect and attachment for me and yet it happens that I am deserted just when I have become invalid with decreased working strength and depressed mood, one who defends himself against extra work and does not feel equal to any trouble. I will not try with this complaint to influence you to take a single step to preserve the lost Committee; I know that what is lost is lost! I have survived the Committee that was to be my successor, perhaps I shall yet survive the International Association. I only hope that Psychoanalysis will survive me. But taken altogether it makes a sad ending to life.

After this expression of personal feeling, Freud gives vent to his underlying irritation with Rank, in renewed criticism of his lack of proper presentation of his material, his abruptness, and his enthusiastic one-sidedness, which is unlikely to make him friends. Incidentally, Freud again mentions his doubts of the new technique and even ventures a word of interpretation regarding Ferenczi's hostile feelings for the Berliners and blames Rank's lack of analytic experience—only in his fourth year—for his overenthusiastic pursuit of new ideas.

How unable Freud was to remain outside the controversy and how strongly he really felt about the new ideas is evident from his frank discussion with Rank of a paper he (Freud) is preparing on the "Passing of the Oedipus Complex" that is openly critical of *The Trauma of Birth*. Yet he also consults Rank about how to postpone its publication because it would be interpreted by the analysts as opposition to Rank, mitigated only by their personal relationship. When Rank asks him why he does not declare his disagreement openly, Freud replies that his judgment should not be final, and in any case the applications to cultural adaptations are valuable.[40] The inconsistency of this attitude cannot be explained logically but for Freud it was essential. He could not go beyond the momentary ambiguity to a position that might mean the end of a relationship on which he had depended. The ultimate disillusionment for Rank was Freud's confession that he had read only half of the book as yet and that he was testing out Rank's technique by giving all his patients[41] *The Trauma of Birth* to read and asking for their impressions.[42]

How painfully this affects Rank, who is nevertheless preparing for his first trip to America, may be guessed from a note to Freud, written on the day after his long account to Ferenczi, in which he reports himself as in bed with angina. But Freud, under the burden of a new prosthesis, and depressed by a head cold, can see only that Rank is unimpressed by his criticisms. Nevertheless he is planning to be absent from the next meeting of the Vienna Psychoanalytic Society and to pass the presidency on to Rank, "I would prefer to do this before the Congress convenes so that you may appear there in your new function." [43]

Rank, who cannot bear that Freud should believe him to

[40] From a letter of Rank to Ferenczi, March 20, 1924.
[41] Chiefly patients in a second year of analysis.
[42] From a letter of Rank to Ferenczi, March 20, 1924.
[43] From a letter Freud to Rank, March 23, 1924.

be unmindful of the criticism, tries once more (March 24, 1924) to let Freud sense the hurt he feels that the criticism has been "not exactly friendly from the start. Otherwise, you would not have failed even to suggest wherein you saw the frequently stressed value of the book, while you expressed, without leaving any doubt, what you saw as its weaknesses." Again Rank tries to give factual proof by citing instances of Freud's underlying attitude, but concludes with a beginning recognition of what lies ahead. "I hope, dear Professor, that you will not take my frankness amiss, for I see in it not only the condition for any personal relationship, but also the best means for an understanding."

Freud continues to give vent to his irritation with the problems Rank has introduced in his letter to Ferenczi (March 26, 1924). He cannot tolerate Rank's lack of formal presentation, not followed by logical proof of his concepts and, by now, finds practically nothing in the *Trauma* that he can approve. But, he adds, "I shall continue to say that he has discovered something important and interesting, but he has not worked it out in an orderly fashion." He sees nothing that he can understand or sympathize with in the technical modifications that Rank relates to the theory but declares himself open to future experience. After expressing his disapproval of the Berliners' behavior toward Rank, he complains of Rank's irritability and the difficulty of becoming a mediator, when there is wrong on both sides. He reassures Ferenczi, and himself as well, in concluding, "I do not need to assure you that my personal feelings for you and Rank remain unchanged. I am annoyed by the weaknesses that appear in both of you, but that is no reason to forget the friendly services and collaboration of fifteen years. But I am also unable to reject the others who could bring similar claims. And a little bit more or less of wrong doing, when one is driven by emotions, gives no ground for condemning people whom one likes otherwise."

Thus the humanity of Freud is still able to overcome logic and consistency. But the irreversible process of growth and change is working through every relationship, however slowly and imperceptibly. Even Ferenczi is beginning to doubt, as he shows in his letter to Rank (March 30, 1924) that encloses his correspondence with the "Professor." He describes his own changing attitudes toward the *Trauma* as he had given them to Freud, including his sympathy with Freud's fear that the *Trauma*, as too total and undeveloped, might harm the "refined and elaborate structure of Psychoanalysis." He tells how his own material, before revision from the Rankian view, had shown neglect of the potentialities of the birth trauma and how he had been impressed with the birth mechanisms appearing spontaneously after setting an ending. He acknowledges his debt to Rank for technical progress and the shortening of treatment. But he does not fail to leave a loophole for he inserts, "I was not and am still not informed about the details of your technique." For Ferenczi, there is as yet no slightest thought of a serious difference from Rank, united as they are in their common relation to the politics of the coming Congress at Salzburg and by the fact that Freud's health, as well as his reluctance to face the inevitable conflicts, promises to keep him away. Rank yields to Freud's desire that Abraham's candidacy for the presidency of the Congress should not be opposed and agrees not to protest publicly, inasmuch as Eitingon has agreed to take Rank's place as secretary so that Rank will not have to work with Abraham.

Out of this stormy situation and the Conference in Salzburg, despite a second spell of illness (as noted in a letter from Freud of April 10, 1924) Rank sailed for America on April 27, 1924, five days after his fortieth birthday. It would be hard to exaggerate the significance of this act of separation in space upon those he left behind as well as upon himself. It is his first completely independent step taken into a world unknown to him and unloved by Freud. He goes entirely on his own, so he says, without invitation from any professional group, as the first intimate associate of Freud to journey to New York with intent to practice there for a limited period. While he still feels himself to be related positively to Freud and will soon be analyzing the majority of the members of the New York Psychoanalytic Association, nevertheless in his first public appearance before the American Psychoanalytic Association in Atlantic City on June 3, 1924, about a month after his arrival in New York, he does not hesitate to explain simply and directly the modifications in his analytic practice that have arisen through his new understanding of the effect of the trauma of birth as revealed in the analysis of every patient where an ending is set in advance. Of course he is accepted in this country at first because, although not a medical man, he comes direct from Freud in Vienna, and has already analyzed Americans in Vienna; but there is also something in what he brings of his own that proves to be releasing as well as intriguing to the New York analysts, especially those whose previous work with Freud has left them dissatisfied or unable to effect cures with their patients.

During this period Freud writes frequently, disturbed by Rank's failure to do likewise. There are business letters occupied with the problems of publication and American rights and with an unpleasant experience that Rank has had in connection with certain relations of Freud who, as Rank believes, had been influenced against him by the enemy in Berlin, or, as Freud surmises, through Rank's own possibly impolite behavior. In any case, Freud must again try to make peace among the warring elements by letter. The first personal letter from Freud, May 23, 1924, is light and friendly, indicating his sympathy for anyone involved with the unreliable ocean and the mad life of New York City where it is well "to sell one's life as dearly as possible." He adds, "Nice that you now have nearly all of my former analysands, whose analyses I recall without any satisfaction." He reports his health as slowly improving but far from satisfactory to him, and ends with a sentence as characteristic of Rank as of himself: "Give my regards to all the squirrels and also feed them with peanuts in my name. The real zoo to be visited is in the Bronx."

Meantime Ferenczi, who also has not heard from Rank except via Mrs. Rank, writes at length (May 25, 1924) of what happened at the Salzburg Congress after Rank left, their offense at his early departure, and some satirical jokes made at the dinner about Otto and his trauma. The rest of the letter is filled with the details of family news and the problems of editorship that have fallen upon Ferenczi. Apparently Rank hastened to reply, for a second letter from Ferenczi of June 7, 1924, full of excitement, reveals a plan evidently suggested by Rank under the spell of his own success in New York, that Ferenczi should join him there. At any rate, Ferenczi seems to be taking all the preliminary steps for a journey with his wife to New York. The intervening letters are not preserved in this collection, but a final letter from Rank to Ferenczi (August 10, 1924) shows that Rank's early enthusiasm had been dampened by longer experience with underlying conditions and that he had evidently advised Ferenczi not to come. To Ferenczi's natural disappointment and probably his reproaches for the hardships resulting from his too speedy change of his own arrangements, Rank replies:

If I have caused you a disappointment, it was done in good faith and to spare you a greater disappointment if you had come. . . . The drove of patients who, as some one jokingly said, lined up along the whole length of Broadway, has so thinned it will be hard for me to fill my daily program next month. Analysts who before were fully occupied have now one or two patients and even Brill, the busiest of all, is here only three days a week. I know, of course, that this is strongly conditioned by the summer, but conversations with some of the analysts have made me doubt that it will be any better for a stranger in the fall. As I could not give or transfer to you any of my cases, you would be dependent on the others who are themselves hungry fish and live from the scraps of the big neurologists and psychiatrists. My own success was somewhat unique and not to be repeated. Even I myself could not repeat it, because I had mainly the analysts who know what such an opportunity means and would make any sacrifice to utilize it. Naturally, they would like to get rid of me soon, after they have learned from me all that they can, and that leaves little hope that they would be eager to take on another stranger. . . . Accordingly it would be necessary to have some capital to cover the expenses of travel and of the stay here in the beginning, for I would advise you not to come here as the guest of an analyst. They have a tendency to exploit us like slaves and as a guest of one you would have to take it. I acted here from the beginning as an independent practitioner on a purely business basis and I believe that only in this way was I able to solve satisfactorily the difficult problem which had to be overcome.

While this unfortunate business did not by any means end their friendship, one could hardly doubt that it injected something negative into the break already made by Rank's departure, while Ferenczi could not have been untouched, generous though he was, by Rank's unrestrained assertion of the success of his technique as compared with Freud's. True, Rank was assuming that his technique was understood by Ferenczi but only his own absorption in the new experience could have made him so insensitive to Ferenczi's immediate situation. While there are no further communications in this collection to tell us exactly what happened later that led to the final break, the forces leading to separation are already strongly in the ascendant.

There remain in this collection the critical letters between Freud and Rank, which I can never read without sadness because of the inevitability of the struggle between two men, so deeply related and so basically unlike. That a man of Rank's brilliance as a therapist combined with his natural tendency to think in philosophic terms could continue to work in complete harmony with Freud, theoretically, practically, and personally, is inconceivable. His deviation should have been anticipated as the natural outcome of an individual's growth away from the parent stock.

The prolongation of the struggle that at worst is attributed by the others to Rank's weakness, or at best to his neurotic or psychotic illness, can be accounted for only by the depth of his love for and obligation to Freud, who had fulfilled his deepest needs—for opportunity, for financial help, but most of all for a living person on whom he could project the ideal self. With every separation in space that demands of Rank increased development of responsibility for himself and independence of Freud, there arises a deepening conflict between the force of his genius and the human need to remain related, secure in the only backing he has ever had, and held by the ties of family, friends, and native city. It would be strange if Rank, who had traveled so little, now suddenly thrown into the midst of an unknown city, without personal friends, speaking the language with effort, had not experienced extreme swings of mood, from elation at finding himself able to help the analysts with whom Freud had been unsuccessful to revulsion against the nightmare of New York in summer, and fear of the lengths to which his own independence was taking him.

It is not strange that he found it difficult to write to Freud under his increasing conviction of his own technique and his growing rejection of classical analysis. From Freud's letter of July 23, 1924, with an implied reproach for not hearing from Rank, one sees that New York also contains unfriendly

analysts who are eager to report back to Freud Rank's every
misstep in the new environment. Moreover, stirred by a request from one psychiatrist for an explanation of Rank's
birth trauma, Freud reiterates more clearly his disagreement:

*In the months since our separation, I am even further from
agreeing with your innovations. I have seen nothing in two
of my cases that have been completed that confirms your
views and generally nothing that I did not know before; the
final birth phantasy seems to me still to be the child that one
gives, analytically, to the father. I am often much concerned
about you. The exclusion of the father in your theory seems
to reveal too much the result of personal influences in your
life which I think I recognize and my suspicion grows that
you would not have written this book had you gone through
an analysis yourself. Therefore I beg of you not to become
fixed but to leave open a way back.*

Thus we have come to the final accusation upon which
every analyst is tempted to fall back when he meets an in-
escapable difference in theory or practice. Freud himself was
much slower to resort to the analytic interpretation of others
than the disciples, but when faced with what he envisions as
Rank's possible destruction, he must do what he can to save
him. The fact that growth away from the father substitute
is never considered as an alternative to the assumption of
neurosis has always amazed me, especially in the case of
analysts whose stock in trade is the desirability of freeing the
patient from fixations on parents. Freud's frank but genuinely
concerned letter was the occasion for terrific conflict, as one
can tell from Rank's repeated efforts to frame an answer.
There are four different versions retained by Rank in this
collection, of which only one was sent,[44] as determined by
Freud's references in reply. For the first time, Rank treats

[44] Rank to Freud, August 9, 1924.

Freud as an equal, not his Master, and does not soften either the theoretical or the technical convictions that are directly opposed to Freud's. Such directness is possible only at this distance and under the necessity of affirming his professional development heightened by the independent experiences here recorded.

The fact is that I have undergone the same experiences as you: I have found in all my work here, which is many-sided and intensive, day by day and hour by hour, nothing but confirmations and even additions to my point of view, which, moreover, has been confirmed here too from different sides. By chance I have had an opportunity to see again in just these last few days how the phantasy of giving a child to the father cannot be resolved analytically and put to use therapeutically except by leading back to the mother and the own birth.

For the rest I cannot understand why you lay so much emphasis on the final birth theory which therapeutically and theoretically is not nearly so important as the basic concept that the transference libido is a purely maternal one and that the anxiety basic to all symptoms was originally tied to the maternal genital and was transferred to the father only secondarily. If you interpret the phenomenon of transference starting from the father, with the male, you get the homosexual fixation, with the female, the heterosexual fixation as a result of the analysis; that is really the case with all the patients who come to me from other analysts. The analysts among these patients have felt it subjectively and objectively; subjectively as they have lost nothing of their neuroses, objectively as with this technique they were unable to cure their own patients. And that is not the fault of the people here who are neither better nor worse than people in Europe, but the fault is in method and technique. When analysts saw they could work more easily with modifications introduced by me and get better results—with their patients as well as in their own analyses—they praised me like a savior. I am not so blinded as not to subtract a good part from these successes as complex-conditioned, but what remains is a bit of truth and reality that one cannot remove from this world by closing one's eyes.

I have the strong impression that you do not want or are unable to see certain things, because sometimes your objections sound as if you had not read at all or had not heard what I really said (I only remind you in that regard that I was able to direct your attention to the fact that you have imputed something to me and Ferenczi which we never had said, it was just the contrary).

Now again you say that I have excluded the father; naturally that is not the case and cannot be, it would be nonsense. I have only attempted to give him the correct place. You apparently bring in the personal relations between you and me, where they do not belong. In this connection it gave me a peculiar impression that you were saying I would never have defended this point of view had I been analyzed. This may be true. The question is only, whether that would not have been very regrettable. After all that I have seen of results with analyzed analysts, I can call it only fortunate. For the rest, you know as well as I do that the accusation that an insight is derived from a complex means very little in general in the first place, and in the second, says nothing of the value or truth of this insight. All the less, as psychoanalysis itself has shown, that the greatest achievements themselves result from complexes and their overcoming.

While I am writing this I feel painfully that through a scientific difference, which one would think could be seriously discussed, a dissonance has come into our personal relations. To a certain degree it may be unavoidable in all human relationships. But I gather from your letter that your personal feelings toward me could still be the same old ones. All the more deeply do I regret that objectively you do me so little justice. I am, for instance, strongly convinced that you have an absolutely wrong idea of how I use psychoanalytic technique.[45] Actually, I have taken nothing from it, I have only added something, which truly I think is very important and which others already consider essential for the understanding of their cases and their therapeutic handling. I do not know how far I can still hope to be able to show you through cases what I can do. In any case, it is more and better than at that time when you talked very highly of my therapeutic achievements.

I do not know either how much your judgment or prejudice against my position has been influenced by some noisy ranters who from time to time feel the irresistible urge to set themselves up as saviors of the psychoanalytic movement or your person, without seeing that they only give full rein to their childish jealousy. In the same way the Berlin plans and plots of which I hear seem to me so foolish in their gesture and so unworthy of a scientific movement that I hope you also will have little use for it. I would like to know what is finally to be achieved by it. If they want to remove me from my official positions to which, up to now, I am tied not by ambition but by duty, care, and toil, they can attain it without any backstairs politics, if you should think it desirable. If they want to refute my point of view, again there is no need for plotting or intrigues. The more light is thrown on them, the more agreeable it will be for me, for the more distinctly the abysmal ignorance of people like Abraham will be revealed. Do you really believe, dear Professor, that an argument by a man like Abraham will impress me, when I am in doubt of your judgment in this matter?

But I think that for these people intrigue itself is more

[45] True not only of Freud but of many Freudian analysts who still tend to believe that Rank began his analysis by explaining the *Trauma of Birth* and setting an ending.

important than to reach certain goals. But this is exactly the point where I shall take no part in the game if the cards are not put on the table on both sides. One cannot expect that I would let myself in for a repetition with concessions and compromises after my experiences with the departed Committee, allegedly in the interest of the psychoanalytic movement, in reality in the personal interest of the participants, who know very well how easily one can burn one's own fingers at the pleasant spectacle of an auto da fe. Perhaps you will tell me that I am mistaken, that, on the contrary, Abraham is ready for peace. That is just the hypocrisy against which I defend myself, that one allegedly makes sacrifices that serve nobody, but that ruin the movement for which the sacrifices allegedly have been made. Do not let us forget that the psychoanalytic movement as such is a fiction and for the people who are now eager to work at a psychoanalytic movement, I confess, I have no sympathy.

As you see, I explain to you my attitude in this whole matter as openly as it can be done, because I see herewith the last hope of clarifying the situation as soon as possible—a situation that has become difficult for you, too, as you have to assume with different persons a different attitude towards my contentions. I feel, also, that you are entitled to learn what I really think and feel in this critical situation that is personally so painful.

I was very glad to hear from you yourself that you are satisfied with your condition and if one can trust the psychology des Dementis, this fine condition will last a long time.

With the best regards to your family and cordial greetings to you,

Your devoted

Rank

After this declaration of independence has been sent there comes another letter from Freud, containing his final plea for a change in Rank's attitude. It would be hard to resist a letter so full of kindness and warm concern. One wonders if Rank would have been able to send his letter, which he had probably held over for several days anyway, if he had waited long enough to receive Freud's letter of August 25, 1924.

Semmering, 8-25-24

Dear Dr. Rank,

Today's mail brought a letter from you, but it contains only an introduction for a superfluous Dr. W. It surprises me that during these months of your absence, in situations so critical for us, for you and me, you have not felt a greater necessity to let me know what goes on with you, inside and out, and it worries me.

Although I now look at most events sub specie aeternitatis and cannot expend violent emotions on them as I did in earlier years, I am not indifferent to the changes in my relation to you. My condition seems to indicate that I have still some life span left and it is my strong wish that during this period you should not become lost to me. You left Europe, I hear, in a state of excitement and distrust. The knowledge that I have turned away to some extent from approval of your last work may have increased your mood. Probably, you overrate the affective importance of this theoretical difference and you believe that, during your absence, I have been accessible to influences inimical to you. The purpose of this letter is to assure you that this is not the case. I am not so easily accessible to others, and the others—I had for some days the visit of Eitingon and Abraham—are equally sincere in recognizing your great merits and regret deeply the rudeness with which you isolate yourself. There is no animosity toward you either with us or with my New York family. There is just time to exchange a letter before your return. I would like you to inform me and reassure me about your present state of mind.

The difference of opinion concerning the Trauma of Birth

carries no weight with me.[46] Either, in the run of time—if there is enough time left—you will convince and correct me or you will correct yourself and separate the lasting new gains from what the bias of the discoverer has added. I know that you are not lacking acclaim for your innovation, but consider how few are able to judge and how strong the desire is in most of them to get away from the Oedipus wherever a path seems to open. Even if much is erroneous, in no case do you have to be ashamed of your product, rich in spirit and content, which brings new and valuable ideas even to the critics. But surely you should not assume that this work of yours must disrupt our relation founded on the intimacy of so many years.

Adding to my cordial regards the expectation of seeing you soon,

Freud

One could hardly exaggerate the effect of Rank's letter following closely upon Freud's with its kindly and even anxious concern for Rank's welfare. It was like a blow in the face from a supposedly loyal friend and adherent as Freud's immediate reply of August 27, 1924 clearly shows.

Semmering, 8-27-24

Dear Dr. Rank,

Had I waited only one day more I could have spared myself the preceding letter. I dare not hope that a repetition of this event is imminent. But your letter was very painful for me. I never would have believed that you could write in such a manner, that surprises actually never cease. One is never prepared for everything.

When you first told me of the Trauma of Birth, I made two remarks to which I can connect two points. (It could be that my memory telescopes two occasions.) The first was: this is not the correct presentation. You answered, almost defiantly:

[46] This, of course, constitutes the core of the problem for Rank.

105

But *I* cannot do it differently. Your presentation has in fact a great share in the critical reserve, which *I* also felt toward your findings, after overcoming the first fascinating impression. It would have been correct to point out where your innovation connects with the established position—which you do not contest—that is, with the libido theory, the Oedipus complex, the role of the father. But all of this was completely passed by in your book, or touched on so superficially that it gives the impression of indecision not yet overcome, or of a polite bow while the argument really leads elsewhere. Such impressions in addition to the failure of your own presentation are very decisive. Consequently you leave, for instance, only two roads open for me, which would lead to a personal judgment: one of observation and the other of weighing my prior opinions, or my prejudices, if you will.

My observation has, as yet, not permitted me to make a decision, but up to now has furnished nothing that would correspond to your interpretation. In the last half year I had six cases, five of them knew of your theory, some were instructed by you. I avoided, of course, any kind of contradiction. The result was that the analyses took their usual course without any magical alleviation or acceleration.[47] Your experiences are different; do they therefore cancel mine? We both know that experiences permit of many explanations, hence we have to wait for further experience.

After all, the right to have an opinion of one's own prevails for me, too. I have endeavored to respect it with each of my friends and adherents, as long as we could preserve a common ground. . . . I was not and I am not in agreement with Ferenczi's statements on homosexuality and with many points of his active therapy. In my opinion he puts a too great store on complete agreement with me; I do not. Suppose you had told me one day that you could not believe in the primordial horde

---

[47] It is hard to understand how Freud could accept this inevitable failure, in view of his own disbelief, as an objective test of Rank's technique.

and the primordial father, or thought the separation into Ego and Id to be inexpedient, do you really believe that I would not have invited you for meals or would have excluded you from my circle? It is true, you were always very reserved in taking a critical stand, probably too much so. And now you seem shattered and offended that I refuse your Trauma of Birth, though you have my admission that it is never easy for me to follow a new train of thought that somehow does not go my way or to which my way has not yet led me.

The second method remains, the weighing of the prejudices. Here I have much to confess: for instance, my inability to understand how the magic formula of leading back all libido to the mother should produce a therapeutic effect, lacking in all the other acts of analysis. According to our theory, every object libido is originally narcissistic. The leading back goes still further but I have never been able to ascribe to it any healing effect. Moreover, you can always distinguish whether the libido has shifted from the mother to another object, or if it simply so happened that the mother was the first object and that other parts of the narcisistic libido have turned to other objects. All this is so dark and undecided that a good measure of tolerance is necessary in making a judgment.

Up to now we have ascribed the healing effect of the analysis to the overcrowding of the resistance to the transformation of the repressed into the conscious. If this is compatible with the assumption which one can surmise in your book, that this effect depends on the success of the abreaction to the birth trauma, then a thorough discussion is necessary. My first impression is that it does not hold together. The whole subject is shrouded in darkness that I have, as yet, not succeeded in penetrating. Your book has brought it out and has done nothing to clarify it. . . . In a letter, even if it has become as long as this one, only samples of the material can be discussed. I would like to continue this discussion with you, dear Rank, for some winter evenings, when you are in the mood for it again.

But now comes my second remark. I said then: with such find-ings another man would have made himself independent. I still cling to this reservation, otherwise I would have to declare the situation as desperate. There are ugly things in your letter. To impute to Abraham "profound ignorance," to call him "a noisy ranter," that presupposes a disturbance a judgment only to be explained by a boundless affectivity, and fits ill with the overcoming of complexes. An evil demon makes you say that this psychoanalytic movement is a fiction and puts in your mouth the very words of the enemy. An abstract thing can be real, too, and is not therefore a fiction. Your acrimonious re-mark that you are glad not to have been analyzed—otherwise you would not have made your discovery, based on the exist-ence of complexes—is not at all justified. You overlook the danger, to which some have already succumbed, namely, of projecting into science as a theory that which moves in oneself, that has really no value as a conquest.

This piece of exegesis becomes very painful for me, but some passages in your letter sound as if you had decided to break up the relation with us and our cause after an intimacy and common work of more than fifteen years and to justify thus the calumny that first had infuriated you so much. If that is your earnest intention, what can I tell you that you would not know yourself and that you must have found in these fif-teen years?

Had my illness progressed further it would have saved you a decision, certainly not easy for you. Since, as it seems, I have to be prepared to continue to live, I am faced with a situation that a short time ago I would have rejected as unthinkable: es-pecially painful because I find the reason for this loss so in-sufficient; hardly a comfort that I cannot discover my own share of the guilt. My feelings toward you have not been shaken by anything. I cannot, as yet, give up hope that you will return to a better knowledge of yourself.

I am in no hurry to mail this letter; I shall find out from your wife when you are expected to return.

> Cordially,
> Freud

The exact date of Rank's return to Vienna I do not know, but it must have been in late October or early November. In any case, it was one thing to express the fullness of a newly realized authority and independence at the distance of New York, and quite another to maintain such a separateness when back in the old familiar situation, faced with the reality of Freud's illness and need, the enormity of his own desertion in the eyes of former friends and of his own family as well. One does not cut off attachment as deep as Rank's to Freud in one stroke. It has to be accomplished by repeated efforts and realization of inevitability until, at some possibly slight but unbearable point, the final act is taken by removal in space. Rank has been accused of running away, of escaping, but how else is such a severance accomplished? Anyone who has known Rank intimately could not doubt that he paid dearly for his freedom, in fear, conflict, illness, and suffering.

From letters written by Rank to the Committee, it seems that on his return to Vienna he could not bear his alienation from Freud, especially as he was faced with Freud's increasing illness; he actually fled to Paris but, with the consequent guilt and depression, he was unable to return to New York at once as had been planned in advance on previous arrangements there. He was driven by the intensity of his emotions to return once more to Vienna in order to yield to Freud's willingness to help and to forgive.

The result of these analytic conferences with Freud is registered in a letter to the Committee (December 20, 1924), which reveals, as nothing else could, the extremity of Rank's internal conflict. Judging from the Rank of the *Daybooks*

109

and from my own knowledge of him, I feel sure that never in all of his life before or since has he yielded so completely to the dictates of emotion, at the expense of his own integrity. That he could so humble himself to the members of the Committee, who took full advantage of their opportunity to put him in his place and exact future good behavior, is inconceivable to those of us who knew him in the years of his maturity. After an introductory paragraph of apology, he writes:

Only after the recent events in Vienna, which you probably know, has my attitude and behavior toward the Professor become clear to me. Obviously certain things had to happen before I could gain the insight that my affective reactions toward the Professor and you, insofar as you represent for me the brothers near to him, stemmed from unconscious conflicts. For these reactions I could only give an account to myself and you, after I had overcome them.

From a state which I now recognize as neurotic, I have suddenly returned to myself. Not only have I recognized the actual cause of the crisis in the trauma occasioned by the dangerous illness of the Professor, but I was able also to understand the type of reaction and its mechanism from my childhood and family history—the Oedipus and brother complexes. I was thus obliged in reality to work out conflicts that would probably have been spared through an analysis, but which I believe I have now overcome through these painful experiences.

From analytic interviews with the Professor, in which I could explain in detail the reactions based on affective attitudes, I gain the hope that I was successful in clarifying, first of all, the personal relationship, since the Professor found my explanations satisfactory and has forgiven me personally. As a further consequence there will be an opportunity for discussion, clarification, and coming together in the scientific field, where I shall be able to see things more objectively after the removal of my affective resistance.[48]

The letter continues with specific apologies to Abraham and Jones, adding in mitigation that he had never carried his criticisms beyond the intimate circle. To Eitingon and Ferenczi he wrote separately. Sachs he had never included in his resentment, but asks pardon for unintentional hurt. He concludes, "I would be glad to hear that my explanations have found with you the same analytical understanding as with the Professor and that they give the satisfaction which, I hope, can afford the basis for the resumption of our group work in a not too distant future."

Only a state of complete submission to his personal devotion to Freud, as well as his rightful guilt for excessively hostile feelings and utterances toward other members of the Committee, however deserved by them objectively, could have enabled Rank to accept the patronizing replies from analysts who admitted no share in the evil but emphasized their need for more detailed information about his talks with Freud, as well as proof by future deeds, with a significant reference to "any future publications." The sense of the Committee is that he has much revision of the old to do before embarking on the new. Rank's unconscious feelings of jealousy and rivalry may have been softened but there is no indication that the others, Ferenczi and Eitingon and Sachs excepted, are less suspicious or less ready to pounce on the first sign of continuing deviation. Probably Freud, who now experienced once more the reality of the personal relationship and the depth of Rank's yielding, was less apprehensive about the theoretical and technical differences, once he had succeeded in getting hold of the hostile feelings

[48] It is important to note that added objectivity and experience only served to confirm the theoretical and technical differences, which could not be wiped out by any repentance or admission of a neurotic problem.

and bringing about the first moves toward reconciliation. The Committee, however, removed in space and outside the experience, were well aware that many differences of theory and practice brought about by *Entwicklungsziele* as well as by the *Trauma of Birth* remained to be settled and they were right to question the possibility of Rank's return to the fold unless he could recant fully and completely. Still, under the relief of the restored relation to Freud, Rank was able to accept the offensive letters and write his appreciation of "the proof of friendship and confidence." [49] He assures them that he knows that this is only the first step but continues:

The next and most important step, the conversations which I have had ever since with the Professor, has yielded to the necessity of starting as soon as possible on my trip to America planned long before—it is true, under entirely different premises and conditions—and so I am going this very week to New York. According to the news from there it seems that confusion has arisen in the heads of the analysts, caused especially by the news of the events here in Vienna, a disturbance to which I have certainly contributed much and which I shall endeavor to make good as far as it is connected with my actions in New York. I will try in discussions and lectures to make them more reasonable by rectifications, explanations, removal of difficulties, and resistances. I will use this occasion myself to make clear my own scientific point of view; to take back, limit, or modify whatever was premature, uncertain, or dangerous, and to bring the new insofar as it is defensible into relation with the already established. This necessary work there will give me, I hope, material and viewpoints for the formulation of my position, for which I shall then of course find an outlet in publication. . . . [50]

At the same time the trip to America offers me an op-

[49] Letter January 7, 1925.
[50] Note Rank's refusal to accept the limitations which the absent committee had tried to place on him as one of the conditions to be met.

portunity to answer the questions in the Berlin letter, at least with a short explanatory remark. My change had started only after my departure from Vienna and after I had returned from Paris in order to be able to talk it out once more with the Professor. It concerned only purely personal or rather human motives. My American activities and plans had nothing to do with it immediately. It was just that it was psychologically impossible for me to leave the Professor thus, to leave him in the lurch as I was able to do the first time in a manic state,[51] which, as direct reaction to his illness, was intended to spare me the pain of a loss. As I found him again I fell into the compulsion to repeat the same action, only it did not succeed this time, as the feeling of guilt came up as depression and forced me to return and to discuss.

Rank had arranged to go back to New York in November, 1924, directly after his return to Vienna, on the basis of his success there. Now, although the current controversy in Vienna as well as the resulting postponement of his return has upset the New York situation somewhat, he reiterates the fact that he would still be bound to return independently of the New York Psychoanalytic Association, as he had done in the first place. Referring to the request for more information regarding his present change of attitude he writes,

I am hoping that the situation may be clarified meanwhile and spare me from touching on details which one does not put

[51] From the time of the *Daybooks*, Rank as in this letter has always understood his own manic-depressive swings, which for him were usually related to the periods of extreme creativity with their aftermath of exhaustion. The intimations of neurotic illness given by Jones in Volume II and reinforced in Volume III by a definite psychiatric diagnosis of "cyclothymia," which he finds to have been recognized by Freud also for a number of years previously, could have been no surprise to Rank who, after he had ceased to exist for Freud and Jones, managed to live for twelve years with a "psychosis" that seemed not to interrupt the creative drive, the therapeutic practice, or the teaching engagements, maintained to the time of his death in 1939.

out even before a circle of friends but which one unveils at
the utmost to an analyst. The Professor, of course, knows the
story in all its details and I hope that will be sufficient for you,
too. It stands to reason that I shall inform you of the events in
America and that I shall start the discussion with you scientifically as soon as possible after I have become a little clearer
myself concerning various problems. In the firm hope that the
New Year will see me again in your circle, I remain, with the
best friendly wishes to you all.

Your
Rank

What Rank experienced in this second visit to New York
is impossible to understand in terms of the average human
being. From a notebook covering the year 1925, it is evident
that he continued to examine intensively his own conflicts,
personal and professional, as they had been brought out in
his recent therapeutic interviews with Freud. At the same
time, he not only carried on his regular work with patients
but conducted a seminar for the New York Psychoanalytic
Society in which through six sessions, with the use of cases
brought up by the members, his point of view and practice
were subjected to every kind of critical question. The synopses of this seminar provided by the Society are available
and give the names of those taking part in the discussion,
with their contributions. They are familiar names to one
who knew the New York psychiatrists of that period, Brill,
Stern, Kardiner, Obendorf, Glueck, Polon, Feigenbaum, Asch,
Blumgart.

From these recordings, it seems that Rank did his utmost
to hold to the Freudian base and to explain his recent innovations as an extension of Freudian psychoanalysis, not a
departure from it. He dealt patiently and sympathetically
with their repetitive questions about the criteria for end-setting in analysis, their desire for a formula. In the final set of

questions presented for discussion at the last seminar, the crucial one is still—Rank's relation to Freud. "To what extent does the Rankian contribution represent a radical departure from the Freudian position so as to make it inconsistent with established Freudian principles, both theoretical and practical?" Rank's answer was unequivocal: "he does not think that the Rankian contribution represents a departure from Freudian positions. He never thought so or said so. He developed new concepts that extended the Freudian theory, carrying it to its biological conclusion." As one reads these revealing synopses, one can see that so long as case material is being discussed, there will be no lack of differences among the analysts present, differences as strongly expressed as any Rank might introduce; their ways of conducting analyses are obviously individual and even temperamental. Let theory, apart from the case, become the bone of contention, and each one will want to assure himself that Freud stands somewhere in the background—that no dangerous deviation is involved.

After this period of self-examination, combined with an even more pointed organization of his own views and practice necessitated by its repeated presentation in the seminar for the New York analysts, he returned to Vienna and all its unsolved reality problems, in May, 1925, where he remained throughout the summer. It is probable that Freud renewed his attempts to help Rank with something approximating analysis, which the Committee, including Freud, felt to be his greatest need and best hope for the future. The impossibility of this situation is so apparent at this distance that one wonders how it could have been sustained so long. Freud, stricken with an incurable illness, needing more than ever to find in Rank one who could be trusted to sustain the psychoanalytic movement and needing also the personal tie on which he had come to rely as well as the practical help, is the last person to be able to take on the objective role of analyst for Rank. While Rank's guilt for his need to escape,

115

to abandon the father figure who has given him everything and is now in need, must be increased by the inevitable resistance to accepting analysis from Freud, since clearly everything Rank believes about the therapeutic value of his own methods would be violated by the Freudian approach. Nor is there any psychoanalyst, certainly none among the Committee, to whom Rank would not now feel superior in viewpoint and technique. How long then can he sustain the illusion that his own development is the result of a neurosis that can be cured? How long will it take him to acknowledge that Freud really does not understand, will not admit the Rankian contribution to be a derivation from his own psychoanalytic formulations, much less an improvement upon them, even if it has been true for Rank?

Whatever the emotional conflicts of that long summer, heightened by the determination of a wife (whose future goal as child analyst was deeply involved with the Viennese connections) not to be separated from the Freudian group, Rank was not only able as always to utilize every immediate experience for theory formation but was even compelled by his irrepressible creativity to continue his writing. Somehow, in this desperately conflicted year of 1925, he completed the first volume of his *Technik der Psychoanalyse*, whose Foreword is dated Vienna, Spring of 1925, when it was published. This volume takes the place of his part of *Entwicklungsziele*, the book from which Ferenczi had already withdrawn his contribution, but it is much more confident and complete, with the added assurance gained from the two periods in New York.

The second half of the book is devoted to the technique of dream interpretation based on a collection of dreams from his practice in their actual analytic setting. There is no evidence in this volume that he does not consider himself a follower of Freud, although he brings out clearly the differences in his practice and their bearing on psychoanalytic theory. This book one can see as quite possible to accomplish at this time, for it involved chiefly the reorganization of familiar, already collected material; but in this same period he also wrote the first volume of his *Genetic Psychology*,[52] in which he utilizes not only analytic material but surely the results of his own self-analysis in New York. In this little volume, which unfortunately has never been translated for publication, he reverses the psychoanalytic approach that begins with the adult neurotic and goes backward into infancy as the source of the evil, in order to look at the normal development of the child positively and constructively.

The first chapter on the "Genesis of Genitality" was prepared in time for presentation at the Hamburg Congress in September, 1925. It traces the movement of the child at birth, from breast to own body, to final genital primacy, with a fineness of detail and of physiological accuracy that is not easily to be found in the literature, even today when the importance of birth, mother, and breast for future relationship is no longer disputed. The chapter headings, "Genesis of the Guilt Feeling," "Genesis of the Object Relation," followed by a section on the psychic mechanisms of "Projection," "Object Relation," "Identification and Ego Construction," "Denial and Adaptation to Reality" all point to something very different from his previous writing. He is going

---

[52] *Grundzüge einer Genetische Psychologie Auf Grund der Psycholoanalyse der Ichstruktur, I Teil.* (Leipsig and Vienna: Franz Deutike, 1927).

Privately circulated translation for use in lecture series, New York School of Social Work, Fall, 1926.

Several chapters from *Genetische Psychologie* have been published in the *Psychoanalytic Review* in English:

"The Genesis of Genitality," *Psychoanalytic Review,* XIII, 1926, pp. 129–144. (Basic chapter summarizing Volume I.)

"Pscyhoanalytic Problems," *Psychoanalytic Review,* XIV, 1927. (Introductory chapter of Volume I.)

"Beyond Psychoanalysis," *Psychoanalytic Review,* XVI, 1929. (Introductory chapter of Volume II.)

Two lectures, one on "Character Formation" and one "The Task of Education," representing two basic chapters of Volume II.

beyond the analytic situation to the purely human relationships on which and by which the individual moves toward
self-realization.

The poem from Tennyson's "In Memoriam" with which
he chooses to introduce these chapters is so characteristic of
Rank's love for the appropriate quotation and so indicative
of a new use of his experience that I include it here.

> The baby new to earth and sky
> What time his tender palm is prest
> Against the circle of the breast,
> Has never thought that this is "I."
>
> But as he grows he gathers much,
> And learns the use of "I" and "me"
> And finds "I am not what I see,
> And other than the things I touch."
>
> So rounds he to a separate mind
> From whence clear memory may begin,
> And through the frame that binds him in
> His isolation grows defined.
>
> This use may be in blood and breath,
> Which use were fruitless of their due,
> Had man to learn himself anew
> Beyond the second birth of death.
>
> ALFRED TENNYSON, In Memoriam, XLV.

On just what day in this long struggle between the personal
self and what Rank calls in *Art and Artist* the "immortal
self" the final break was consciously made or impulsively
accomplished by movement in space, I do not know. But it
is significant that in his 1930 account of his works he says
that Freud's final rejection of his position was precipitated by

Volume I of the *Technik*. This book, again probably printed without consultation or warning, was exactly the kind of outcome that had been anticipated by the Committee in their emphasis on no more publications until his reformation was established to their satisfaction. Rank had never for a moment acquiesced in this condition, as he intimated in his final letter to the Committee. Thus Freud and the others were once more faced with a *fait accompli*, a more complete and far-reaching presentation of the very views and practices that had previously brought down the accusation of deviation and/or neurosis.

It was obviously in response to reactions to the *Technik* that Rank acknowledges at last Freud's refusal to understand, for in a foreword to Volume I of *Genetische Psychologie*, dated Paris, Spring, 1926, in the second paragraph referring to the *Trauma of Birth*, he says, "However disconcerting it is that the founder of Psychoanalysis, out of which my conception had developed, opposes it with an attitude affectively conditioned, it could not disillusion me nor confuse me in going on with subsequent work." It is interesting that in this small volume with its psychoanalytic terminology the process of differentiation from the Freudian base, which is indicated in a new emphasis on the ego and the beginning of a constructive human psychology, has taken on a greatly increased momentum.

That Rank had already established some connections in Paris is indicated by a bulletin of the Groupe d'Etudes Philosophique et Scientifiques pour l'examen des Idées et Tendances nouvelle, for the year 1924–1925, preserved among his papers. Rank is scheduled to give a lecture on February 22, 1925, on "La Psychoanalyse et son influence sur l'evolution intellectuelle." Whether he ever gave this lecture is doubtful as he was in New York at that particular time, but it seems definite that by May, 1926, if not earlier, he had taken up residence in Paris. At any rate I have a letter

119

from 31 Rue de Chazelles, dated May 18, 1926, in answer
to my application for analytic time in New York in the fall.
A second letter from Zurich, dated July 18, informed me
that he would be in New York by October. Thereafter his
address remained Paris until he settled permanently in New
York.

It is not surprising that the Committee considered Rank
a traitor, disloyal to a benefactor, unfaithful to his friends,
a deserter who weakly ran away. As Sachs puts it, "He (Freud)
had done everything in his power to make Rank's way
through life smooth and to bestow on him a leading part in
the psychoanalytic movement. Then came the time when
Rank broke away from psychoanalysis, doing it not with a
clear-cut decision, but alternately renouncing all his former
opinions and then again half-heartedly turning back to them.
Yet, when after many ups and downs the final rupture came,
Freud did not show the soft regret that I felt at the loss of an
old friend. He said sternly, 'Wenn man jemandem alles
verziehen hat, ist man fertig mit ihm.' (Now after I have
forgiven everything, I am through with him.)" [53]

It is strange that a psychologist or a psychotherapist should
so fail to understand the separation process in human relationships, even when taking part in it personally. Yet Freud
himself, the very source of modern psychology, apparently
could not allow for a developmental process that led away
from himself and psychoanalysis and involved a relinquishment on his part. Rank at least was following his own forward movement, while for Freud it was a forced yielding, a
loss not chosen or accepted as right. Perhaps physical or
natural scientists are able to maintain personal relationships
despite intellectual disagreement, but a psychology of the
individual is like a religion: one may admit difference as a
right; one cannot embrace it.

[53] Sachs, *op. cit.*, p. 149.

III *Years of fulfilment*

THE thirteen years of life remaining to Rank after his formal severance from Freud and psychoanalysis in 1926 may be designated years of fulfilment only if one views human experience as potentially a process of continuous rebirth in which more inclusive selves may emerge, however painfully, from preceding levels of incomplete development.

The compulsion to write that characterized Rank's years of residence in Paris was at first primarily his necessity to free himself ideologically from the shreds of his psychoanalytic past, to redefine himself in the light of his increasing rejection of the very theory and practice to which he himself had contributed actively. Hence the argumentative tone of the second and third volumes of his *Technik der Psychoanalyse* in which he subjects to merciless criticism not primarily Freud, Jung, and Adler, but the position of an old self now

123

opposing the emergence of the new. One may ask how Rank escaped the curse of a permanently embittered personality, more than justified by the professional isolation and nullity to which the fiat of the inner psychoanalytic circle had condemned him. Nothing that he published thereafter was ever to be noticed since a priori it was the expression of a neurosis, if not a psychosis. The answer is to be found first of all in Rank's deep-seated belief in himself which, from his earliest years, had always returned to save him from periods of depression and secondly in a tremendous creativity never to be denied for long. To my knowledge the only real resentment he ever held against life was against the necessity to earn a living in ways that left no time or energy for creative expression. Multiple physical ills he bore with increasing patience. If being a Jew was a problem to him, no sign of it escaped him in the *Daybooks*, or in any form recognizable by me in thirteen years of acquaintance. Moreover, there was an important source of sustenance in those eight years of residence in Paris interspersed with lengthy stays for practice in the United States that has never to my knowledge been understood or appreciated, that is, the remarkable development of his ability to help the patients who still sought him regardless of the Freudian ban. Not merely the brilliance and speed of his evolving therapeutic skill, but its humanity, its acceptance of the emotional reality of the helping relationship, must have increased his self-confidence and provided a warmth of immediate human response even within the professionally limited situations psychotherapy permits.

At all events, in the practice of psychotherapy Rank moved out of the classical tradition into a completely reversed conception of the role of the therapist as secondary, leaving to the patient the active role of the creator in the therapeutic process. Rank's use of a greatly shortened treatment period, evolving out of his growing understanding of how to limit time and utilize ending to the patient's advantage, resulted in a degree and quality of therapeutic skill that has probably never been equaled and could be known only to those who had experienced its magic. It was unique, not to be taught or passed on through formula, as much the expression of his peculiar genius as was his music of Mozart. Yet even Rank's therapeutic gift was finally to become an almost fatal obstacle to self-development, although its renunciation threatened economic security and the loss of an increasingly restricted professional self.

The prolonged compulsion to write that characterized the eight years in Paris culminated in two books. *Art and Artist,* his final organization of the problem that had absorbed him from the time of his first book, *Der Künstler,* brought to an end a deeply ingrained aspect of the old self in a spirit of renunciation, together with an affirmation of the value of the artist's personality and its development as the real focus for the creative impulse. The second book, *Psychology and the Soul,* gave evidence of a new, socially motivated interest, going beyond individual psychology to the race and the supreme motivation underlying every stage of its development in the depth of the human longing for immortality, however disguised today as scientific psychology.

The developmental crisis, expressed creatively in *Art and Artist,* had to be lived through by Rank in a desperate struggle to give up the ambitious, competitive striving of an earlier period, together with the acclaim of accepted achievement. Months of prolonged conflict and depression were experienced before he finally came to an inner acceptance of a new self that could forego for a time the old media of creative expression and utilize constructively, actively, and with humor the outlets still remaining to him.

There were only five years left for his life in New York and the continued cultivation of a personality ever more human, spontaneous, and socially responsible. His own delight in new-found aspects of the impulsive self that had been so severely restrained in youth and even in the period of Freudian adherence breaks through repeatedly in letters to me. Despite overwork, illness, insufficient income, and professional ostracism, Rank could always find, as he says, "worlds within himself" yet to be discovered. It is in that meaning of continued self-discovery and self-integration that I have called the years that finally produced *Beyond Psychology*, his last book and his first to be written in English, years of fulfilment.

IN PARIS, 1926-1934

I T IS doubtful that the year 1926 could possibly have felt like fulfilment to Rank as he began his life in Paris, where psychoanalysis has never flourished. Perhaps he had patients who followed him there from Vienna but that he would find new applicants at first, apart from his American contacts, seems unlikely. One wonders how long it took for him to measure the extent of his loss, or did he, as was his wont, realize in one instant the fullness of his isolation? At all events there was to be no more turning back. At one stroke, he has finally severed his connections with Vienna and medical psychoanalysis, although it is the only profession for which he has had training. As a nonmedical analyst he must practice without the protection of Freud's sanction. No longer can he expect patients to be referred by European analysts, once they become aware of the changed relation to Freud. It is only a matter of time until the blight of Freud's rejection will begin to affect the psychiatric source of supply in New York. Cut off from all his friends, facing the possible loss of livelihood as well as the alienation of his wife, it would not be strange if Rank had succumbed to depression.

However, there is some evidence of his condition in the fact that he was at least able to assemble under the title *Sexualität und Schuldgefühl*[1] (Sexuality and Guilt Feeling) some papers that had earlier received favorable comment, and publish them in 1926, as well as to bring out the first volume of *Genetische Psychologie*[2] and a revised, enlarged edition of *Inzest-Motiv*.[3]

Whatever he may have suffered from neurosis or depression throughout the spring and summer of 1926, he was quite able to return to New York in October, establish himself modestly at the Hotel Holley on Washington Square, and begin a full program of analysis and lectures. He was still analyzing a number of younger psychiatrists, some of whom I came to know in passing. Whether he conducted a seminar for any medical group at that time, I do not know. There is no record of it. But there were psychiatrists as well as social workers included in the audience that tried, for the most part vainly, to follow the lectures that he read painfully from the English translation, one evening a week at the New York School of Social Work. As far as I was able to judge in my heightened emotional state, the response of the audience was largely in terms of personal resistance to or pleasurable excitement about the possibility of being analyzed, plus the postanalytic reactions of those who had already experienced analysis. The fact that Rank represented or would soon represent an anti-Freudian form of psychotherapy was hardly glimpsed by this younger, unsophisticated group. It is amusing to recall

[1] Internationale Psychoanalytische Bibliothek XXI, Vienna.
[2] Franz Deuticke, Leipzig and Vienna.
[3] Franz Deuticke, Leipzig and Vienna.

that two of the most prominent social workers in New York, who sat back of me at the lectures, selected me as the guinea pig to be observed before themselves venturing into any analytic relationship. The results cannot have been encouraging for (as far as I know) they never risked themselves beyond adopting and promoting Freudian theory as far safer and rationally preferable. The acid test they left to others as rash as the guinea pig.

On my return to Philadelphia full of enthusiasm for my own experience in New York, I stirred up the latent interest of my friends and professional associates to such a degree that several of them were ready to apply for a Rankian analysis. Consequently, guilty though I was for my own selfish motives, I wrote to Rank in fear and trembling about Philadelphia as a suitable place for his next visit.

The awe in which I held Rank, my realization that for the second time in my life I had met genius, made it impossible for me to think of him as needing anything I could provide. Indeed, it is only now in old age that I can appreciate the courage and self-confidence with which Rank tried out any opening that gave promise of fresh opportunity to work outside the range of direct Freudian opposition. Philadelphia in 1927 was still just discovering and disapproving of Freud. There would be little if any recognition of Rank's presence and certainly no conception of his difference. Only his lack of medical degree might provide ground for special criticism. Moreover, at that time the conservative Philadelphia psychiatrist would hardly have considered an analyst of social workers a threat to his own practice.

I was overwhelmed with joy on receipt of a letter dated January 28, 1927, from a new Paris address, 19 Rue de la Tremoille, indicating his interest in Philadelphia as I had described its possibilities, and closing with this sentence: "After a short semirest I am working again on a full 'New Yorklike' schedule to which the same cold seems to belong."

129

Evidently I had referred to a cold from which he had suffered in New York and for which he had undoubtedly been reproached by every patient looking for the weak spot in the analyst's armor. Thus encouraged, I must have put my energy to work on further ways in which to add to the attractiveness of Philadelphia, for I find a letter, dated February 28, in which he says that one of his medical friends in New York advises Philadelphia rather than Chicago (from which he has apparently had applications) and that he is about ready to decide on Philadelphia for the fall. He carefully states his responsibility for staying as long as the analyses require and his usual fee, with a reduction for some social workers if necessary. He also indicates his readiness to give a lecture course in Philadelphia (which I must have suggested) and says it would be "easier to follow and understand but also of more practical value" than the New York lectures of the previous year. These lectures he says he is now writing as Volume II of *Genetische Psychologie* of which the New York lectures formed Volume I, the theoretical part. A letter of June 6, with a new address, 9 Rue Louis Boilly, which was to be his permanent address in Paris, speaks of a number of applications from Philadelphia. He adds, "I am answering now that I can't promise to take anyone definitely and will have to make the final choice after I have seen all the people there and selected the most suitable ones. I also had a letter from Mr. Pray (then Dean of the Pennsylvania School of Social Work) regarding my lectures. He says, as I had expected, that he would prefer a series of more popular lectures. I am afraid I have to leave open this question too till I come to Philadelphia. I expect to be very busy all summer long and therefore to stay in Paris all the time."

Nothing in this letter betrays the undue eagerness of a man in need, nor does it promise anything in advance that might add to the certainty of an unknown situation. There is no hint of self-protectiveness, no apparent fear of risk. By

July 28, I felt obliged to write to him again as I had been approached by the person who had first told me about Rank, with an offer that I was asked to transmit.

July 28, 1927

Dr. Otto Rank,
9 Rue Louis Boilly,
Paris XVI*

Dear Dr. Rank,

I have been commissioned by Miss X, whom you may already have seen by this time, to offer you the use of her rooms while you are in Philadelphia. I am writing you about them now because I am using them and if you want them, I should like to know it if possible by September so that I can get other rooms—which would be perfectly simple for me. So don't hesitate to take them on my account.

I told Miss X that I did not think the rooms would be very suitable for your purposes but she was not convinced, so I give you the facts and you may decide for yourself.

There are two rooms of medium size on the ground floor of a very small apartment house. The front room has two windows which open on a narrow street, rather noisy but with no street car. The back room has one window opening on a quiet court. There is a direct exit to hall from both rooms, so patients need not meet. The rooms are suitably furnished.

The objections as I see them are as follows: There is no telephone service in the building—no telephone in the rooms at all at present. There is no maid service. The walls are very thin so that persons in the outerhall seem to be in the room and if patients are waiting in the front room they can hear anything above a whisper. The rooms are almost directly across from the social service building, where everyone knows everyone else, and would be profoundly curious about your patients.

If these rooms as described are not what you want, and if

131

you will give me an idea of what you consider essential and what you expect to pay, I might save you time and effort by getting together a list of possible places for you to look over when you come. And will you please tell me about what time you expect to arrive.

Great interest in our coming has been expressed by Y—, the executive secretary of the X— Council in Philadelphia. He will probably approach you for lectures. May I suggest that you do not commit yourself until you have talked over the situation. This organization is given to propaganda at any cost. Perhaps if I tell you that they considered Adler perfect and are getting him for a course this year, it might indicate some of the factors to be considered.

Fall seems very near with only a month of vacation intervening—at least for me. I hope you are going to get some rest between groups other than the trip over and that there will be no trace of a cold when you arrive.

With cordial greetings,
Sincerely,
Jessie Taft

My directness was matched by Rank's, who writes on September 12 as follows:

September 12, 1927
9 Rue Louis Boilly
Paris XVIe

Dr. Jessie Taft
311 South Juniper Street
Philadelphia, Pa.
U.S.A.
Dear Doctor Taft:

Thank you for your letter of July 28, which I only had answered by cable before going on my vacation.

I told you in my cablegram that I could not accept the offer made by Miss X.

I would appreciate it very much if you would be kind enough to look for a place for me. I think you know exactly what I want (or rather what I don't want and cannot take). The price does not play any role at all as long as the rooms are comfortable and suit my purpose.

I expect to sail in the first week of October and start work in Philadelphia about the middle of the month.

Everything else I think we will talk over when I arrive.

With cordial greetings, Sincerely

O. Rank

The arrangements were made by me with a willingness that had never before accompanied practical chores involving outside excursions, and as a result Rank took up his first residence in Philadelphia in a suite at the Benjamin Franklin Hotel, with a distant view of the Delaware River.

As I have stated in the Introduction, I had been attending, in the winter and spring of 1927, the weekly seminar carried on by the Rankian medical group in New York, devoted to earnest efforts to comprehend and use the lectures just completed at the New York School in the fall. This seminar was to be continued in the fall of 1927, under Rank's guidance. It was at their first meeting in the fall, held on his arrival in New York, that I faced in the flesh the demonic forces I had been responsible for summoning. If I felt guilt for the will I had exerted, it was swallowed up in the well-nigh overwhelming fear with which I entered the lovely room where our meetings were held. Only a desperate courage and Rank's simple kindly greeting brought me through that evening. The next morning, after what was probably a sleepless night, I met Rank in the Pennsylvania Station as he had requested, so that he might utilize the trip for a discussion of the Philadelphia situation.

Only someone who has had the experience of trying to relate postanalytic emotion to the reality of the analyst will understand what Rank's first Philadelphia sojourn cost me and what it gave me in self-discipline and development as a therapist. Although no one could have known better than Rank the personal nature of the motivation that inspired my activities in his behalf, never for a moment did he put me back in the role of patient, never did he utilize his knowledge of my innermost make-up to interpret even the most obvious aspects of my behavior. I was like the rest of the New York group, a learner, and free to bring him the current problems of my practice. From the start he never failed to maintain a relationship which, although it deepened into friendship, was always a reality relationship, never a taking advantage of postanalytic transference. He gave freely the reality of what he had to give, but nothing more, even when he had to disappoint unrealistic expectations. On the undeviating honesty of his friendship I learned what apparently he had understood always, the meaning of inner growth which develops on relationship that tolerates but refuses to reciprocate undesirable projections.

In the period between Rank's arrival in Philadelphia in October, 1927, and his departure for Paris before Christmas, he carried a full schedule with analysands, lectured for the Pennsylvania School of Social Work on Monday evenings, and went to New York once a week, probably on Friday or Saturday evening, to lead the seminar for his group there. A conference with me on my current practice was worked in when possible, sometimes at an odd hour in Philadelphia, sometimes on the train to New York. The Philadelphia lecture course consisted, as he had intended from the first, of the six chapters that constitute the body of Volume II of *Genetic Psychology*. Difficult as they were and are, they are far more human in feeling and content than the theoretical presentation of Volume I, which had formed and continued to form the core of our work in the New York group. I do not recall that the content of Volume II was ever made the center of discussion, probably because it departed from the daily problems of analytic technique into a philosophic yet practical contemplation of "Character and the Self," "The Significance of the Love Life," "Social Adaptation and Creativity," "Education and Domination," "The Emotional Life," and, finally, "The Possibilities of Therapy." These analysts, medical or otherwise, as I soon discovered, were no different from a group of social work students. They cared only for cases and chiefly their own. If there was ever any discussion of theory on the level of Rank's interests, I cannot remember it. Yet his patient and courteous consideration of every problem brought up in the seminar never failed. If he was bored with our lack of understanding, he did not show it, nor did he try to push the group beyond the level of its real concern.

In Philadelphia, he had only one opportunity to speak directly to a medical group, at whose suggestion is not recorded; but among his papers there are the notes in German that he used for an evening lecture at the Philadelphia College of Physicians, on February 25, 1928 (after he had left Philadelphia) on "Therapeutic Approach to the Neuroses." I remember attending the meeting and later hearing Rank express satisfaction that he had been able to speak from notes instead of reading a paper translated into English. At the time I did not know that he had used German notes for his speech but I did realize that he was speaking more freely than I had ever heard him speak in a formal situation. As I look at the outline of his talk, I can see that it must have been a feat to reorder for use on the spot without retyping, as he evidently did, the three main headings, putting Number 3 in Number 2's place, extracting as Number 1 a part of Number 3, at the same time expressing their substance in a different language. It reveals the completeness with which Rank organized his thinking, combined with the richness and immediacy of his associative processes, which were never blocked even by a language handicap.

After a brief stay in Paris, Rank had returned to New York to complete the seminar and remained there at least into April, for there is among the papers a quaint printed announcement of "a meeting of the Boston Society of Psychiatry and Neurology, to be held on April 19, 1928, at the Medical Library. Address by Otto Rank of Paris (by invitation), "Beyond Psychoanalysis." A note from a Boston member of Rank's New York seminar betrays the source of the invitation.

One might question the wisdom of presenting, to a group of conservative Boston psychiatrists and neurologists, a purely psychological approach intended to encompass as well as to go beyond psychoanalysis itself. The Boston of that period, in my recollection, had little regard for psychoanalysis as an approved therapy for the neuroses and would probably have failed even to appreciate, much less to oppose, Rank's way of going beyond it. His emphasis on the social and ethical factors important in therapy as in living would surely have appealed to them, but might well have been outweighed by his inclusion of love and the emotional life as legitimate material for a genetic psychology.

The New York Mental Hygiene Committee, led at that time by a member of the Rankian group, ventured to bring out in pamphlet form for distribution two chapters from this volume, "Character Formation" and "The Task of Education." Although the titles sound sensible and useful, they do not make for popular reading.

Sometime in the spring of 1928, Rank went back to Paris and did not return to this country until January, 1929, when he distributed his time between Philadelphia and New York. There has now begun for Rank the period of his most intense creativity. Everything seems to be forming in his mind at one and the same time and with a force that compelled him to write. He says that *Wahrheit und Wirklichheit* (Truth and Reality), the third volume of *Genetische Psychologie*, was written simultaneously with the second volume of his *Technik* as its philosophic accompaniment. Once in Paris, he described to me his way of writing. Everything flowed from his pen, already organized and complete, almost compulsively, as he once described it in the *Daybooks*. He could hardly get it down fast enough to hold it. This does not mean that he was careless, for his manuscripts bear witness to much editing and his references to other authorities are voluminous and meticulous. What it does mean is that Rank, from the time of the *Daybooks*, has never ceased to work on the concepts that even then seemed vital to him, and has returned to them at each new level of his own development and experience in an ever-deepening and more inclusive comprehension.

Although he brought *Truth and Reality* to public notice in his lecture series of 1929, given in New York and Philadelphia, I cannot recall reacting with shock to his use of *will* in that volume as a basic concept in his psychology nor can I remember that its content was ever brought up for discussion in the New York seminar. Only the second volume of the *Technik* could have made the impact on me and on the group that I have already referred to in the preface. Philosophy one can keep at a safe distance; practice comes straight home and cannot be ignored. One objective indication that the concept of will was not projected into the New York group until 1930, although Rank himself had already begun to alter his own therapeutic technique by 1929 (if not before), is found in a remarkable address entitled "The Psychological Approach to Personal Problems" [4] that he gave for the Mental Hygiene Department of Yale in Sterling Memorial Hall on February 28, 1929. It is probably his first long

[4] This address is included among Rank's papers in typed and teletyped forms but was not published.

speech in English and was evidently taken down in Teletype at the time, with all the errors of a spontaneous talk, for an audience with which he seemed to feel at home. With the utmost simplicity, he freely describes his early relation to Freud and his present conception of the failure of psychoanalysis as a psychology or therapy for the future. He characterizes briefly the one-sidedness of Jung and of Adler in their efforts to overcome Freud's biological conception and says about his own problem with it:

But neither Freud, nor Jung, nor Adler sufficiently considers the creative part of our personality, namely, that which is not purely biological as Freud sees it, nor purely racial as Jung conceives it, nor yet purely social as Adler thinks, but which is purely individual.

It may interest you to know, as it also interested me, when I had a chance to look back on my own development, that already in 1905, when I first came in contact with Freud and his theory, my first reaction was a little book, a pamphlet, in which even then I pointed out this lack in the Freudian theory. What I called "the artist" was something other than the man who actually paints; I mean by that the creative personality and I tried to explain this creative type by using Freud's psychology and his terminology, but I found that I could not do it without going beyond Freud.

At the end of this talk, he takes up a number of questions that had been prepared and presented to him in advance. The first one: "What are the criteria for selection of an individual suitable for analysis?" Rank handles with a freedom that could well have shocked his audience as well as amused them. He says in part:

I think in order to decide whether an individual is suitable for psychoanalysis, if you don't mind my putting it paradoxically before I explain it, he should be analyzed first. In other words, you have to have a complete understanding, not only of this individual's psychology, but also of the general situation, of all his external and internal problems.

I will give you an illustration just from my own actual experience: A woman comes for consultation; what's the matter with her? She suffers from some kind of intestinal symptoms, painful attacks of some kind of intestinal trouble. She has been sick for eight years, and has tried every kind of physical treatment, she has been X-rayed, examined, dieted, everything under the sun. She came to the conclusion it must be some emotional trouble. She is unmarried, she is thirty-five. She appears to me (and admits it herself) as being fairly well adjusted. She lives with a sister who is married; they get along well. She enjoys life, goes to the country in the summer. She has a little stomach trouble; why not keep it, I tell her, because if we are able to take away those attacks that come once in a fortnight or so, we do not know what problem we shall discover beneath it. Probably this defense mechanism belongs to her adjustment, probably that is the price she has to pay. She never married, she never loved, and so never fulfilled her role. One cannot ever have everything, probably she has to pay. After all, what difference does it make if she occasionally gets these attacks of indigestion? I get it occasionally, you do too, probably, and not for physical reasons, as you may know. One gets headaches. In other words, it is not so much a question as to whether we are able to cure a patient, whether we can or not, but whether we should or not.

After some elaboration of this answer, he takes up the second inevitable question about the shortened time and cannot refrain from beginning his reply facetiously:

I analyzed first according to Freud's technique and then gradually developed a shorter one, a technique that is getting

139

shorter and shorter, so that I am almost afraid that soon I won't have to see the patient at all. (Laughter.)

There follow a number of questions that Rank answered at some length and finally a few questions were asked from the floor and discussed briefly.

I have introduced these quotations from the Yale address for two reasons: first to support my own memory that the "will psychology" was not launched as such in New York until 1930, and second, to show the distance Rank has traveled in freedom to express himself before an American audience, without the necessity to read a paper laboriously, or even to depend on notes. He is obviously at home and even enjoying his relation to his audience. When I think of the serious "German student" of my first contact, it is hard to believe that such painful reserve and constriction of delivery in English could ever eventuate in spontaneity. It also seems fairly conclusive that if Rank were using the word "will" as basic to his thinking, which he did the following year, it would not have failed to present itself here in the free flow of this description of his own development.

Rank's reaction to the Yale address is recorded in two letters. The first, a note just before he left for Paris, reads:

March 1, 1929

Thank you for your kind note, Dr. Taft! Experience and Nature (John Dewey) is being published in a new and revised edition by Norton today! I arranged to have a copy delivered from the book-binder directly to the boat. I can't avoid being efficient! It's a curse.

The Yale speech they tell me was excellent. I had a stenographer to take it down and will probably publish it later on.

The chimpanzees with whom I spent two hours are simply lovely. They are making a thorough study of the psycholo-

140

gists around them and know already how to please them in their experiments. They don't know anything about time but are experts in regard to space because they spit right in the middle of your face from any distance. That's their way of lecturing.

All good wishes for you and your friends whom I appreciate also as mine.

O. Rank

From this last reference, one sees what inspired in part the outgoing, informal beginning of the Yale address, his appreciation of the University setting in which he had spent the afternoon.

A second letter later in the spring refers to "my new book," the third on which he has worked within the year, and indicates also that I must have been disturbed by our seminar discussions after his departure. My guess is that someone was equating Rank's increasing distance from Freud and psychoanalysis with a departure from the scientific; in other words, from medical backing. Rank is certainly not oblivious to this trend. He writes in a letter dated June 10, 1929:

June 10, 1929

Dr. Otto Rank
9, Rue Louis Boilly
Paris XVIe

Dear Dr. Taft:

Your kind letter arrived when I was just in the midst of finishing my new book of which all but the last chapter is written. Since I left everything concerning "physics" to this last chapter and took up only the much easier aspects of "metaphysics" so far, I am sorry not to be able to satisfy all your curiosity about the future of science in general and psychology in particular. My chief impression, however, is that physics

141

consists of at least as much speculation and interpretation as psychology, only it seems to be (even) less real.

I am glad you liked the lecture. I liked it when I gave it, which I not always do. I think Dr. X—, from whom I haven't heard about it, doesn't know what to do with it and I can see it is difficult: shouldn't be published as it is and shouldn't be rewritten, probably shouldn't be published at all—it was just a talk!

Thank you for all the news from Philadelphia, including your "unconscious" poem. I wish (sometimes) I could write poetry instead of—what I have to write, or rather not to write at all. But I am afraid such a "Samoan" life might be unreal—for me! As things now look I rather think I won't be back in the States until next January.

The group's reaction and behavior does not surprise me. I have seen groups for twenty years and that's the reason why I don't want a group of my own or to be the "leader" of a group, although it is difficult to be all alone and all by yourself. On the other hand I may go so fast in order that no one can catch up with me—not only myself—

My best greetings to you and all your friends and all good wishes for a pleasant summer.

Yours
Rank

The new book is explained in the next letter of September 4 and indicates his plans for the following year.

September 4, 1929

Dear Miss Taft:

Thank you for your kind letter of August 8, which has been forwarded to me to the southern part of France where I was staying a short time with my family. Now I am back in Paris waiting to get ready for work.

I am inclined to accept the invitation to Chicago, which I

owe to your thoughtfulness. I am planning to come early next year and stay over till the International Conference for Mental Hygiene (the beginning of May).

I congratulate you heartily on your permanent teaching job because it is something one needs (we need). I wish I could do something of that kind, but I am afraid I never will. I am too much ahead of the current thought and—of myself. Or—as Dr. X in one of his recent letters put it politely: I am a kind of Einstein in the field of psychology and therefore people don't understand me (of course with a few rare exceptions!)

I was doing some analyses all the time—up to the end of July—the book I finished within a few weeks and now it is in print. The title is Seelenglaube und Psychologie, showing how our scientific psychology grew out of the belief in the Soul (Immortality) and still represents for us the same although it denies the existence of the Soul. In one word, psychology being our religion. This idea is carried through all the stages of human development from the magic world view of the primitive to psychoanalysis and of course to my own concepts.

The Trauma of Birth appeared finally in England. Since it will take several weeks before the American edition will be ready, I am sending you a copy of it.

I am glad you have (or rather had) such a splendid vacation —mine was somewhat spoiled by ill health in the family—but now we are all well again.

With cordial greetings to you and Virginia,

I remain

Yours

Rank

By February of 1930, Rank, accompanied this time by his wife, was back in New York at the hotel on Gramercy Park, carrying a heavy load of control analyses, as well as private patients. My own hour, once a week on the day of the evening seminar, usually the latest possible before dinner, was subject to sudden cancelation with a note like the following: "I am very sorry to find it still impossible to see you on Wednesday; after ten hours of work, I know you understand and I appreciate it." When I did see him he was often so tired that I had not the heart to bring up one more problem from my own cases, however pressing, but did my best to provoke the ready interest that could always respond to an objective stimulus and, momentarily at least, lift the burden of fatigue. Yet I was not selfless enough to spare him that extra hour.

On the first meeting of the seminar, February 5, there was an introductory statement by Rank on the function of will in analysis. I do not believe that *will* as the central force in the therapeutic relationship had ever before been made the focus of his teaching in this group, although *Wahrheit und Wirklichkeit* as well as *Technik* II was already in print and the implications of a new recognition of the critical value of the will psychology for therapy had already been thought through by him both technically and philosophically. As I recall his feeling for Schopenhauer's will, expressed in the *Daybooks*, and the ever-developing emphasis on the individual as creative, thoughout all his previous writing and analytic practice, I can hardly understand how and why this presentation of the will came as such a break with the past. Certainly it was not foreign to his own development, but it proved in the end to be unassimilable by the group constituting this seminar. I have no way of knowing what were the real feelings of the group members. The minutes of those meetings show only conventional, rationalized responses. I do know that my own sense of shock was temporary. As soon as I overcame what I perhaps rationalized as traditional prejudices inculcated by my academic training in psychology, what ensued for me was a revelation that lit up my whole way of thinking and working. Perhaps Rank himself came to such a moment of sudden enlightenment, dif-

144

ferent in its revelation from his previous insight, for he says in the first paragraph of Chapter II in *Truth and Reality*: "My reintroduction of the will concept into psychology solves a succession of problems in such a simple and satisfying way that it may seem to some a *deus ex machina*. But I know too well that I have not brought it in as such; on the contrary that I have busied myself long and intensively in an attempt to solve certain problems which psychoanalysis had brought up anew without coming to a satisfactory solution. Only after a struggle against prejudices of every kind did the acceptance of will as a psychological factor of the first rank seem unavoidable but soon also became a matter of course, so much a matter of course that I had to say to myself that only a tremendous resistance could have hindered the complete recognition and evaluation of will as a great psychic power."

At any rate, the "will" focus liberated Rank finally from his Freudian past, from the biological, developmental details of family history as the core of analytic procedure, and from the old psychoanalytic terminology. It was, of course, the result, not the cause, of his internal development as he gradually overcame creatively through his writing and thinking the trauma of his separation from Freud, with its prolonged conflict between two powerful wills, and took upon himself full responsibility for decisive difference. With new language and a dynamic technique that cannot be learned, any more than one can determine in advance what the impact between two personalities will be, the usefulness of his teaching relation to a medical group as varied as this one in mental and emotional development will be increasingly diminished, and his own dissatisfaction with results heightened.

There is nothing in the minutes of this seminar, during which he actually assigned chapters from the second volume of *Technik*, and himself read whole sections aloud as a basis

145

for discussion, to show that the group was reacting to change and newness. They seemed to accept "will" placidly, with the usual questions about its effect on beginning and ending with their patients. Just one recorded reaction in the middle of the nine sessions may be significant. Suddenly, as if Rank had not been doing exactly that, someone asked if he would please devote the next session to an explanation of his will psychology and one member put in frequent nagging questions that seemed to betray an underlying resistance rather than any desire to be answered.

If I did not know, from many years of presenting "will" to students of social work, how slow they are to admit its existence, particularly in themselves, and how impossible it would be to hold them to it without the functional control of a training process in which each must take responsibility for the impact of his own will on that of the social agency client, I would not be as skeptical about what this group of Rank's was able to take in. They were already psychiatrists who had a professional status to maintain, who were obliged to be above and beyond the student level. Rank had no basis for holding them to the inner development that would have been necessary for real understanding. They could question and discuss on a rational, externalized level in terms of their patients of the moment, but how free were they to follow a nonmedical leader into dangerous divergence from their orthodox Freudian background with its claim to scientific validity, especially since in themselves they did not respond to this introduction of "will" either with excitement or with active resistance? Moreover, they were doubtless already under pressure from the older established Freudians in New York City—their fellows in the Psychoanalytic Association.

The full extent of the enmity to which Rank was subjected in Europe probably never came home to his New York circle until they were exposed to the virulent attack made upon him at the First International Congress on Mental

Hygiene in Washington on the morning of May 8, by various Freudians who took part in the unplanned discussion at the end of his program. The paper that Rank had submitted in advance to be distributed to discussants and made available in various languages for the use of the Congress was the one he had given in Chicago in February entitled, "The Training of the Will and Emotional Development."[5] This profound analysis of a problem that lies at the root of all child training and child development received scant attention from any of the formal discussants except myself. But the brief paper he actually delivered as a summary made a perfect target for the onslaught that followed when it was opened to discussion from the floor. I am inserting a copy of this so-called summary, which I find among his papers and which was not included in the formal papers published afterward, as was the real paper.

Paper Read by Rank at the First International Congress on Mental Hygiene, Washington, D.C., May 8, 1930

(*Rank's original typed copy dated Sunday, May 4, 1930, New York*)

I like the idea of a ten-minute summary instead of reading the paper, not only because the latter is rather boring but chiefly because it gives me a chance to talk newly, almost to give you a new paper, the original one having been written back in the fall and not especially for this conference either but as part of a book on education and world view.

[5] Otto Rank, "The Training of the Will and Emotional Development," Chapter III of *Modern Education*, New York: Alfred A. Knopf, 1932. Originally delivered as a lecture at the Mid-West Conference on Character Development, Chicago, February, 1930; printed in their Proceedings entitled *The Child's Emotions*, Chicago: The University of Chicago Press, 1930. Also submitted as a paper to the First International Congress on Mental Hygiene, Washington, May, 1930, and printed in Volume II of papers of this Conference.

So with your permission I will use my ten minutes to give you my discussion of my paper or rather the world view back of it and furthermore a glimpse of the personality expressed in this world view. In doing so I intend to introduce myself to the part of the audience which does not know me and at the same time relieve some doubts and correct some misunderstandings on the part of those who think they know me or knew me in the past. Because my views and ideas have changed considerably during the twenty-five years of my work in psychology and its applied fields of human science.

On account of this, my undefinable position, there was some difficulty in placing me on the program of the Congress. I am no psychiatrist, no social worker, no psychoanalyst, not even an ordinary psychologist, and to tell you the truth I am glad of it. Because I have gone through all the phases of the development of scientific psychology and its practical applications within the last twenty-five years, my extensive experience and study both theoretical and therapeutic has led me to the conviction that the scientific approach to human behavior and personality problems is not only insufficient but leaves out the most essential part of it, namely, the human side, the characteristic of which is just that it can't be measured and checked and controlled. And yet it is the only vital factor not only in life but also in all kinds of therapy, mental hygiene in the broadest sense. What helps is not intellectual knowledge but human understanding, which is emotional and hence cannot be schematized and utilized. The main trouble with the scientific approach to human nature is not so much that it has to neglect the personal, so-called subjective, element but that it has to deny it in order to maintain the scientific attitude. This is clearly seen in psychoanalysis, which could not help recognizing the high importance of the purely human side and yet had to stigmatize it scientifically as being only a transference phenomenon. In interpreting the human element scientifically, psychoanalysis had to deny it and so defeated its own scientific ideal, becoming unscientific by denying the most essential aspect of the personality.

I don't want you to misunderstand me! I am no longer trying to prove that Freud was wrong and I am right. I realized definitely for the first time in my book Truth and Reality, published two years ago, that it is not the question whose interpretation is correct, because there is no such thing as the interpretation or only one psychological truth. Psychology does not deal primarily with facts as science does but deals only with the individual's attitude toward facts. In other words, the objects of psychology are interpretations and there are as many of them as there are individuals and even more than that, also the individuals' different situations, which have to be interpreted differently in every single manifestation.

So the battle is really on, not between different schools of psychoanalysis but between two world views, which have been in conflict with one another since the dawn of science with the early Greeks and even long before as I tried to show in my last book, The Belief in the Soul and Psychology. What I want to emphasize here is not the superiority of one interpretation, that is, of one psychological theory over another, but the difference in world view underlying all the ardent discussion about psychological values which is now going on with an emotional conviction comparable only to the religious wars in the so-called darkest medieval times. This conflict will not be lessened until we admit that science has proved to be a complete failure in the field of psychology, i.e., in the betterment of human nature and in the achievement of human happiness toward which all mental hygiene is ultimately striving. The result of scientific psychology can be summed up today as the recognition that it is necessarily insufficient to explain human nature, far less to make the individual happier.

The error lies in the scientific glorification of consciousness, of intellectual knowledge, which even Psychoanalysis worships as its highest god although it calls itself a psychology of the unconscious. But this means only an attempt to rationalize the Unconscious and to intellectualize it scientifically. But just this attempt has proved to be the main test for a scientific comprehension of the individual and its failure is clearly shown in the complete lack of the essential part of the Unconscious, namely, the emotional life, as I point out in my paper. Intellectual understanding is one thing and the actual working out of our emotional problems another, as I brought forward for the first time in 1922 in a pamphlet on the Development of Psychoanalysis.[6] This was my first parting, not from Freud, but from his whole ideology, which is erected on the fundamental importance of intellectual understanding as a curative factor. The second step beyond the materialistic viewpoint of Psychoanalysis I made in 1923 in The Trauma of Birth with the emphasis on an Unconscious absolutely inaccessible to any intellectual grasp; at the same time I was still trying to carry the scientific approach to human problems even further than Freud but I realized that in doing so I was carrying it ad absurdum. It is only within the last two or three years that I have gradually overcome, with the increasing acknowledgment of the purely human factor in psychotherapy, the intellectual ideology that worships knowledge for the purpose of controlling and predicting human behavior. For in order to pretend that control and prediction are possible, one had to deny the individual's own will, his emotional instability, and the large part chance plays in the sphere of our psychical life even more than in our cosmic life. The scientific approach with its artificial emphasis on one truth and its aim to control and to predict strives ultimately only for security, but it is a false security which does not do away with the cosmic fear of the individual and hence does not make us any more happy. Experience has taught me that understanding and explaining do not get you anywhere unless it comes as a result of personal experience

[6] The part of *Entwicklungsziele* contributed by Rank (Ferenczi co-author), translated by Caroline Newton.

through suffering that the scientific ideology tried to spare the individual from childhood on. I don't believe that the individual can really develop and grow up without having a chance to go through emotional experiences and conflicts of all kinds. My life's work has convinced me that real knowledge, insight, and human understanding only follow the emotional and actual working out of a problem, not vice versa as psychoanalysis, and for that matter all scientific ideology, maintains. The educator, the social worker, the therapist, can only use their own knowledge, gained by their own personal experience to let others experience their own knowledge and understanding of themselves. But it cannot be thought out intellectually and transmitted by purely mental processes such as learning, teaching, study, instruction, and so on.

And now I have said what I have to say. Let me only at the end refer you to an example for it is what you have right before you in this conference itself. Almost everybody to whom I have spoken about it said there is not much use in attending any of those big conferences for the purpose of learning anything. The most valuable factor in a gathering of a crowd like this from all over the world lies in the human element, in the meeting of people, in the contact with the personalities themselves and not with their written and read words. So I hope I have been true to the real human spirit of this conference in pushing the personal element into the foreground, not without feeling greatly obliged to the broadminded attitude of the leaders in Mental Hygiene who offered me the opportunity to do it.

Nothing could be a better index to his own state of mind and to a world view that would forever separate him from any school of "scientific" psychology, Freudian or otherwise. The atmosphere was electric. Here was the opportunity eagerly awaited by the Freudians to slay Rank publicly before an international audience. Chief among the attackers was Dr. Franz Alexander, later to become a power in Chicago. I was too excited to be able to register anything but the emotional turbulence and to marvel at Rank's calmness. He seemed actually to enjoy the situation and, when he was allowed a last word, quietly affirmed his satisfaction with the new and his willingness to carry it. For him, too, it must have been a relief to meet the opposition face to face at last, to assert an independent self, and to relinquish publicly the last shred of the Freudian halo.

I did not see Rank again until I met him in Paris the following July but his farewell note foreshadows the ill-fated "book project."

> HOTEL GRAMERCY PARK
> 52 Gramercy Park North
> New York
> Monday, May 12, 1930

Dear Dr. Taft:

In the course of our discussion in Boston about the book they are planning I suggested that you should contribute a chapter on the emotions. Of course I don't mean to impose a task on you but I thought you might like to do it—there is plenty of time and no hurry about it. They all would like it very much if you did it and I would highly appreciate it.

Needless to express again my gratitude to you for your paper in Washington; not because you supported me but for your understanding.

I was sorry not to have had a chance to say good-by to Virginia.

> Au revoir à Paris!
> Yours
> Rank

Why Rank ever let himself believe in this plan sufficiently to outline, for those proposing it, the thorough-going, ac-

curately documented list of his works up to 1930 that he
later produced with copies for all concerned, is hard to
understand, for self-deception was never his besetting sin.
He must have felt at the moment a need for group support
strong enough to blind him temporarily to the guilt reaction
which, as I can now realize, gave the illusion of on-going
creative enthusiasm for this point of view. As for myself,
since I had no idea of separating either from Rank or my own
point of view, there was no pressure to take part in such a
pretentious undertaking and I doubted my ability to write on
a subject that has baffled psychologists from the beginning,
even though Rank had opened up the way. Moreover, knowing
the difficulty that Rank's books present for any reviewer and
not having much faith in the depth of understanding attained
by the members of the seminar, I was deeply skeptical of the
outcome, although I accepted the assignment. The "book"
committee never called a meeting that included me nor sent
me any communication and to the best of my belief this
utopian scheme was, in fact, the dying gesture of the New
York Rankian group as such.

My first experience of Europe during the following summer
was memorable, not only because of Paris, the Black Forest,
Munich, and Oberammergau, but because for the first time
Rank appeared in purely friendly guise, anxious to welcome
American friends. He had written in June: "This is only to
let you know that we all quickly recovered from the last
'trauma' of America and are looking forward to seeing you
and Virginia soon. Will you please let me know what we can
do for you here before you arrive. That is, making hotel
reservations or preparations for your trip, etc. We shall be
glad to do anything we can, so don't hesitate to ask! Also
let us know in time the day of your arrival."

My friend and I were touched to find awaiting us at the
Hotel de l'Univers, St. Malo, the following unexpected
greeting, "Welcome in Europe—to both of you! I hope you

will enjoy your first stay in this country although the weather just now does not seem to be what it should! Will you please let me know when you expect to arrive in Paris. Au revoir—Rank."

It was almost too much for two Americans as untutored as we were to be met by an invitation to dinner and the theater for our first evening in Paris. Mrs. Rank, whose English, unlike her French, was far from fluent, joined nobly in offering the hospitality of their modern apartment at 9 Rue Louis Boilly, for whose interior decoration she had been responsible, and later suffered for our sakes a visit to Versailles. No one who has been there will ever forget the beautiful, stately room in which Rank received guests and patients, with a photograph of Freud still in evidence, nor the small but perfectly equipped library that was his especial pride. Most of all, I remember the emergence of a boyish, mischievous Rank, who could enjoy with abandon a window-shopping excursion through mysterious Paris streets and make the ordering of lunch an adventure.

His underlying absorption of this period came through in a letter of August 6, which reached us in Munich:

> The Analytiker[7] is coming to an end, but I don't feel it is a happy one, not only as far as he, in the book, is concerned, but also inasmuch as I am concerned with the book. The last but one chapter that I wrote yesterday is not as good as the previous ones and the last one I will finish to be done with it. It is probably the last book I shall write on the "Neurotic," analytic situation, and the like. There is not anything to say about it any more. (I enclose a table of contents, which is almost as good as the whole book; each chapter has about twenty typewritten pages.)

The table of contents reads in English translation:

[7] Third and last volume of *Technik der Psychoanalyse, Die Analyse des Analytikers.*

154

Therapist and Neurotic as Complementary types. I. Ideological versus Dynamic Therapy. II. Life Fear and Death Fear. III. Total Ego and Partial Ego. IV. Illness and Healing. V. The Role of the Therapist in the Therapeutic Situation. VI. The End Phase and the Therapeutic Agent. VII. The Individual and the Social.

Not long after our return to Philadelphia, I received the following letter indicating that he still felt a concern about the group's proposed book and reporting on his own newest writing:

October 15, 1930

Dear Dr. Taft:

Let me first tell you how much I enjoy your letters because they are real ones, just as you are real and also a real friend of mine of which I have only very few!

I am glad to see that you have the same viewpoint inside yourself and so it doesn't matter whether I have formulated this or that already or not. I probably have but I myself am the last one to be asked where, I have the hardest time to look up references to myself in my own books and I would rather write a new book than bother to look up a former one! I can't really tell you where I spoke of physical pain as being a form of emotional pain but I think I did somewhere.

What you say about fear apropos of Freud's book (Symptom, Hemmung und Angst) is certainly my opinion too and you will find it expressed beyond doubt in the 3d volume of the Technik, which is now in print. This will settle the fear problem for the time being. As far as the emotional life in general is concerned, I have also a few new ideas expressed in that book that I am not sure will be accepted by you readily (but you will see yourself).

As soon as I have some clean proofs I shall let you have them. About the time for translation I don't know yet. I

155

was also wondering whether it wouldn't be only fair to Mrs. Moxon to let her also translate the 3d volume, since she did the first and second,[8] but you will go on anyway with your translation, which you have to do apparently for yourself and by yourself and in case you are willing to let the Boston group use your translation I shall be only too glad. Although I am afraid they won't wait either or probably every one of them (except Dr. Y who does not even pretend to know German) will start a translation of his own for himself.

This state of affairs gives at the same time a picture of the Boston situation. I had recently letters from Y and Z showing considerable lack of organization in the whole matter despite a sincere willingness to contribute to the book. I wrote to all of them frankly what I thought was lacking in the whole enterprise and asked Dr. X and Dr. A (who was willing to finance the preliminary work) to help them toward organizing the whole enterprise. (I also suggested they invite you to a New York meeting in case they feel at all inclined to arrange such a meeting.) That seems to me all I can do now to further the work beyond what I had already contributed.

Besides, I wrote lately (I mean in this the last year) three books that round out my whole philosophy of life as it should be presented in the Boston book. The book on education is still unpublished, the 3rd volume of the Technik is in print and The Artist is almost finished. Within the last month I wrote twelve chapters and I have only two more to do now.

Meanwhile the chances to publish some of my books in America have increased. Mr. Knopf, who is publishing a more popular book of Psychoanalysis by Dr. Y, became

---

[8] Why Mrs. Moxon's translations never appeared I do not know. *Modern Education*, her translation, was published by Knopf in 1932.

interested in the Genetic Psychology, which he wants to publish. Mr. Lewisohn, who is a good friend of his and who admires my work, wrote immediately to Mr. Knopf urging him to bring out all my works, particularly my last ones. (Keep this to yourself, please!) I am sure the book on education and even more the Artist will interest a wider public although they are by no means popular. Both will turn all educational fashions of the present day and all literary and art critics of the past and present upside down.

I had a rather satisfactory talk with X the other day when he came to visit me on his way back. He expressed himself about Mrs. Deutsch's book that he found it too "mechanistic" and although she seems to know what it all means, it didn't mean anything to him. I took the opportunity to point out to him that as soon as he accepts the dynamic point of view, which he seemed inclined to do, he would have to give up some of his rigid "scientific" ideals because Dynamism leads very soon to the limitations of science, the aim of which is to predict and control. He saw that for the first time and it seems to have made some impression on him because Mr.——, who is his most intimate friend (and now in Paris for some time) told me afterward how pleased he was with X's attitude toward that problem; at the same time he was afraid (and so am I) that X won't be able to defend this viewpoint on his own against the psychiatric and analytic crowd when he gets back to New York.

I myself feel that it will be a big job for me to stand up —with some help from a few friends—for the defense of this dynamic and human viewpoint although there is no use in making a martyr of myself in fighting for it. I am glad I am beyond that, but just the same I feel I have to come to America sooner or later to do what I can. Perhaps Mr. Knopf will help a great deal if he really becomes interested.

I am glad you feel much more confidence in your work now with patients, and I also wish to congratulate Virginia on the printing of her book.[9]

But I realize that apparently I am trying to outdo you in writing a longer letter! So the rest—later!

With warmest regards to you and Virginia,

Yours, Rank

P.S. You saw of course my discussion of Freud's Hemmung in the first part of Genetic Psychology.

The next letter of December 5 shows the inevitable reaction after this period of concentrated creative work and a corresponding disgust for everything connected with it.

December 5, 1930

Dear Dr. Taft:

A few days ago I mailed the first clean proof sheets to you and I hope they will answer some of the questions that seem to have been on your mind lately. So in this respect my present letter will be shortened, leaving all the discussion (surely one-sided) to the book. I think at least two of its chapters live up to the second part (the one on fear and the one on partial Ego). The last chapter is somewhat sketchy. It ought to be worked out into a real social psychology, which I may write one day if I get old enough.

Meanwhile I finished The Artist (about which Virginia is right, I think, although what one needs of the artist's psychology in order to understand the creative side of the "neurotic" you will also find in the new volume of the Technik).

As to the Boston book I am at a loss what to think. Dr. Y resigned definitely from the leadership and neither Z nor W declared himself as to what his part is going to be. I don't think there was any conference though Y spoke to X and A

[9] Virginia P. Robinson, *A Changing Psychology in Social Case Work*, Chapel Hill: The University of North Carolina Press, 1930.

158

spoke to them when she was in Boston. But I haven't heard of any results yet.

So you'd better do this also for yourself whenever you feel like doing it. As far as I myself am concerned I lost all interest in publication, be it in German, in English, or in French. The book on educaton is still unpublished and the Artist will remain so for some time, I am afraid.

Please don't think that I am not interested in your translation, but I have a horror of looking at any of my books again after they are written, no matter in what language it is.

With my best wishes for Xmas and the holidays to you and Virginia,

I am as ever
Your
Rank

My contact with Rank in 1931 was confined to the letters that follow.

January 26, 1931
Paris

Dear—what? I feel inclined to say "friend" but you may substitute anything else you like when reading this!

I will tell you as much as one can in a letter what is the matter with the New York group as well as with myself. As a matter of fact I never have been invited by them. I just came on my own account and they made use of it. But now I also feel less (word illegible) and less determined, chiefly for internal reasons that are exaggerated by the external situation. By that I mean I feel no longer the need to push my matter and fight for it and if I only had enough money to live on I would give up the whole work and only write (which then I should like much better too). But as it is I feel forced by financial needs to go to America because I cannot make a living otherwise. I always have a few hours here—had so far—but as soon as people stop coming I shall starve. What adds to my unwillingness to come to America are at the present moment two things: (1) the conditions over there, which may make it difficult for me to get sufficient work so as to pay even the heavy expenses of my stop and stay and (2) the growing antagonism of the Freudians in New York who, under the circumstances, may even be able to prevent me from practicing. (They tried to upset or offset Mr. Knopf, who wanted to publish some books of mine.) The authorities seem to make it difficult anyhow for foreigners to enter the states and for their sakes as well as my own I shall have to have some assurance for getting work (lectures, courses, etc.)

As far as X himself is concerned, I don't expect him to do very much now for me; first he is in need of patients himself and naturally shouldn't like any heavy competition, secondly he wants to remain on friendly terms with the Freudians, who already have reproached him for his connection with me. Last May before I left I realized his attitude (which is personally still very friendly) and told him frankly that he could give up the group if he felt like doing so, which seemed his position then.

Of course I could always go to some other place—once I was asked to come out West, which almost seems the only place left since Boston is too uncertain. I would probably do it if I were a few years younger, but now I don't know.

This is the not very perspective [his word] picture of 1931. Here I have a few hours that fill the morning and in the afternoon I write or read. The present cases I shall probably finish by the end of February or early in March and then I don't know? I do this too well too!

I hope you don't mind my having talked so much about myself but you asked me and I felt like telling you what I thought.

160

Meanwhile you have been probably going on with your translation and have found what you were looking for.

A couple of weeks ago I read Virginia's book in one evening from cover to cover and had in mind to write to her telling her how much I enjoyed it. But I waited for a happier mood to turn up—and am still waiting. So will you please give her the message meanwhile!

With cordial greetings to both of you

Yours

Rank

February 19, 1931

Paris

Dear Friend—

Just a few lines to thank you for your kind words. Please don't force yourself actually to do anything that you don't like to do. Nevertheless I appreciate your decision to write the review of the 3rd volume. Shortly before your letter came I came across Lewis' review of Seelenglaube in the Psychoanalytic Review and felt that either he hadn't read the book at all or not gotten the slightest idea what it was about. I would not have asked you to review the Technik, however, because I know what it means. But if you do it I will be thankful for it.

You seem to be getting on rather quickly with the translation, I think; the chapters after "Illness and Healing" are not as good as the previous ones, I feel, and the last chapter is only a rough sketch of what should be developed into a "Social Psychology," the key to which I found the other day.

Meanwhile I also received Y's famous book and found it quite flat! Not because it is purely Freudian but maybe because it is, since I am fed up with a new presentation of the development of psychoanalysis—and I am afraid the public is too.

Last week Knopf turned up in Paris, had a very friendly

161

talk with me in which he expressed definite interest in my whole work. We decided to start with the last books and then work backward or forward as it may be. So he contracted for the as yet unpublished Education as well as for the new book on Art, which is almost finished. I was very much tempted to suggest you as translator for the Education but didn't quite know whether you'd like it or curse it (and me), maybe both. But then he seems to be in a hurry to have the books translated (the Education having about 60,000 words, the Art more than 120,000) and definitely said that he prefers his professional translators who, he said, were considered good (they did Spengler, Keyserling, and other celebrities). So that's settled, although I must confess it did not help my resistances to publication, because since he left I have not touched the books that I have to go over.

Your chapter on emotions I am afraid—or rather glad— you will have to write for yourself or for me (or for White)[10] because it seems to me that the Boston group has failed with it completely.

Don't worry about patients for me, because it is as bad as if not worse than with the books: I am in need of them to make a living but I don't want them. I am just as glad if a patient does not turn up as if he does.

But enough of my "bad" self—the other one that still exists sends you warm thanks and greetings.

Yours
Rank

Paris—Easter Sunday

Dear Jessie,

I have to say this this time—which may mean more or less, but is different anyhow from "friend." Because your last

---

[10] Wm. A. White, at the time Superintendent, St. Elizabeth's Hospital, Washington, D.C., and editor of Psychoanalytic Review.

letter makes me feel a little different toward you in emphasizing your difference from me—which is good!

Whatever your argument about "illusion" may mean it certainly means a difference between us that I am glad of. Maybe that's why I expected you to disagree and maybe that's the reason why you disagree. So for the time being let me have my little "illusion," which may be just my way of interpreting certain things and just as much a part of myself (though a "complex") as the rest of my book about which you happen to feel alike.

As a matter of fact I think you are right in your argument —using my own weapon against me—and all you say about it I agree to when I read it. If you can find a way in translating it into your meaning please do so (maybe "objective" will do instead of "illusionary").

I realize how hard you must work for the translation and the review but you know how much I appreciate it and some day I hope to see your translation too. Meanwhile I feel a little coerced by publishers, also here in Paris, which is just the last thing I can stand.

Just today I received a letter from Professor Kronfeld in Berlin (you remember the man who drew such an excellent picture of my work last year) telling me how much he was thrilled with the 3d volume. Early in March he gave a lecture on it at the "Medical Society for Psychotherapy" in Berlin at which the most prominent psychiatrists and psychoanalysts were present. He emphasized as new and very important what he calls the "anxiety-structure of the personality," i.e., fear as an active drive (an impulse) and its significance for therapy and theory. He says only the very orthodox Freudians made some stupid criticism but others got up in defense of my ideas.

Here in France it is beginning too, two books now in the process of translation will be published this fall and another publisher wants to bring out the Inzest-Motiv, which I have to rewrite almost completely. So you see—too much work still (even in Europe) and the beginning burden of so-called "fame"!

As you see my mood is still the same—fundamentally at least—although my cold is gone after a few days' vacation in the South.

I hope you had some pleasure too at the Easter holidays and didn't spend all the time on writing. Don't allow yourself to become completely "demoralized" by your friend.

                                                            Rank

Cordial greeting to Virginia!

When I look at the bulk of the material, manuscripts, notes, clippings, reviews, and references that was accumulated during the years of writing and revising *Inzest-Motiv* from 1905 to 1931, I begin to appreciate his resistance and to marvel once more at his capacity for grinding work.

His next letter reminds me that I, too, must have been able to work beyond myself, when sufficiently motivated, although I have never understood how I was enabled to do what seemed to me then and now so clearly beyond my powers, unless it was the realization that if I did not, no one would.

                                           Paris, Easter Monday

Dear friend Jessie:—

Just after having mailed my letter to you I received yours from the Europa with your review.[11] I think it is an excellent summary not only of the book in question but of my whole therapeutic philosophy. Of course you had to limit yourself, but this, I know well, was just the real difficulty that you

[11] Jessie Taft, review of Otto Rank's *Die Analyse der Analytikers*, in *Psychoanalytic Review*, Vol. XVIII, p. 454. Reprinted in *Mental Hygiene*, Vol. XV, No. 4, October, 1931.

overcame in a masterly way. I am glad White took the review and I am sure it will help in some way (at least us!).

At any rate I was glad that you liked doing it and that it was helping you too. I think you have a right to be proud of this "partialization." From the few sentences of your translation that you inserted I feel that you have re-created my ideas rather than translated them. But it sounds well and strong!

The social psychology is still in its embryonic stage, i.e., sleeping but not passively, rather growing quietly. It is an outgrowth not only of the last chapter but also of all my last books on Education and Art as well. It probably will be, when finished, a synthesis of all my previous attempts at synthesizing. Now I have to revise a few former books of mine for French translation, amongst them the Inzest-Motiv, which I am planning to rewrite completely from a social (anthropologic) point of view; after that I shall be ready for the new book.

I hope you did enjoy your well-deserved vacation after the hard work of the last weeks—

As ever yours

Rank

A brief note dated May 25, 1931, speaks of the possibility of coming to the States, perhaps in the fall or winter, and refers again to his work on preparing his former books for French translation, especially *Inzest-Motiv*. Of the Social Psychology, he says it "is still what it was when I wrote you about it, i.e., is finished in my head and only has to be written!" [12] The note ends:

I have been very well lately and am amazed at my productivity: it comes so easily and goes so well!

[12] Little did he guess how long this ready-to-be-written book would linger over the years before it emerged just before his death as a final affirmation of his belief in life.

Most of the summer, at least up to August, I shall have to spend in Paris because I have a number of cases just beginning now.

With warm greeting from all of us to Virginia and you

I am yours always

Rank

Paris, July 14, 1931

Dear Friend,

It is quite some time since I heard from you and I really feel sorry if it has been my fault (not writing myself). But since the late spring I have been terribly busy and last month and this month I am working from 8 to 9 hours at analysis! At least no financial worry now! Besides, I had to prepare two former books of mine (Doppelgänger and Don Juan) for a French translation and have a contract to rewrite the Incest volume for the same purpose. Last week an English publisher asked for the rights of the Incest book and now he and Knopf are fighting for it (I never thought this could happen to my books). The sociology book is asleep since you last heard of it but I am recasting the Inzest-Motiv from a sociological point of view and all I have to read for that purpose is a good preparation for the new book. (The Artist and Education will not appear before the beginning of next year, it seems).

I am sending a little review[13] of Dr. Baudouin, the famous (Swiss) psychotherapist, of the 3rd part of the Technik that might interest you.

Meanwhile plans for my coming to Philadelphia have proceeded—at least your plans. Virginia's letter gives me at least the opening to come and as far as the program is concerned I think that's just what I want right now: social case work material and no analytical or psychiatric discussions!

As to the financial end, I feel I ought to get more out of

[13] Action et Pensée, May, 1931, p. 248.

166

it (of my trip, not of Philadelphia) and therefore am trying to work out a scheme that would enable me to go for a while to New York too just to make some money (in spite of the hostility there). On the other hand this implies a longer absence from home and since Mrs. Rank does not like to come to America I find it difficult to reconcile all the factors in the situation. But somehow I hope to be able to work it out and come. (I hear Alexander is going to be in Boston!)

With best wishes for the summer

Yours always

Rank

In the letter of July 27 he is more doubtful about coming to Philadelphia, saying:

With Alexander in Boston and Nunberg in Philadelphia I am afraid there will be again only New York left for me— if I come at all! I still must confess that I have no real desire although I would like to see some of my friends.

He is staying in Paris this summer with nine patients and supervising some French translations:

I take it easy just the same, I am not going to be run any more by anything or anybody (including myself!) So don't worry! The new book will come in time, I don't hurry!

The next letter, even with the spur of a vacation, betrays his reluctance to face New York as well as a growing disinclination to write or revise anything.

Antibes, November 3, 1931

Dear Jessie,

Your letter reached me here in the South of France where I was staying a few weeks after a rather heavy summer's

167

work and a severe cold—I am returning, however, to Paris in a few days where several patients are waiting for me.

Beginning the season comparatively late makes it unlikely that I shall come to America this winter and I must confess I haven't a great desire to come in spring either.

I haven't done any writing lately but a great deal of thinking, which clarified and confirmed the feeling that I am "fed up" with psychoanalysis and with America as far as it is concerned with it.

I foresaw, if you remember, a Freudian wave, which necessarily will last some time since it represents the "mechanistic psychology" which mechanistically trained minds only are capable of grasping!

That's one reason for my not being in any hurry, neither for teaching nor for writing. I feel I am a few generations ahead anyway, so why widen that distance?

But if or when I write the new book on human relations (*Social Psychology*) I want you to translate it for publication—if you want to—

Your review of the *Technik* looked to me in print even better than in manuscript and I am glad that *Mental Hygiene* is reprinting it with your signature.

I shall be glad to see and read anything you send me, especially as I am expecting not to be too busy.

With best greetings to Virginia and yourself

Yours always

Rank

P.S. Please keep the French review.

Paris, December 6, 1931

Dear Friend,

As I told you in my previous letter (which I hope you received meanwhile) I was glad to see your paper[14] and when

---

[14] Jessie Taft, "An Experiment in a Therapeutically Limited Relationship with a Seven-Year-Old Girl." *Psychoanalytic Review*, October, 1932.

it came the other day I read the main parts (introduction and conclusion) the same evening (the case material I couldn't bring myself to read yet).

I find your presentation simply excellent! The presentation of the case, of my viewpoint, and last, not least, of the whole problem confronting education and especially child guidance.

It shows—what I knew anyhow—that you are well prepared to receive my book on education, which is expected to be released in February. There I carry that whole problem to its roots in human dualism and show that it is the outgrowth of our whole civilization! I am glad your paper presents that fundamental problem in the concrete form of a case and yet shows all the implications to those who know to read and want to see. White seems to be one of them and I am glad your paper will appear in the Review.

As to myself—I feel still the same (as my last letter shows)—if anything a little worse since I am back at "work." No plans yet made but I will let you know—and it is good to know how you feel: I appreciate it and am grateful for it.

With best wishes to you and Virginia from the whole Rank family,

Yours always

O.R.

In January Rank writes that he will probably return to the States very soon, and asks about the possibility of a lecture course or patients in Philadelphia if New York should prove to be impossible. The course was a good possibility but of prospective patients in Philadelphia I could say little. Finally he decided to try New York regardless of conditions, as he had the final editing of Knopf's publication of *Art and Artist*, with its numerous illustrations and references, to oversee. His state of mind on arrival is revealed in his first undated note from New York, probably some time in February:

HOTEL GRAMERCY PARK
52 Gramercy Park North
New York
Thursday

Dear Friend,

Thanks for your kind welcome! I have been hiding here for a few days—to get adjusted—but didn't succeed—at least not in hiding! Everybody seems to know that I am here and America is just as terrible as ever! But also I am not so well now—I have difficulties with myself—apparently the usual crisis that one reaches sooner or later.

I hope to see you later on when I have gotten more of a hold on myself! In any case if you should happen to come to New York will you let me know ahead of time?

With greetings to Virginia and yourself

Yours
Rank

As I responded with anxiety for his problem and an irrepressible desire to help, he wrote even more frankly of his unwillingness to see me. It was late March before I could induce him to give me an appointment on a Saturday morning. I shall never forget the pain and shock of seeing Rank, for the first time in my acquaintance, unable to conceal his inner mood, which was a depression so deep that it was evidently an effort for him to speak at all. All my innate impulse to help came to the fore and I found myself in the incredible role of trying to give back to Rank, the human being, something of what had been given to me by Rank the therapist. His mood lightened enough to permit him to show me the proofs of Art and Artist, but there was no real change. I soon saw that I was dealing with forces beyond my powers and I left with a heavy heart. A short note from him followed.

HOTEL GRAMERCY PARK
Thursday, March 24

Dear Friend—

Your visit the other day was not only a pleasure but also a help.

I would like to see you this week end but I have already made other arrangements for Saturday and Sunday that I cannot cancel.

But I shall keep next Saturday (April 2nd) morning free if you let me know that you want it.

Yours

Rank

I did go to New York once more and found Rank in a somewhat better state, although far from his usual self, so that the lunch to which I had looked forward was a painful experience for both of us. I was deeply disturbed but should not have been surprised by a telegram dated April 6 saying: "I have left New York. Please cancel all engagements." It was evident that Rank had reached once again a personal crisis, one that had to be met by actual flight from a situation that had become intolerable. This was the kind of blow that could have severed my relation to Rank permanently, since I had to endure for two months his continued silence, my anxiety about his condition, and my own deep sense of injury, together with the effort to conceal from others the enormity of his behavior.

Finally, it came—the letter that expressed simply and frankly at whatever cost to his innate reticence his realization of the pain he had caused and the inner necessity that had motivated it. Only the personal development, which I owed in large measure to the help I had received from Rank's therapy, enabled me to meet and overcome the disruption that follows the discovery of the therapist's frailties as a

171

mortal. Of the helper one demands perfection in mood, physical health, and behavior, everything that is unattainable, impossible, and even undesirable for the living human organism. The greater the genius, the more difficult the problem for the individual who harbors it, especially when his make-up renders him sensitive to others in direct proportion to his awareness of self.

Paris, June 4, 1932

Dear Jessie:

I not only feel that I ought to apologize first for the disappointment and trouble I caused you but I really regret deeply the pain you must have felt on account of me—even before I left so abruptly. I knew you were my friend and you showed it more than ever before in our talks and especially in your letters to New York—and yet you couldn't help me then because you stood for something (at least with one part of yourself) which I had to get away from at that time.

Now I can turn to you again—to your human self and your friendship, which I don't want to lose if I can still have it, i.e., if you still keep it for me.

What I did was terrible in a sense—not only to others but also to myself—but it was a necessity to my inner truer self, the human side, which is now free to turn to you. It was too bad that this need for a radical operation on myself occurred just in the midst of my activities in New York—but apparently otherwise I wouldn't have known how sick my soul was and what I needed for a remedy.

Since then I worked constantly on the rescue of my spiritual Self—which was endangered—and now when I feel free, a new Self, I want to tell you at least how much I appreciated your loving-kindness, your desire to help, and how much I thank you for your friendship, which remained the clearer and cleaner in me since I didn't use it (although you kindly offered it).

I am clear in myself now as to my personal problem, which I hope to work out in the right spirit to my own satisfaction soon; it doesn't bother me nor does money worry me (although I have not a cent); I am sure of my attitude toward life and this will take care of everything else.

Meanwhile (besides finishing a few patients to whom I had previous obligations) I am writing a few things as a working out but also as an outgrowth of my deepened experience and don't particularly care whether they will be published or not (nor whether they will shape themselves into books at all—although one publisher wants me to write just on a subject which interests me now tremendously.)

That's all I wanted to tell you today. Tell me about yourself and also about me—if you can or when you can.

Yours as ever

Rank

P.S. After I had written this letter an inquiry came from the Child Study Association for an article on the "Crisis of Birth" (how well I know that now!) as the first contribution in a special issue—the last article is by you on the pain of loss through death. Isn't that strange? Or rather not.

How I managed to reply to this letter or what I said I do not know, but the problem was certainly not solved for me and was undoubtedly increased painfully by the time that elapsed until I heard from him again.

Paris, October 8, 1932

Dear Friend,

I haven't written to you—or anybody else for that matter —because I am not well again this summer as you heard from——.

I am just now coming out of a crisis that lasted over a year and I don't quite know where I am at present although I feel well and am working.

173

I am sending you by the same mail the book on Art and Artist, which has come out well.

The next book I am supposed to write (I just received a note from Harpers urging me on) is on "Psychoanalysis and the Jew" in which I venture to "analyze") in a spiritual and cultural sense) Freudian psychoanalysis as a product of Jewish mentality.

But meanwhile I am playing around with other things: the re-writing of the Inzest-Motiv for a French translation and the book on human relations, which still fascinates me most but is too difficult to approach at present.

Cordially yours,

Rank

The account of Rank's recovery from the crisis that brought him to the breaking point in New York is revealed in the several letters of 1933, ending in the emergence of a powerfully active, humorous, and somewhat scornful self, sufficiently separated from the past to make deliberate use of the present for its own ends.

It is apparent from the first letter that writing has not been easy for him or for me.

Paris, February 8, 1933

Dear Friend,

It was good to hear from you after a long period of silence (maybe on my part?) and to learn that you are working and planning actively. I myself am trying for a change the other way and don't do very much—to which present conditions are very seducive (or seductive) anyway—

I am glad you got hold of D. H. Lawrence of whom I read a few things early this winter that gave me the same impression—that his philosophy is close to mine with the advantage (on his part) that he has no scholarship and

174

disciplined experience. While I was reading him (mainly *The Fantasia of the Unconscious*) I felt that he was the greatest psychological philosopher since Nietzsche because more human (but certainly greater than Freud and all the rest of "fiction-writers"?). (Of course you know Middleton Murray's *Son of Woman*, a book that gives the whole Lawrence because it adds to the known one the unknown one.)

About Melanie Klein and Anna Freud, I think you are right. Together with other phenomena in the world (for example Karen Horney who is now in Chicago) it seems to me that this is the natural revenge of women against the "masculinized" psychology. Horney is the clearest and simplest example because she does it openly and in that sense it was a very clever move of Alexander's to bring her to Chicago first of all to get the following of the women-groups and secondly to get the chestnuts out of the fire for him (as we say in Europe) without burning his own fingers thereby. Freud is trying his best to accept those things, evidenced by an article on female sexuality (or sexuality of the woman), which he discovered only now to exist (I think the article has been or will be translated for the Psychoanalytic Quarterly). About Bernfeld at present—the present Bernfeld, I mean—I know very little. He is much more broad-minded than the medical men in the field (he is a Ph.D.) and was primarily interested in education as such. In his psychological outlook he is hampered by an absolute fixation on Freud (he was the one who has been quoted as saying in an interview that Freud is not only 100 per cent right but 200 per cent, i.e., not only every word he has written is the truth but every word he is going to write in the future). This reminds me to answer your question—(is it seven?)—in telling you that for the time being I gave up writing—there is already too much truth in the world—an overproduction which apparently cannot be consumed!

175

Nevertheless I am glad that your book is going to be published and I hope to receive a copy regardless of any promise on my part.

Could you let me have the review of Modern Education from the Prof. Magazine and also a review that is supposed to have appeared in the Nation in August: I am not curious but my German publisher would like to see it.

The Child Study article I am afraid I can't write any more. With warm regards—also to Virginia

Yours
Rank

Paris, May 12, 1933

Dear Friend,

It was good to hear from you again, and a long letter too, because I hear so little now about what's going on in the world—and I have so little to say about myself either!

Your book[15] is a real contribution and although I knew most of the material contained in it already I looked through it. The last few pages (last chapter) are an excellent presentation of the fundamentals of all therapeutic processes to which nothing can be added.

It is some time ago that I lost all interest in any kind of therapy (although I will have to do it to earn my living), but so far I haven't been interested in anything else. Least of all in writing, particularly for the same reason you gave for your resistance to the Artist! You will see to what extent I agree with you when I tell you that about four weeks ago a Viennese publisher became interested in a German edition and suggested that I would revise the book. The first thing I did was to eliminate the chapter on "Game and Destiny"! But when I came to less radical alterations I was unable to (dis-) entangle the thing—and now it rests.

[15] Jessie Taft, The Dynamics of Therapy in a Controlled Relationship, New York: The Macmillan Company, 1937.

The best part of it, however, is that I seem to enjoy that lack of interest in books and writing. I only feel badly if a publisher or translator approaches me and tries to coerce me! and the irony is that with the decrease of my interest their demands increase; there are about half a dozen books of mine that are at present being translated in France and England and that I don't like to be published in their old form without being able to give them a new one! This seems also to be blocking the new books: I still have a dozen to write but I can't write in the former manner and haven't found a new one; and it's doubtful whether I ever will! But since it doesn't worry me in the least (i.e., I am not struggling at all with it) it may well be that I don't want to find any new form and just let it go at that.

Philadelphia seems to be still very active and moving on. It's good to know the share you have in it.

With all good wishes for the summer to Virginia and yourself

Your
Rank

Paris, August 8, 1933

Dear friend Jessie—

I didn't write earlier (although if I remember correctly it was your turn!) because I was waiting till I could tell you that I am definitely out of the crisis—not only of the last two years but of the last ten years, that is, since I left Vienna in 1923.[16] Now this second period seems to be over and I am spiritually and emotionally ready for the next step. The only difficulty I can see is a practical one, i.e., I have to use my position and my abilities to earn a living that will enable me to live and carry out some plans for writing. To give you an idea of my present state of mind: I put aside the book on

---

[16] This seems to be an error, although it is the year of *The Trauma of Birth* and his beginning estrangement from Freud.

177

the Jews (and Religion) that Harper's are urging me to do and am writing a humorous (not bitter) satire on our present civilization in which I am making fun of everything people take (too) seriously, including myself.—If I can judge from the main ideas and the few things I put down already it is going to be a great book in the manner of Rabelais or rather of Cervantes, who killed a whole literature by one book. At any rate while doing it and reading some of the great humorists (the greatest, because most human, being Mark Twain) I am enjoying myself and I am laughing a great deal. Fortunately, in that mood not even the economic crisis (I mean my own!) seems to bother me very much—although I have to do something about it—as well as for my former Self whom I am afraid I shall have to support for the rest of my life.

The enclosed announcement will give you an idea of the kind of clarity I lavish on it (the former self). Dr. Bailey, who studied with me, is a young, ambitious therapist who is willing to do the "dirty work" for what he himself can get out of the show. What I have in mind is really to train a few people to carry on my ideas—not when I am dead but as of now so I can gracefully withdraw without hurting him too much (always the old Self). The little money I need for that enterprise I am trying to raise now—a thing which I never could do but which I feel now capable of accomplishing just as efficiently as any American business man—although a little more gracefully—perhaps.[17]

(The above correction reminds me of two things I wanted to tell you: first that I am writing this humorous book[18] in English, which to me seems the language of humor; secondly that nobody is supposed to know about it since I am

---

[17] Although Dr. Jones hints at Rank's ability to make money, which he could probably have done if he had ever really tried, to my knowledge he never had more than enough for current expenses on a generous but not luxurious scale. [18] In the material in my possession there are clippings and notes on Mark Twain, but only beginning outlines and ideas for a book on humor.

going to publish anonymously (this not for the sake of the old Self but for other reasons that you will find in the book.)

All this doesn't prevent me from carrying on a little practice, just enough to keep me financially afloat, and I found that doing it this way, as it were on the side, has improved it considerably. Whereas I was unable to handle a certain patient[19] last year (she might not have been ready yet, though) I feel that this time I did a perfect job on her.

From a Philadelphia patient I heard that you strained your shoulder in a fall, but that you were on your vacation and even painting, so I thought you must be all right again. I should like to have that confirmed by you as well as to hear other news from you, Philadelphia, and the States, the lost country of the former Self, which just the same is sending you the best regards together with the friendship of his newly discovered

Twin

Don't think I am crazy—Maybe I was in the past but I never was saner and "weller" (my private English) than now.

I must have been somewhat apprehensive about this new self of Rank's that seemed to be leaving behind much that was still vital to me humanly and professionally. I was far from having separated from psychotherapy or the importance of Rank's contribution to philosophy and practice, and I was fearful of losing the only Rank I had known. The letter of September 18, 1933, is evidently an answer to my expression of doubt about himself and the new plan now rapidly expanding into a definite project with all his newly released energy and genius for organization behind it.

September 18, 1933

Dear Friend,

Your two letters arrived together as you wished them to and were read in their order. It was good to have the second

19 A friend of mine.

one—not only good for you to have written it but also good for me to read. Don't worry! This, my old Self, is not so different from the one you knew in Paris—in fact it is just my natural Self as I always had it only overlaid by all sorts of superstructures—also with the one you thought I had never developed! namely the putting in of the whole self in terms of a person.[20] Although I realize the difference, I think I came very close to it in my relationship with Freud that I only now so completely outgrew that my old natural Self (which even Freud always recognized as a "roguish boy") came back into its own. This new Self is therefore the real identical twin of my old natural Self, and what I exaggerated as the new twin was only in contrast to the former Self you, and everybody, chiefly saw (the opposite twin).

I also realize now that in spite of the fact that the Institute idea is developing rapidly under my hands into a big scheme (International Exchange of Ideas on Educational Psychology) it really is a kind of mausoleum of this past self, which in this way gets a beautiful and honorable burial whereas my natural Self is amused (that is the humorist) at seeing people believe it is in the Institute.

For the last few weeks I have had no patients but was happily busy with all sorts of nothings (translations, revisions, etc.) and conferences with people interested in the Institute. Within the last few days I happened to see Dr. Godwin Watson, from whom I got valuable information about the training of psychological advisors for schools and Dr. Allen[21] whom I shall see more of this week. He incidentally said that he thought you are interested in "historical" therapy although you are getting good results from the automatic working out of the present emotional relationship in the therapeutic situation. I tried to correct his misconcep-

---

[20] A reference to my reproach that he had never been analyzed.
[21] Dr. Frederick H. Allen, Director, Philadelphia Child Guidance Clinic until his retirement in 1957.

tion of your attitude but do not know whether I succeeded. Maybe you can talk it over one day with him.

I should be delighted to see you arrive with a group of selected workers and students at the Institute next summer.[22] In fact, I wish you would go ahead with preparations now. Just as your letter came I was sketching out a program for the Institute and as I went on writing I had to attach a bigger sheet of paper because there was no room for all the ideas! I shall send you, perhaps in a couple of weeks, a fuller plan—the chief idea of which is a kind of an international (and yet nationalized!) center for the development of educational psychology. That is to say that lecturers from all parts of the world and all kinds of schools would be welcomed—if they care to come—not to put over their ideas on others but to participate in a mutual working out of ideas for the various groups in each country. The center of this Institute is supposed to be the students, not the professors, and the workers with their particular problems and needs in their field. In simple words they should tell us what they want and need and if this is sound we shall try to help them to work it out (we don't pretend that we have it already) but not try to tell to them our outdated stock of worn-out ideas. In one word, a living dynamic center instead of a Sunday-school-class where first the Old Testament (Freud) and then the New Testament (Jung) are taught mechanically.

And now it's Sunday morning, a lovely autumn day, and I shall treat myself (or rather my twin) to a drive in the country. I am alone (my family is returning next week) and I'll drive myself.

Good-by

Yours

O.R.

---

[22] The economic depression in the United States, as well as the traditional lack of means of students of social work, is overlooked.

After thoughts. Dr. Y. from whom I didn't hear all year wrote me just before sailing to Europe that he couldn't read my book (which I had given him last summer here) because he feels he has to complete first his elementary (Freudian) education. Although I think he is right (for himself) and I understand it, yet I wrote him in a somewhat sarcastic vein that he shouldn't bother to read any of my books save the very last, because only then he could be sure that all the trouble of trying to get what I say wouldn't be wasted, since I couldn't possibly develop any change when I am dead. He had said in his letter that he goes to Germany for the whole summer and should probably not have enough money to spend for a trip to Paris!

Now I am not going to attach a new sheet to this epistle. The sun is too tempting!

The next letter was on a letterhead in which a name for the new institute was being tried out.

THE SOCIAL HYGIENE CENTER
Training Institute for Practical Psychologists
Paris—France
November 5, 1933

Dear Jessie,

It is almost a month since you sent your last letter but I (a combination of the old and new Self) have been so busy these last few weeks that I postponed writing to you until a comparatively quiet Sunday on which the weather doesn't permit driving out! So I am taking you for a drive (not for a "ride") and tell you briefly some of the news.

The Institute developed from the planning stage that was still pleasant into the difficult and rather unpleasant stage of getting something started with all the stupid, slow, and self-possessed people who populate this world. I naturally agree with what you say about the psychologists in general and X—

182

in particular; but this is one more reason for the Institute (I confess though that I think that only in a few optimistic moments—otherwise I am just as pessimistic as you are about it.) However, I don't see any other way—or any better way for that matter—but to invite some of the leading people in various fields to co-operate in an attempt to improve matters.

But there are brighter aspects too. I am looking forward with pleasure to a group from Philadelphia next summer and hope, of course, that you and Virginia may come. One of the sponsors connected with the Baltimore Steamship line will enable me to secure excellent accommodations at a reduced rate. So just let me know!

I should also like to hear about your course on Lawrence and the creative personality: that's where real therapy comes in—if at all! Also tell me more about your new scheme of work.

All my other interests and literary plans are pushed into the background, for the time being. I don't like that—that is the twin doesn't like that and very often rebels against it.

I haven't read Gertrude Stein's new book (neither do I know any of her former ones). I only read a review of it in the New Yorker and I am not ashamed to confess that I liked it very much without any further desire to read the book. I think she is too sophisticated for me—and I crave simplicity (the other I have myself).

With warm greetings to you and Virginia

as always yours

Rank

P.S. I'll let you have more (soon to be printed) circulars for distribution.

As the organizing of the new project continued with ever-increasing speed, the proposed title, "The Psychological Center," met with objections from the interested Philadelphia group who later cabled their suggestions. On December 8 Rank wrote the following note:

Dear Jessie,

This is only to acknowledge your letter—arrived yesterday —and to thank you for your willingness to let me have the translation of the Technik.

You are right about the title; we had already had similar criticism. What would you suggest? If you have a good idea, please cable it.

I am going to publish an article about the Institute soon in New York (I don't know yet where).

I wish you would think it over and would come next summer; A. is not coming anyway and besides you are more important to me than all the rest of them. I want to see you and also talk over with you a number of things—especially co-operation in the training program. In case we have money the Institute will finance your trip![23]

I wrote to Mr. Pray some time ago about the new plan!

There are plenty of cases here among the American students and artists and very interesting ones concerning vocational problems.

About Dr. Bailey I can't tell you yet. So far he has been very helpful on the practical side.

Curiously enough P. is the only member of the New York group with whom I am in touch. He seems at least honest and loyal.

With kind regards to Virginia and yourself,

Yours
Rank

My experience with mixed groups and institutes for social workers had made me skeptical of the success of this international project that was being developed so rapidly by Rank

[23] Unnecessary to note that there never was enough money, nor did I expect it.

and his immediate American associates, Dr. Pearce Bailey, a psychiatrist, and Dr. Harry Bone, a psychologist. The word "center" itself, chosen by them, was received critically by the Philadelphia group who actually voiced their opposition in a cablegram suggesting other titles with "Institute" as the substitute for "Center."

At this date my friend, Miss Robinson, and I had decided that we would at least go to Paris for our summer vacation but we were hesitant to commit ourselves to a six weeks' session, not knowing what we could possibly contribute to such a gathering beyond what would come far better from Rank himself or the psychiatrists who would be there.

His reply to our doubts and reservations follows in the letter of January 7:

THE PSYCHOLOGICAL CENTER
Paris—France
January 7, 1934

Dear Jessie, We changed the title, as you see; we couldn't avoid "Center." I am sorry, because Institute has a bad connotation here in France. But I don't think it matters now!

I was very glad that you decided to come next summer although I would have liked to have more of you here in Paris and at the Institute. But it will be good anyway to see you here.

I wish you could bring a selected group with you (including students and workers from the clinic). I am going to write to Allen and Pray and will ask them to come. Pray said in his letter to me that he would like to come anyway; Allen thought it might be difficult for him to get away since he was absent so long last summer; but I will urge him to come.

With the London group we will soon establish contact— Dr. Bailey will go over there at the end of the month. I would have liked to go myself but I have so much to do that

185

I can hardly breathe and so for the last two weeks at least I didn't do anything except enjoy my vacation in Vienna and in Switzerland! There I renewed former contacts with the educational group at the Institute Jean Jacques Rousseau, especially with Claparède, Baudouin, Piaget, and others.

But upon my return I found my desk full to capacity and the daily work is absorbing all my time and energy so I can't even read Mark Twain, to say nothing about writing!

So I must cut this letter short although there are many more things I could and want to say. But that for the summer—

Meanwhile all my best wishes to you for the New Year— and to Virginia too.

Yours always

Rank

The next letter a month later shows how much more clearly and fully than I he had understood the conditions of the world and the probable futility of any such effort, even his own, to bring educational, psychological, and psychiatric interests together. I could but accept that for some reason he had to go through with this project and that with his experience in organizing groups, editing journals, and handling authors he could create almost out of thin air a genuine group experience on however frail an international foundation. For regardless of every handicap, the first and only session of the Psychological Center was to be a success.

February 28, 1934

Dear Jessie,

Your letter dated Feb. 11th arrived today just in time to give me a very much needed cheer-up! I was so glad to hear you talk again and to listen to you—almost your voice—after all that "tommy-wrott" (my own spelling but also my own meaning) that I encounter otherwise. There is no worry about my getting too absorbed, in fact lately I have been fearful of getting less and less interested in it all the time. Of course times are difficult too, all over the world: people in America have no money to come over and besides Europe seems to be threatened by war!

Since Xmas I have been doing very little! I had only a couple of patients from whom I could barely make my living and neither writing nor reading nor anything else did interest me. I even doubt whether it is an advantage (or a virtue) not to be depressed in such a situation, but I wasn't —nor am I—although I almost wish I were! I would like to go away for a few weeks and just do nothing but so far I haven't gotten the money to do so. If some debts are paid to me soon I shall go away next month and stay away over Easter, otherwise I don't see how I can go on working through the summer when I didn't have any vacation last summer either.

About the Institute and my changing attitude toward it I have talked to you; maybe the fundamental trouble is that I haven't anything to "teach" and can't have any kind of a "school"—even not an undogmatic one—whereas most people (and "good" people for that matter) want that, need it!

Last week I started a small seminar group of five (Miss Ward[24] included) and the few discussions we had so far made me aware of that; this feeling was accentuated by the presence of Dr. W. from Boston who represents the—to me— friendly type of American analysts. And yet how pathetic it is to see him struggle to match my theory against the Freudian when I haven't got one and he couldn't understand it anyway, because he doesn't know (what you know) that it is a question of being that theory oneself, of representing

---

[24] Miss Jane Shaw Ward, a Y.W.C.A. secretary on her way back from many years of teaching in China. Her fluent French and long administrative experience proved to be an invaluable help to the Center.

that viewpoint in one's attitude towards life. The message is as simple as was Christ's, but you get crucified before they get it!

But enough of that! I was glad to hear that you are going to teach next fall—and sorry to hear about your trip to Chicago. But evidently that's the way life comes—mixed! I shall enjoy talking over with you the possibilities of teaching although I don't know where I could come in. On the other hand I have enough of analysis and would like to (probably have to) start something else. The other day I received a letter from Brazil asking permission to translate all my books into Portuguese and publish them as a complete edition. Maybe I can find a place there near the Jungle: Europe's dying anyway!

Just today I was reminded that I have to finish reading your translation of Technik; I started on it right away and did three fourths of it before Xmas—but nothing since. It is very lively and dynamic (expressive) but seems to need some polishing for publication (there are a few errors with regard to the German). Of Wahrheit und Wirklichkeit there appeared only a few days ago a French translation a copy of which I am going to send you.

I shall also let you know shortly about the dates of the Institute that my collaborators will fix in the course of next week.

I will also send you two typescripts of articles not yet published: the one for publication in America, the second, the French one, a lecture I am giving here at the Sorbonne on March 15th.

The English I wrote myself (not the French) although it has been polished, maybe a little bit too much, by my collaborators. Of course reading Mark Twain—as I do right along—does not make it any easier to write English; it was rather bad luck to choose as my favorite author a writer whom I think is the greatest word artist in modern times (only comparable, as far as the art of verbal expression goes, to the Bible and Shakespeare).

So there I am!

Give my best greetings to Virginia and write again soon to yours

Rank

There follow two letters that intervene before he concentrates on the organizational problems of the summer, undeterred by the economic collapse in the United States and the shadow that Hitler is already casting over Europe.

March 17, 1934

Dear Jessie,

This is just a word to let you know that I am leaving tonight for a three weeks' Easter vacation to the South of France, where I expect to just do nothing at all. (Mail will be forwarded, so write, please!)

I am also writing to Mr. Pray asking him to come over for this summer's session (15 July—end August) a program of which will be ready in about a week's time.

In case we use your name later on in connection with the Center's activities, what title or official position can we add? Please let me know.

I hope Chicago was not too hard and you didn't lose your sense of humor! The other day I gave here at the Sorbonne a "revolutionary" lecture[25] on psychoanalysis as a bourgeois ideology that has been killed by the failure of democracy and individualism. It was a big audience (in French, mind you!)—very much interested and keen—that applauded me. Only some friends thought it was too radical.

With best wishes to Virginia and you

Rank

[25] Groupe D'Etudes Philosophiques et Scientifiques Pour L'Examen Des Tendances Nouvelles, established in 1922. Sorbonne 46 Rue Saint-Jacques V. "La Psychologie et Le Milieu Social Jeudi," March 15, 1934. M. le Dr. Otto Rank.

Easter, 1934

Dear Jessie,

It was so good to get your long (good long) letter while I was on my vacation down South and to find Virginia's letter and the book on my return this morning.

I have no more objection against reading Gertrude Stein (evidently I have from the mistakes I am making while writing it but I might just as well finish the sentence) than I have against reading most "modern" books; I have no need for them; I am "modern" enough myself. Incidentally I can see an affinity between Gertrude Stein and myself, particularly in a talk she gave here in Paris the other day on her ideas (emphasis on the present, on the difference of everything); on the other hand I can think of no greater difference than between her and Mark Twain: it is like the Niagara and the electric lamp (you see!) lit by the current from the tamed water towers; He is the most spontaneous writer I ever read, she the most self-conscious (and somewhat snobbish). Maybe I'll send you a volume of his, but anything of his—almost every line is genuine.

Meanwhile I am sending you as my Easter egg a French translation of Wahrheit und Wirklickheit (under the French title La Volonté du Bonheur), which just came from the press. It may help (or hinder) you in your struggle with the German.

I also enclose with the book a copy of an article I wrote for American consumption (which has not yet been consumed, though!) and will send later on a translation of my French lecture at the Sorbonne or a copy of the original French. I have no copies at hand and only enclose the announcement.[26]

I am glad for you that Chicago is over. I am anxious to see how Allen reacts to my invitation (and Pray? is he coming?)

26 No copies identified as such in his papers.

I would like to talk to you about your future plans on teaching. If you and Virginia come over we will arrange things so as to suit you best, although in case we need you at the Institute (for a little while) I hope you won't object; as a conpensation we may spend one or two week ends outside Paris and "go native."

About your using your translations of my German books, I think it will be all right to have a limited number of copies for restricted use of the students in school; but we may also try to get them published; I should like to see your translations in the hands of American readers.

About Germany and other European things we might better talk than write. I can see in Hitler and his Germany a very interesting proof of my ideas on psychology being necessarily ideological. Admittedly they do only what all the rest of them do, while denying it: namely, use psychology to indoctrinate their favorite ideology (be it religious, or political, or scientific).

But maybe this is too much for you to swallow at once.

So I close
As ever
Your "same"

As the next two notes indicate, my friend and I had finally capitulated to the extent of promising to participate in the first two weeks of the session, leaving the last weeks free for others from New York and Philadelphia. That there was fear as well as humility governing our behavior, I would not deny.

April 30, 1934

Dear Jessie,

This is only an urgent note asking you definitely whether we can mention your name (and official position) on the program of our summer session. If you want to participate at all you would be free to do so in any way you wish (lecture, discussion, case work, supervision, control analysis, etc.) and for any amount of time (from one day to six weeks).

The question is whether you want to participate at all.

You may know by this time that Allen has decided to be here the last two weeks in August and you know, of course, that Miss Dawley[27] is coming. That's all from Philadelphia. Pray sent a nice note regretting he couldn't come this year.

I would appreciate it if you would let me know by cable your decision since this last announcement has to go to print next week.

I understand your hesitation and please feel perfectly free to say what you want. It won't make any difference in our relation, although I would naturally like you to teach us something.

At any rate I shall be very glad to see you in the course of this summer and I am looking forward to talking things over with you.

If you don't want to see the Institute you can see me, apart from it.

As ever yours

Rank

P.S. I went through your Technik translations, which are excellent: we are using them now in our seminars.

May 3rd noon

Dear Jessie,

This is only to acknowledge with thanks your letter that arrived last night after mine was mailed; this one I am taking to the boat train so it will reach you at the same time.

I was very glad to hear that the reservations are made and that you and Virginia are planning to participate at least two weeks in the Institute. The rest of your summer plans sounds even better than that. (Do you want me to do some-

---

[27] Almena Dawley, Chief Social Worker, Philadelphia Child Guidance Clinic, until her retirement in 1957.

thing at the American Women's Club for your reservation?)

About the rest don't worry—I am not either!

As far as group co-operation is concerned I am, of course, of your opinion—and you know it anyway!

As always yours

Rank

May 31, 1934

Dear Jessie,

This is just to wish you and Virginia bon voyage for your trip on the Ile de France, sailing June 16th.

If you have time before leaving I should appreciate it if you and Virginia could make some arrangements with your publishers to have them send over to the Center several copies (I think about 6 each) of your books to be on sale here during the session. The question is whether they would accept returns in case we don't sell them (the Center will buy one copy each anyway for its library).

As ever

Yours

O. Rank

We arrived in Paris on June 22, well in advance of the dates set for the "Psychological Center," July 15—August 31, and established ourselves at the American Women's Club, 61 Rue Bossière, in a room so large and high-ceilinged that it would have contained a small apartment. The huge wardrobes that took the place of closets made little impression on it. The bathroom was of similar proportions. A balcony overlooking a charming court provided the last touch of magic for two Americans who had hardly ever seen a palace, much less lived in one. How much our palatial residence added to the charm and ever increasing excitement of that summer I shall never know, but the memory of the Fourth of July celebration there, with President Roosevelt's aged mother as the center, giving her talk in French clearly and fluently without notes, brings back the pride we shared with other Americans present.

As I had not seen Rank since his abrupt departure from New York, there was a gulf between us to be bridged despite the many letters that had intervened. On my side there was no lack of apprehension. What Rank felt I do not know but he arranged for a meeting the day after our arrival so that the uncertainty need not be prolonged. Knowing him as I did, I realized that there would be no talking over of the past. He had written all that he could express and I knew well that he would never refer to it again. Whatever was to be between us had to be immediate and present, without explanation, recrimination, or apology. I am not naturally reticent and usually any grievance I have demands full verbal outlet. I did not know whether I could let the past be past but I also knew that if I could not, there might be an end to friendship. To my surprise and relief, there was no problem for either of us. Communication was established on sight with an ease that only Rank in his new freedom could have made possible and we went on from there to all the exciting problems ahead.

We had arrived in time to join the last week of a seminar Rank had been holding for a number of Americans, including the minister of the American Church in Paris. It was a delight to see Rank so at ease in his own situation and to share in the discussions with the small group of men and women that met in the beautiful room at 9 Rue Louis Bouilly whose memory I had treasured. I was glad to find it just as beautiful as I had thought, but this time with no lingering photograph of Freud in evidence. It amused me to see how Rank had sharpened his teaching methods in the interval, involving my friend, happily not me, in an assignment the very first day. He had a gift for making people work when he wanted something, perhaps by virtue of his own example.

As it turned out, I was not to escape scot free, for almost before I knew it I was caught up in Rank's desire to learn something about working with children, in which I had only recently had a limited but successful experience. I had been aware that my therapeutic experiments with children were probably motivated in part by my desire to do something Rank had not done first but having had enough experience to satisfy my own need and to show me that Rankian therapy could be used with children as well as with adults, I was only too glad to "teach" Rank anything that I knew.

There was under discussion the problem of a five-year-old girl, whose mother had evidently appealed for help to someone in Rank's seminar, probably the minister of the American Church. Rank asked me if I would be willing to work with the child if the mother was willing. At that time I had not learned sufficiently the meaning of limitation for myself and, eager to do what Rank wanted, I rushed into a situation that might well have been my undoing. The absence of any related setting, of a socially sanctioned agency, of the office environment to which I was accustomed, did not deter me. The American Church offered a room to use as office, my friend Miss Robinson agreed to carry the role of social worker with the mother, and after a hasty trip to collect toys suitable for a five-year-old, an appointment was made for me to meet Christine. The utter falsity of this situation is so apparent that I can hardly credit my failure to see it in advance. Christine proved to be too much for me as she had been too much for her mother and there was nothing in an empty, meaningless church to hold either mother or child to the responsible commitment that application to a child guidance clinic involves. Two strangers in a foreign church do not make a socially responsible or even a sensible situation and Christine felt it on sight. Only the fact that Christine was already developing whooping cough saved me from a prolonged experience of failure. As it was, my gratitude to her for getting sick in time was tempered by the fear that I might have caught the infection. It would have served me right.

Out of this folly there came a new conviction for me about the impossibility of helping in a vacuum and I was able to give Rank genuine enlightenment as to why he had never been willing to take on work with children.

The Psychological Center, as it was finally designated, utilized for its first institute the accommodations provided at the Fondation des Etats-Unis, Cité Universitaire, which included lecture and reception rooms, with living quarters and a cafeteria available for those who wished to use them. The atmosphere was enhanced by a charming garden and the beautiful Parc Montsouris, just opposite, where we sat to watch the children and work off the excitement of the morning discussions. As the opening day drew near, Rank was everywhere, seeing to the final copies of the translations,[28] announcements, and programs, fixing dates for the prominent French and Swiss lecturers, arranging for the opening reception and tea, apparently in complete possession of himself and unruffled by the multitudinous details on which everyone wanted to consult him. He seemed not to have a care in the world and to be free to give time to his American friends with such genuine pleasure that it felt more like a vacation mood than the prelude to a hard-working six weeks in which he had to carry the basic lectures, although supported by Dr. Bailey[29] and Dr. Bone. After giving our limited contribution from the theory and practice of a training school for social

[28] In addition to my translations of the three volumes of the *Technik* (on which I was still working up to the last minute) Dr. George Wilbur had provided a translation of *Seelenglaube und Psychologie*. See his paper, "Soul Belief and Psychology—Some Remarks on the Recent Publications of Rank with Special Reference to the *Seelenglaube und Psychologie*," read before the Boston Psychoanalytical Society November 11, 1930; published in the *Psychoanalytic Review*, Vol. XIX, 1932, pp. 321–326.

[29] Dr. Bailey's lectures were published as "An Introduction to Rankian Psychology," in the *Psychoanalytic Review*, Vol. XXII (1935), pp. 182–211.

workers and of a child-placing agency, Miss Robinson and I yielded place to Dr. Frederick Allen, and Miss Almena Dawley, who represented the most enlightened practice of that period, in actual help for parents and children.

Our return from a trip to southern France on August 17 found the Center in full swing and Rank still full of energy and able to find spare time for his friends. After experiencing two more stirring sessions of the Institute and greeting many newcomers from America, we found it hard to take the *Paris* back to New York on August 22, and could well believe in Rank's final appraisal of the Center in a letter of August 29: "The Center was a real success to the very end. I am afraid you really missed something because I may never be the same again." [30]

He wrote more truly than he knew, for although the program for the 1935 session of the Center was already in print, Rank was about to leave Paris and Europe for good, on his way to become an American. The rapid exit of Americans from Europe was becoming ever more conspicuous and the threat of war could no longer be ignored, at least by Germany's neighbors. So despite a far from favorable economic situation in the United States plus a hostile psychoanalytic association in New York that had already begun to influence Philadelphia, Rank decided to come to the States in the fall provided he could get an official invitation from some recognized agency that would be acceptable to immigration authorities as assurance of future employment. At the close of the Center, he had received numerous requests for lectures and courses as well as applications for therapy, but something had to be made definite and formal. The Dean of the University of Pennsylvania School of Social Work sent the request for a lec-

[30] There were glowing reports of this first session in the French magazine *Action et Pensée*, January, 1935, and in the *News-Letter* of the American Association of Psychiatric Social Workers of the same date. In the latter there was included Rank's opening lecture entitled "Psychology and Social Change."

197

ture course and to Miss Robinson's letter of amplification he
replied in a letter of September 27, 1934.

Paris, September 27, 1934

Dear Virginia,

Thanks for your kind note just received this morning and
the cordial invitation to Flourtown.

As I have already written to Jessie, I am planning to sail on
October 8th on the City of Norfolk and expect to arrive in
Philadelphia on the 18th, going straight to the Benjamin
Franklin (I may drive up from Baltimore in Bailey's car
which I am taking over).

I should like to make as many contacts as possible in
Philadelphia before proceeding to New York, which I still
dread somewhat for various reasons (to be explained later
—maybe the same reasons you are going to give me for
abandoning the word PSA).

At any rate I shall enjoy spending the week end in Flourtown even if I have to share the room with Puffy and her
family.[31]

I am in no hurry for New York so I can see people if necessary on Monday or Tuesday following the week end for I
want at least to make sure of my work in Philadelphia.

Helen is leaving on Saturday for a college just outside
Paris and Mrs. Rank will be busy with packing and breaking
up the house for the next few weeks. In the midst of all that
and the "triste" reports from America I naturally feel somewhat uncertain about the building up of a new life. But
with the help of such friends as you and Jessie there is certainly hope.

Yours
Rank

[31] Our yellow Persian, always with beautiful kittens of varying parentage.

198

Thus Rank took up his new life in New York to face its active hostility as well as the ambiguous attitudes of former members of his own group. Knowing the many unfavorable factors, I expected the old reaction of disgust and aversion on his part but I was mistaken. I had underestimated the zest for living in the new self as the letter of November 10 so plainly shows:

THE ADAMS
Eighty-Sixth Street
at Fifth Avenue
New York
Saturday, November 10th

Dear Jessie,

I intended to drop you a line all week but was so busy with all sorts of activities—plus all the little things that I attend to myself—that I actually found no time.

I don't hate New York at all—I suppose because I am different, probably hated myself before in it; in fact I like it —was always attracted to it—and if I had a little more leisure I could probably love it.

I am glad to hear that the storm is over in Philadelphia. B—'s letter is a shame.[1]

Tomorrow I see Miss S—who is interested in financing the Center. She is a member of the School group.

Will you please lend me your book and Virginia's for the social workers' seminar, which will begin November . . . ; I'll bring the books back to you later on.

Yours
Rank

His new life as a teacher of social workers, particularly psychiatric workers, began at once. He plunged into three courses, two in New York for The Graduate School for Jewish Social Work (now discontinued) through the invitation of Dr. M. J. Karpf and his wife, Dr. Fay B. Karpf, the directors, who had attended the Center in Paris. Mrs. Karpf's continuing interest in Rank's point of view, begun in her first contact with him in Paris, has been expressed in several pamphlets much used in social work bibliographies and, as recently as 1953, in the appearance of a small volume entitled *The Psychology and Psychotherapy of Otto Rank.*[2] This support among the many conflicting forces in New York required no little courage on the part of a small school dependent upon the good will of the Jewish community, and Rank was not

---

[1] The general resistance in Philadelphia to psychoanalysis of any kind, especially as practiced by a nonmedical psychologist, was finally being directed to me. As long as I had not known how to help, Philadelphia psychiatrists were friendly and frequently referred cases that were annoying to them; now that I began to know what I was doing, a few were suspicious and even hostile. The antagonism of New York Freudians to Rank was also penetrating Philadelphia with the recent advent of a Freudian analyst, the first to enter the conservative psychiatric circle.

[2] New York: The Philosophical Library, 1953.

unmindful of the problem. The third course, probably arranged by the leaders of the Hartley-Salmon Clinic (who had also taken part in the Center's summer session) took him to New Haven once a week. In an early letter he reveals his characteristic concentration on the new experience.

New York, November 19, 1934

Dear Jessie,

Just a word to thank you for the books and to let you know that things are going quite well. I am extremely busy. —but even this is outside—doesn't tire me and I don't mind.

The teaching experience is a new revelation to me, and probably a revolution to the students. There is too much to say to begin at all and particularly in writing. But we'll have a chance.

Now I must go to bed. I am writing after having returned from New Haven where I gave them a good start!

I am still reading Huck³ every night when I go to bed and enjoy it tremendously.

As ever
R

The fall passed quickly for Rank, absorbed as he was with the new teaching problems. Christmas brought the following letter:

New York, Tuesday evening, [December ?]

Dear Jessie,

You don't know what your thoughtful gift⁴ means to me. Not only because it is the first volume of a first edition of Mark Twain I possess and not only because it is Tom Sawyer.

But also of what you say about Huck. I am through with

---

³ Mark Twain's *Huckleberry Finn*, which we had given him.
⁴ A child's worn copy of *Tom Sawyer*.

reading *Huck* (which *I* take the liberty to keep because it meant so much to me) but *I* am not through with Huck! Through *Huck* I discovered a new and yet age-old philosophy that is my own, my very real self, and that made me happy.

I must have known it when *I* saw the first page of Mark Twain (before *I* ever read Huck) and *I* found it out.

You don't know how many thanks to you and Virginia for the most precious gift.

Your
Huck (?)

1935

His first three courses for social workers completed, Rank was free to accept in February an invitation from Dr. Lovell Langstroth to visit the San Francisco Bay region and lecture before groups of interested psychiatrists. He delivered four lectures in all, one of which was arranged at Stanford University through the courtesy of the late Dr. Ray Lyman Wilbur. The after-effect of that brief contact has only recently emerged in a book by Dr. Langstroth, entitled *Structure of the Ego, an Anatomic and Physiologic Interpretation of the Psyche, Based on the Psychology of Otto Rank.*[5] Dr. Langstroth and I exchanged views by letter several times in 1950 and 1952 with the discovery that I was too philosophic for him and he too anatomical for me, but he writes with real insight on March 13, 1950: "I surmise that we are not so far apart as you indicate on Rankian theory but the movement of our individualities is in an opposite direction. . . . I seem to sense that you seek to find 'redemption,' if I may call it that, in feeling. . . . I on the other hand find my release in objectivity, in trying to make things concrete. It is just a matter of which direction the individual must take to find 'redemption' in the sense of Rank's chapter on 'Happiness and

[5] Published by Stanford University Press, 1955.

202

Redemption.'" In September, 1952, Dr. Langstroth reports a finished book, which he says "is constructed on the basis of an Ego structure I devised from study of Rank's genetic and will psychology and this finds an almost exact counterpart in brain anatomy. To my mind it fully substantiates most all of Rank's views and I believe its publication will be a big step ahead in our knowledge of the psyche. My only regret is that he is not alive to help me with it and to see this justification of his work which has meant so much to some of us . . . but more than that it has been a very developing experience that literally rocked me back on my heels when I found I could identify all these structures in myself."

That I have felt no need for anatomic justification of my point of view is perhaps to be deplored, but for me and, I think, increasingly for Rank, psychic experiencing, in other words, living, is and must be its own justification. At any rate Dr. Langstroth has performed a labor of love, carefully related to the psychology he derived from his study of Rank and based mainly on the first three books that Rank wrote during the period of his differentiation from Freud, i.e., the three volumes of *Genetic Psychology*. He finds Rank's later work becoming too "vague" and "philosophic," something he attributes to carelessness, than which nothing could be further from the truth. Rank may sometimes have seemed to speak "off the cuff," as it were, but the underlying organization of his thought was ever present, however colloquial or lacking in polish the words he employed. The depth is always there, in him, if not, as frequently happened, in his audience.

Following this first glimpse of California, which ever after became for him a future goal—the promise of peace and relief from the burden of psychotherapy—Rank established himself at the Chateau Crillon on Rittenhouse Square in Philadelphia, with the usual schedule of patients and the prospect of his first course for the Pennsylvania School of Social Work

in his new character as teacher. For his three earlier lecture
courses of 1927, 1928, and 1929, in which he read from prepared manuscript, there had been little if any preparation
by the School and no follow-up of results. At the Psychological
Center he had been again the lecturer; although freely accessible to question and discussion, he had no knowledge or
control of the outcome and no experience of the responsibility
the teacher feels who sees in student papers where he has
failed or succeeded. This time there was to be at least
the beginning of a different experience as far as the school
faculty could make it so. In the years since Rank's first lecture course in 1927, our psychological understanding had deepened and our teaching had improved accordingly. From our
alumni and related social agencies we could now draw upon
an advanced group already prepared to understand something
of Rank's psychology because they had *already* found it valuable in casework practice.

This course, entitled "Theories of Personality Development," was planned to give a broad catholic base of ten
lectures open to fifty qualified persons in which a variety of
viewpoints should be presented by authorities in their field,
to be followed by a credit course of seven conference sessions restricted to twenty-five advanced students and conducted by Dr. Rank alone.

These introductory lectures, presided over by Dr. Frederick
Allen, included distinguished names in the history of American psychiatry: Dr. William A. White, the gifted superintendent of St. Elizabeth's Hospital in Washington, whose
books, *The Mechanisms of Character Formation* and *The
Meaning of Disease*, were on every social work reading list of
the period; Dr. Adolf Meyer of Johns Hopkins, with his respect
for social work and education, representing the best in the
training of psychiatrists, and in the analysis of personality
structure and development. Even psychoanalysis was given
full opportunity for expression in the person of Dr. Franz

Alexander of Chicago, Rank's late opponent at the First International Congress on Mental Hygiene. When the time came for Rank's seminar conferences, which extended into June, 1935, he could count on a group of students prepared and attuned to his teaching, such as he had not experienced before. He was free at last to talk about what interested him and was not held to questions about psychotherapy or his difference from Freud. There was a reading list and a final paper that helped the students to stay related to "personality" as a psychological problem regardless of the always present, purely subjective interest, however disguised. Certainly the absorbed attention they gave was due in part to the aura that surrounds a famous therapist and the potential applicability of psychotherapy to self as well as to professional practice. But Rank held them finally by virtue of the vitality and immediacy of his own thought processes and his complete freedom in their expression. Organization was so fundamental with him that it required no effort on his part to combine it with spontaneity.

By the summer of 1935, after several weeks in Paris, Rank had moved to an apartment on Riverside Drive in New York where he could look out on the Hudson, and in that neighborhood he remained. Two events lightened his burden at that point, one the advent of a highly skilled secretary, Estelle Buel, a multilingual American, reared in Europe and America, a college graduate, with postgraduate work in philology and the history of art in Switzerland and Italy, followed by library training in Paris. No one could have provided more exactly and agreeably the help Rank needed, and to her cheerful efficiency and editorial skill he owed much of the comfort and satisfaction to be obtained from daily living. The second addition to his happiness arrived in the form of an Airedale pup (the gift of a patient) Spooky by name and even by temperament, for he was no ordinary dog. He had a long pedigree that made him eligible to membership in the American Kennel Club and a highly nervous individual temperament, sometimes requiring all the therapeutic skill of his master. In a letter of August 28, Rank writes, "I enclose a picture of Spooky who is a very nice fellow and good friend." Later, from a summer address in Connecticut, he registers his satisfaction in his two acquisitions. "Yes, I brought Spooky and my car and am really here for the first time, the secretary being the symbol of that. Yes, Spooky is a darling! He knows everything without having to be told and he likes the car too . . . he gets his meals daily, delivered from the Canine Catering Corporation in N.Y.C." He actually took Spooky to a dog show at Bear Mountain that summer and in the fall notes that "he goes through the usual disease period and needs lots of attention. However, he is in good spirits and likes horses as much as I do." But later in the month when he had other troubles, he writes: "Third worry, about Spooky who was two weeks in the hospital very ill and when he came back the other day threw nervous fits of a strange sort which I understood and handled accordingly, so today he is much better and probably out of danger." Rank's tenderness for Spooky and Spooky's devotion to him never waned. Despite his sensitive, highbred constitution, Spooky survived all the hazards of youth and grew into a very large, handsome, obedient animal who rarely left Rank's side and lived on to survive his master.

While Rank, his application for citizenship attended to, was "bringing up" Spooky in Connecticut and staying there in order to be in the neighborhood of a very difficult patient, my friend and I had rented a summer cottage in New Hampshire and were using our brief leisure time for writing. I was facing the challenge of writing an introduction to my translations of the *Technik*, looking forward to publication. It is one thing to generalize about an authority who is dead, quite another to expose your interpretation of his work to the living author who must know better than you what he meant. I was exhilarated by my own daring and yet full of apprehension. Who can take another's estimate of himself or his work? But I had to do it even if it meant complete rejection. In working through my understanding of Rank's thinking in relation to therapy I came upon the original stumbling block, the word *Illusion*,[6] the use of which in Rank's final formulation I resisted and still do, even today. His reply to what must have been my protest against a word that threatened belief in the reality of my own experience disarmed me completely:

THE TOKENEKE INN
Darien, Connecticut
Saturday, August 17, 1935

Dear Jessie,

First of all I want to thank you for your beautiful poem, yes, it was a poem, whether you intended it or not: look and listen:

The man at the plough has a more real experience
Than I who look on—but I feel it more than he does.
Is a moonlight night like last night
More real if one does something in it
Than if one aches with not being able to respond to it?

Is reality just where one is not
Or is it where one is?

[6] A single paragraph from *Will Therapy* will illustrate my problem:
"This inner illusional level of our modern human type is the emotional life itself, which permits an inner experiencing without outward living, but when it comes to the expression of emotion, as a rule it is confined to one of the socially provided planes. Emotions, therefore, as the neurotic shows, can simulate living, without the individual's becoming conscious of their illusional aspect; the neurotic longs for a normal emotional life as his ideal, without knowing that the normal person uses his emotions much more as protection from actual experience than as means thereto." Jessie Taft (trans.), Otto Rank's *Will Therapy* and *Truth and Reality*, New York: Alfred A. Knopf, 1945, p. 174; also, Jessie Taft (trans.), Otto Rank's *Will Therapy*, New York: Alfred A. Knopf, 1936, pp. 244–245.

207

All I can grant you—apart from that—is that I might not have known exactly what I really meant when I wrote it! But later on (last winter) I realized that it was the beginning of the play-idea: that is to say we like to make everything illusory in the sense (and with the purpose) of making it ours! Play is everyday creation, we make reality illusory, that is playful (if we can't, then neurotically so) because then we make it or can believe that we do even if we don't. This is certainly so with the emotions in the - - - - (word not legible). Aren't they (not) supposed to be ours and don't we keep them anyway!

Tell me how you like my "poetry."

> Your
> Rank

Regardless of all misgivings and in spite of Rank's repeated expression of lack of interest in the publication of the translation, my own determination, which would brook no obstacle, finally penetrated his indifference for he admitted in a letter of August 26: "Your last two letters sound so enthusiastic about getting that book into shape that I am really curious to see it (or rather myself in your presentation)."

I mailed him the material after I came back from vacation and waited anxiously for his reaction, which came on September 12:

Dear Jessie,

I read your preface and introduction at once and want to thank you for the excellent job you have done.

There is nothing more to be said about it and nothing to be changed because it stands as it is as a whole and is written in one full stream of expression which is yours and you!

I like it very much!

> My best to Virginia and you
> Yours
> R

Do you want it back?

Nothing could have been nicer but nothing could have matched the depth of emotion that surcharged this assertion of independence on my part, an illustration of Rank's point on the nature of emotion. It was clearly my own experience, but far from remaining on any plane of illusion, it provided the motive power for many years of objective realization.

Back in New York after Labor Day, Rank writes that he is again tied to the nine-hour schedule with patients, but says he won't keep that up although he needs money for moving his goods, especially his library, from Paris, and for "starting a new place in the states (still California)." With the usual worries of return from vacation, Rank had before him a request from Cleveland to give a series of lectures at the end of October. Under the depression of his chronic back-to-work-cold he says: "I don't know where to begin! So I began last week to outline the later formulations of therapy: they seem very clear to me (in a sense new) but don't sound at all Clevelandish! (or fit for any group for that matter except Philadelphia!) So I have to proceed to Cleveland." In a few days, however, he was saying: "I am not down and was not for that matter" (evidently in response to my mistaken expression of sympathy); "it may sound strange coming from *me* but I have no other trouble now except money—if it were not for that I could afford to work less and more pleasantly! I was all the time in good spirits and well. (The cold didn't really bother me.)" Nevertheless Cleveland was on his mind and he prepared to come to Flourtown to discuss it, writing, "Apart from seeing you, even for a short time, I want to show you some of the new formulations and to discuss in the light of them the Cleveland lectures. Again I feel so much ahead of myself and I feel sure you and Virginia can help me on that by discussing it." We had some social work connections with Cleveland that could help to make real the level of their interest. What he planned to present there I do not remember and no notes of his lectures are preserved beyond the letter that he wrote from there.

HOTEL STATLER CLEVELAND
Wednesday, October 20, 1935

Dear Jessie,

Thanks for your note which I received before leaving New York.

I knew you couldn't write—and yet I expected a word from you for Cleveland—it was good to have it!

It is—or has not so far been—not bad at all; the success was easy because I had it before I came!

When I arrived I learned that besides the two groups of 40 each there have been 37 people refused, because they couldn't form a third group. I suggested throwing them all together and so have only one large group.

This group includes, interestingly enough, the leading psychiatrists in town although it is arranged by social workers. It is—or seems to be—rather a good group, as you know, some very good people. I spoke to Miss T., who told me how much she enjoyed meeting you and Virginia this summer.

What I am telling them? I can't tell you; the first evening I improvised a lecture on the general situation in the fields of Psychology, Therapy, and Social Work; last night I spoke on the meaning of different psychologies, tonight, I think on illness and cure, then activity and passivity, will, and so on.

I am telling you this partly because I may forget and I won't be able to come to Philadelphia.

As ever yours
R.

After Cleveland, there loomed the next advanced course for the Pennsylvania School and meantime a lecture for the student organization of the New York School of Social Work which, like other student organizations, probably enjoyed bringing in a lecturer out of harmony with the main trend of the faculty, which was Freudian. In a letter dated December 3, written from "The Master" apartments, 310 Riverside Drive, which was to be his permanent address thereafter, he writes: "Over Thanksgiving, I slept for two days, so tired was I and now I am fully awake again. Last week my mother died in Vienna at the age of 80—the last tie there gone when I came here for good." This is, I think, the only reference he ever made to any member of his family and yet a poem in his early notebook, "An Meine Mutter," indicates the depth of his attachment to her.

My task at this point, not entirely easy or pleasant, was to organize a second course of lectures and seminars that should present a broad outlook and create the best possible setting for Rank's contribution. My choice of a general title was "The Organization of the Self." The lecturers in the first half of the course were Dr. Kurt Koffka, a Gestalt psychologist, the anthropologist, Dr. Ruth Benedict, and, on the psychoanalytic side, Dr. Karen Horney, now established (independently of Alexander) in New York. Rank was to conclude this half of the course with a single lecture to be followed by eight seminars for which credit could be obtained by a reading assignment with a final paper. I am amazed as I reread the correspondence of this period by his acceptance of my topics and titles. In response to my first presentation of a subject for his single lecture, he writes the following:

December 16, 1935

Dear Jessie,

As far as I can see the dates for the lectures are O.K. now and as to other suggestions nothing occurs to me at the moment. I shall, however, think the matter over and will let you know within the next few days whether anything came to me in the way of titles and subjects, etc.

The subject of the Double still does interest me and I shall probably like to go back to it once more.

As to Philadelphia—I don't think of practicing there this spring but I may be available for consultations on Mondays (with a chance of week ends too!)

As ever

R

1936

This was not definite enough for the School's purpose and my reluctant urgency about the general subject for the seminars brought the following response:

January 3, 1936

Dear Jessie,

Your "special" reached me in bed with a cold, and although I confess I haven't given much thought to the business yet with that heavy head I seem to be unable to think at all.

One reason why I didn't worry about the title was the hunch that if I once put myself into it—probably at the eleventh hour—it will be something else anyway. But I think "The Dynamics of Self Integration" would cover almost anything I may say: it certainly characterizes my present inclination to regard neurosis as an accompaniment (not substitute) for creativity.

I wish myself I knew what I think about various things! As soon as I know—something—I'll tell you!

Meanwhile I wish to tell you how much I appreciate your help in the matter, knowing that without you I wouldn't even think of it. I can only hope not to disappoint you in the end!

If I should leave New York later than I planned I may come to Philadelphia; my California plan became quite uncertain, i.e., the visit this winter and I may go South for a short while on a real vacation.

> About all this as soon as I am back
>
> As ever
>
> Your
>
> R

With the pressure of work, present and future, upon him (The Graduate School for Jewish Social Work wanted another lecture course in the spring) one finds him turning to the thought of California if only for a brief visit but it does not materialize and he is obliged to consider the south as a substitute. However, he is not too tired for Christmas greetings and his appreciation of the Struwwelpeter book we sent him is in terms of its application to Spooky whom he is trying to teach the "I'll go out but you stay here lesson."

Sending him a printed announcement of the course brought back the following response of January 18:

Thanks for the program which looks very nice—and did inspire (or at best push) me to start an outline of the whole course. I seem to have some ideas how to tie in various things and build up something new. But more work has to be done on it before I can tell you anything. . . . My vacation is still in the air. Now I guess about the last two weeks in February down south.

By February 1 he says:

There seems nothing left to go and yet I am planning to leave in a week. . . . I take some work with me and hope I'll get to it sometime. . . . I saw a lot of Philadelphia recently and altho I thought of you quite frequently (not only by way of association) I am rather glad I haven't seen you *in between. You belong somewhere else and if I can't see you right, I'd rather not at all—and I know you feel the same (total) way. My best to Virginia.*

Meantime I had reached the last steps involved in publishing my translations and Rank cabled the Vienna publisher to obtain the necessary rights. By March 11, he could assure me in the following note:

This morning I received the letter from the publisher from which I see that I can easily arrange matters with him myself—so you won't have to bother with it—nor Mr. Knopf.

Finally in a note of April 2, 1936, came the reward I had never expected. I needed no other.

April 2, 1936

Dear Jessie,

I just read over the week end your introductory chapter to the Technique and want to tell you that I felt this was the justification for the publication.

This is not just a compliment for the excellent presentation—what I mean is that it shows there is somebody who understands it and knows what I mean.

I can see in that way that the fact of your publishing it makes it worthwhile publishing it at all.

Your

Rank

The Philadelphia schedule that began March 23 with the lecture on "The Double" was far too strenuous to combine with a full program in New York. He came to Philadelphia at noon on Monday, spent the afternoon on appointments, conducted a class of fifty intensely interested social workers, the best to be found in Philadelphia, from 7:15 to 9 P.M., and either took a train back to New York or, when he was too tired, stayed overnight at the Hotel Crillon. There was seldom a free moment; someone always wanted to be seen and he could not afford to refuse. Yet tired though he always was, there was never a trace of weariness in the seminar. Something in his personality always took hold of the group and held it without apparent effort. He spoke directly, simply, without formality as if he were immediately related to every person present. He gave his best. His thinking was alive, as if generated at the moment and for that occasion, yet it welled from a depth of experience not to be exhausted and carried for everyone the sense of universality. Perhaps no one in the group had the background or capacity to understand more than a fraction of what he heard, but for every individual there was an experience of meaning, of value, beyond anything he had expected.

Although the Philadelphia course lasted until the end of May, June 10 found him in Rochester, New York, in response to an invitation to give a brief seminar. He writes from there:

June 10, 1936

Dear Jessie,

I really enjoy my stay here—it is a very nice and quite good group of about 45 people from the fields of Social Work and Education.

Yesterday I gave a general lecture somewhat like for the students in Philadelphia. There were over 100 people although the lecture was not advertised. Some people came from Buffalo (University, Sociological Department) and asked me to come there in the fall and the Rochester group wants more too—later on! . . .

It is as though any change of place or external stimulus gave him a needed relief from the fatigue generated by the deadly eight or nine hours a day of psychotherapy for this letter continues surprisingly enough to describe his relation to his own writing:

The book takes on form and shape in my sub- or pre-conscious, a state that I like best and from which I have to force myself into the actual writing. I usually do that by getting a new notebook, scrapbook, pencils, and all the paraphernalia I've liked since my school days (when I stole them). But sometimes I don't get beyond that stage, as for example in the last five years. Maybe this time I'll go further. It will depend on finding a nice place for the summer to do the writing in—but not too nice either or I won't do it.

I announced the books[7] here too and am sure that most of them will get them. I think we ought to be able to do good business.

Yet by June 19 comes the inevitable aftermath: "Rochester was interesting and successful but I am tired."

The "book" was very much on his mind and he plans to get some vacation on a farm in Connecticut where he can write. The following letter from Cleveland reached us in California where we were spending our vacation.

THE LAKE SHORE
Cleveland, Ohio
July 28, 1936

Dear Jessie,

Since the Farm won't be ready until August 1st I am here for a week on a visit (and partly discussing another small-group seminar here for the fall). . . .

The book—a book—is coming along—not so much in writing yet as in spirit! (It's going to be different from what we might expect; I'll try to do the writing in August.)

[7] The books referred to are the translations of *Will Therapy* and *Truth and Reality.*

216

Thanks for the books—they look swell and by the way those copies you kindly sent were the only ones I got since Knopf refused to let me have some for my personal use. . . .

The only review I saw so far was in the Nation, blaming me for not being Marxist! That encouraged me to elaborate my lecture on the different psychologies into a psychology of revolution against "pseudo-revolution" (using psychology as a political tool).

Otherwise life is not too simple either. My daughter is coming over the second week in September, trying still to enter college if possible; Mrs. Rank is not coming yet for various reasons! One being my unsettled plans and what to do with the furniture, library, etc.

I haven't enough money to experiment any more with moving without knowing where I am going to be—on the other hand I want and need my books and manuscripts and —here I am! Anyway I'll try to forget about it all during August and then plunge all at once into it!

With best regards to your sister, Virginia, and yourself

As always

Your H

The summer in the Connecticut farm house seems not to have been the opportunity for peaceful writing that he had anticipated. As I read the letters of the months that followed, I can see that he was already oppressed by the domestic problems about to be precipitated. His daughter arrived in New York on September 12, which was late for applications for college entrance, but with help and advice from Philadelphia friends she was entered as a junior at Swarthmore College just outside Philadelphia. Mrs. Rank followed shortly and we joined them in late October in a visit to Helen. It was evident that they had come together only temporarily on Helen's account for Mrs. Rank was planning then to go to Boston where she had made connections once before, but with strong reservations and even dislike. Shortly after this visit, Rank writes that Mrs. Rank is about to leave for Boston feeling decidedly better toward America and seemingly determined to take hold of it. It is interesting to note that Cambridge became her permanent residence and that she has been highly successful as a child therapist and associate director of the James Jackson Putnam Children's Center, a child guidance clinic and nursery school for preschool children.

Throughout the fall, Rank continued to be depressed and seemed to find a needed outlet in his letters to me. Early in October he writes despairingly:

I felt lately what I told you last time I saw you: namely, that I am dead! That's the way people act now toward me and the sad part is that they somehow seem to be right because I feel dead too! If I can't go out to California and start a new life there I probably will die anyway.

Alas, he was closer to the truth than he knew, for the treadmill of the endless daily hours of psychotherapy was beginning to undermine his health as it also defeated the inner pressure to create at leisure.

It was at this time that I began, with the help of the Dean of the Pennsylvania School and Miss Robinson, to work on a plan for giving Rank a position on the faculty in the hope that he might derive therefrom some sense of community backing that the New York environment did not provide. He had a capacity for enduring an aloneness that few men ever experience and survive but when the active hostility of a former professional group is added to the burden of earning a living in their midst, even the extreme individualist may sometimes yield to depression. After a visit to Flourtown in which we evidently broached our plan, he writes gratefully:

November 7, 1936

Dear Jessie,

Just a word that I have to say to you of thanks.

Your coming toward me at this point as you did saved my SELF—at least for the time being—and if something concrete can be worked out on the basis of your feelings about the new plane (not plan) I hope it can be saved altogether: by giving me a place where I can be my SELF.

Incidentally X— called yesterday (about a course) and made it easy for me to decline definitely by putting a sort of ultimatum up to me. Thank God that's over and done with!

What you say about Helen is so true and human and simple—I think you can help her in finding a new relationship to me—at any rate I am thankful too that you care enough for her to understand her so well!

I'll probably come next week end although I have to work on Saturdays—but we'll see—and I surely like to see Helen too!

Tell Virginia how much I appreciated her writing to Mrs. Rank.

More than always
Your
Rank

By November 12 he can refer to the "book" again although it takes illness to release him.

Thursday, November 12

Dear Jessie,

I don't think I'll come this week end because for the last few days I have had a slight cold that seems to develop into some sort of influenza (at least that's what it feels like).

I am taking care of myself and rest a great deal, using part of the time to get back to the book again; I went over the first two chapters written during the summer and am pleased with it (maybe I'll bring them along when I come the following week).

As ever
Your
Rank

What happened on the promised visit to call forth the note of November 24 I no longer remember but it went far beyond his usual reserve:

November 24, Monday
Jessie,
You really are a dear person—and Virginia is an angel! That's all I have to say!

Your
Rank

P.S. Today, Tuesday, I received word from Buffalo that a course is arranged there for the last week in January, which suits me well because I may after that go out West.

Perhaps the very idea of Buffalo and the ever-recurring thought of the West were sufficient to ease the pressure of New York and his problematic family responsibilities for on December 1 he reports on the book:

Monday, December 1st
Dear Jessie,
Thanks for your two letters received before and after the holiday!

I had a peaceful week end and read and wrote (Chapter III).

You are right, the second chapter is full (too full?) of material—but the double and the twin belong together—it is the main theme of the book; the other chapter won't be as packed.

As far as the theory is concerned I don't want to present any, as such, although the book will show it. The idea is the reader should get it himself (or whatever he or she can get), not for big sale—I know!

I am glad you enjoy Helen as you do and I am sure she enjoys being enjoyed!

As to the lecture title I think it's excellent (any of your versions!)

At any rate (again the book) it has to be taken "total" and I have to put it out first anyway, before doing anything else with it! The task looms up in front of me.

But it all feels good—for the time being—and I am glad you do too.

Your Rank

In a letter of December 9, he tells with evident relief of seeing Mrs. Rank who feels rather good in Boston and is enjoying the first "trickles of success." Apparently, oppressed by a mood myself, I had waited to feel better before writing—without success, as his letter of December 12 shows plainly: "Sorry you feel that way —I know what it is and have barely moved out of it myself—can't give you much strength although something else. You better get strong and be strong for both of us (for the time being)."

At Christmas time he has the parent's vacation situation to handle but seems more equal to it.

Sunday, December 20

Dear Jessie,

Yes it was I who sent you and Virginia the two pieces for your house—and I am glad you like them—they shine like the moon.

Helen has arrived and it is good to have her although one does not quite get together here in N.Y. She'll go next week (23rd) to Boston and I'll go away for a prolonged week end, to be back for the week after Xmas and before New Year. Maybe I'll come back when Helen goes back, that is the week end Jan. 3rd. I'll let you know. I don't know much now because, besides being tired, I am somewhat disorganized.

Your title sounds good and I surely don't know any better one.

I discovered the other day a Miss Shaw here who has a school for finger-painting and the most marvelous material for both therapy and creativity in children. I must tell you about her work. Then we also talk finances (for the seminar) but I think last year's basis will be all right.

Helen got your letter here and thanks ever so much for your thoughtfulness. She sends her best along with my heartiest wishes for you and Virginia for the coming year.

As ever your
Rank

In an effort to provide a little Christmas cheer, we sent him our idea of a Christmas box full of little things, including some carved animals but the futility of such a gesture is only too evident in his reply.

Tuesday, December 22

Dear Jessie,

I like the little book—and do you remember I had the ape on my mantelpiece in Paris!

The tobacco pouch is the softest I ever saw in my life, and I like softness!

The trouble is I am too soft myself for life.

The duck reminds me at present, in my present mood, of Ibsen's "Wild Duck," which used to be my favorite play—for various reasons.

The wild duck when wounded is supposed to go all the way down to the ground, bite into it and stay there till it dies.

222

It was nice anyway to get so many different things—it was like a stocking!

But at present I am going to the ground and I hope you'll wait till I come up again or till you fetch me.

My best to you and Virginia.

Rank

"Huck" likes the cabin in Vermont! I really wish I could retire and live a peaceful life-end. I had enough of the "world" and I have worlds and worlds within myself. I want to talk to you about the cabin in Vermont—please remind me if I don't when I see you.

With my real love to you

Rank

1937

With the approach of the second semester, I was again in the position of having to organize a lecture course and a seminar, long before Rank could bring himself to think about it as concretely as a school demands. On the basis of the success of the two preceding courses I decided on the rather elaborate title, "Growth, Learning, and Change in the Development of the Individual," which interested Dr. Koffka so much that he was willing to come from Smith College three weeks in succession with a fascinating account of memory and a theory of traces. Dr. Frederick Allen introduced the course with his famous chapter on the "Dilemma of Growth," [8] followed by the zoologist, Dr. Herbert S. Jennings of the Johns Hopkins University, whose relatively popular books *Prometheus, The Biological Basis of Human Nature, The Universe and Life,* had inspired every beginning social worker in the Pennsylvania School. Dr. Arnold Gesell of Yale University brought films to illustrate his lecture on "Maturation and the Patterning of Behavior," and Mrs. Lucy Mitchell, the educator responsible for

[8] Frederick H. Allen, *Psychotherapy with Children*, New York: W. W. Norton and Company, Inc., 1942.

223

the Bank Street School in New York, long synonymous with progressive education, provided a realistic connection with children's learning. Finally, Dr. Rank was to take over the problems of growth and change in terms of personality development.

However impressive this program sounded and actually was in its realization, it put pressure on Rank who was still seeing a daughter through the holidays, but he managed to write on January 3 not about the course but about the plan for a closer association with the school.

Dear Jessie, 	January 3, Friday

Thank you so much for figuring out that new plan, which feels so much easier and smoother.

The material is interesting if I only knew how to use it. Would you mind sending the other piece along.

I am glad that you and Virginia feel that way about my participating in the school: it is the only logical conclusion from the development of my work and besides (but mainly) gives me a feeling of security by placing me in a community position.

Sorry I couldn't write sooner and had to resort again to a telegram but I was in bed with a kind of grip—up again today.

My best to both of you

Rank

As I continued to consult him about titles and topics that had to be definite for the printer, his irritation and feeling of being coerced finally broke through in his note of January 11.

Dear Jessie, 	January 11, 1937, Monday

It was really mean of me—you are right—but I didn't mean it! This is the worst part of my nature which always gets me into trouble!

224

Please forgive it!

I know that without your help nothing would have happened and I know that I still need your help—and I will ask for it.

I am glad you like the book!

Thanks for the papers.

I got two inquiries from Philadelphia. You probably know about them.

Then an official letter from Virginia which I shall answer shortly.

As always

Rank

The last week of January he spent in Buffalo giving a seminar for the Department of Sociology of the University of Buffalo. From there he acknowledges the printed announcement of the course.

Tuesday, January 26

Dear Jessie,

Thank you for both your letters and the enclosed program, which looks very impressive! . . .

I wish I had a little bit of your enthusiasm—but maybe I have too much wisdom for that and so have to counteract it by being foolish!

I also have no sense of perpetuation—that's why I don't like my books or my success with people nor any big following! But I am more willing to let things come as they do and at least won't oppose it as I used to do! I can't even get myself to buying a new suit of clothes that I need or anything like that. But I'd love to see you in your new outfit! How swell it must be!

Isn't it strange that I should just be away from New York while you visit! I can't promise to be there in time so don't plan to postpone your return until Tuesday, which might rush and tire you. But I expect to be back in New York on

Monday in the later part of the afternoon and will call you up immediately upon arrival. Will you please leave a message at the Essex where you can be reached in case you should be out.

In Buffalo I thought I'd show them how simplified (naïve) things started (with sexual repression and the like), how complicated they got because nobody knew what it was all about, and that therapy can begin anew, simple, that is, direct, after what we experienced in the last 10 years.

Now I must go over my material for this evening.

My best to Virginia and you.

Your Rank

Apparently negative feelings to which I am no stranger had been mounting in me to the point where I actually put them into a letter, something I had never dared do before, since personal acquaintance had never for a moment blinded me to the fact that I was trying to relate to genius, a difficult undertaking to say the least. So I got back the only unpleasant letter ever to come to me from Rank and it cleared the atmosphere. He wrote in part:

HOTEL STATLER
Buffalo
Friday, January 29

Dear Jessie,

I don't see why you had to write me that terrible letter, unless you are at moments just as unreasonable as I am. But this time I didn't deserve it at all. My letter was written —though apropos of yours—out of my mood here which it reflected and in fact I felt very good about you while I wrote it.

Feeling my lack of enthusiasm in spite of the fuss people here are making over me I realized that I never had a real

226

sense of perpetuation or continuation and was glad you had it for me. . . .

So, I propose we shouldn't be so silly and a little unreasonable since we don't seem able to be wise.

Things here are going all right, the group is not so bad and discussion is quite lively. On the other hand, the more people I talk to the more hopeless it seems really to get them any further. But I don't deplore this nor do I blame them nor do I feel badly about it.

Professor X—who is a hyperintellectual and therefore feels the need for the other side—emphasized again how contrary my viewpoint is to the whole mentality of our age and if I could complete my work (for which I need two lifetimes he said) that I will be called in the future the Kopernicki of the social sciences. Curiously he started his discussion with your pet "Illusion"!

I hope you have enough time in New York and that I did not spoil anything—or that you don't let it spoil whatever you and Virginia may get out of it.

Still your R (incorrigible)

For three months before the Philadelphia seminars began on April 19, Rank was busy with the usual heavy New York schedule, which was lightened for him by two discoveries; one he describes in a letter of February 11.

Thursday, February 11

Dear Jessie,

Thanks for your notes and letters and—what was in them! I am glad you enjoyed N.Y. I did too that evening!

Since then I have been too busy with too many various things and also somewhat "dazed" by a book, which doesn't often happen to me. But—believe it or not—I've found a book that does the same thing with (or to) law that I did

227

for theory and education: that is first separating all content from dynamics and then stating the fundamentally dualistic principle inherent in the dynamics: showing what it is and pointing out why it has to be that way, good and bad. It's profound psychology although he doesn't know it and calls it "anthropological approach." . . .

What else is there to tell—maybe too much to write any further.

So I'll do it next time.

My best to both of you

Rank

The book, as I learned later, was Thurman Arnold's *Symbols of Government,* which proved to be the precipitant of Rank's final course in the Pennsylvania School. The other discovery arose from an opportunity to see a number of the Shaw finger paintings and to hear about their relation to the problem children who had produced them. Later he made active efforts to interest Dr. Allen and Miss Dawley in the possibilities of finger painting for the Philadelphia Child Guidance Clinic, which finally resulted in a demonstration for the clinic staff by Miss Shaw. [9] He had in his own apartment a number of these pictures loaned by Miss Shaw and took great delight in showing them to us on our New York visit.

He was also becoming more involved with the inside problems of social casework and reacted with distaste to a new word in social work theory for which I was largely responsible. In a letter of February 28, he says, "As to 'function' I get more and more suspicious of words (or terms). It seems that they also besides clarifying something, contain (or create) a new problem. I am afraid you have to tell me whether I am 'function' or 'need' (and which of the two Freud is)." Rank was the last person to understand function as used by the so-

[9] Ruth Faison Shaw, *Finger Painting,* Boston: Little, Brown, and Company, 1934.

cial agency, for he himself had never been in the position of representing any agency. The only function he knew was a professional one but in his case self-oriented and self-maintained. Its importance as a support for the social worker was hard for him to realize or to conceive of as allowing for a truly helpful relation to the client. At any rate Rank should not be held responsible for the functional approach in social work, which has been a bone of contention in social work discussions and often identified with the Rankian influence on the Pennsylvania School.

By the end of March he was hoping for a brief respite before beginning the course in Philadelphia. I had been aware of the strain he was under and had apparently written with real consideration for he writes on March 21 with an expression of feeling rare for him:

March 21

Jessie,

    You are a darling.

    You are an angel!

    That's what I wanted to tell you in response to your last two letters—even before you told me not to bother to "write" but just to say a word!

    I didn't because—I don't know!

    Anyway I didn't write before because my plans were uncertain. As it looks now I will leave New York the middle of this week and go for a few days South—not very far—just to see a little of Carolina and Virginia. Before coming to Philadelphia I am going to be in Richmond for a couple of lectures which I promised more than a year ago. This way I can nicely combine it with a little rest over Easter that I need very badly.

    On Sunday the 4th of April I'll meet Helen in Philadelphia, who is coming back from a visit in Boston. I don't know whether you can do anything for me about the course,

*except to have somebody start it with some material! Or do
you think it's better to leave that to me too? Do as you
think best.*

   With love to you and Virginia

                                                   Your
                                                   Rank

The Philadelphia schedule proved to be a genuine strain
this year, for under his new responsibility as a member of the
faculty, in addition to the evening seminar for the large group,
he had undertaken to teach in the afternoon a small group of
advanced caseworkers who would present their own case material for discussion. Although he usually arrived on Monday
noon there was seldom a free moment, with the usual requests for appointments and often a need to see his daughter
at lunch. Since he left for New York immediately after the
evening seminar there was little opportunity for me to enjoy
any personal contact, a deprivation that I bore with difficulty.
It is only now as I look back over the records of this term
that I can see how much we asked of him and what he gave.
I did not attend the afternoon class but my notes from the
evening seminar bring back vividly the deep excitement that
animated the whole group—actually the same persons who
had attended the two preceding courses. Here was a new
Rank, who was willing to bring to the group the factors in
growth as he conceived them concretely, in terms of actual
cases, and to illuminate for social workers and educators the
dynamics of the growth process out of his rich experience.
The response of the group never failed to provide the needed
stimulus that called out the brilliance of Rank's thinking
about any given case as well as his understanding and acceptance of human frailty. No one who had the good fortune to be
present will ever forget the evening in which he exhibited a
number of the finger paintings supplied by Miss Shaw with
the child's explanation of his picture and a brief account of

each child's symptoms and general family situation. To the remarkable revelations of a young child's effort to put out his problems, Rank's sensitive comments only added wholeness and validity. One felt that he might have painted every one himself, so internalized was his understanding.

On the last evening of the course, discussion centered on training for social work and the kind of growth that can be expected or required of the social worker. One could not ask of a training school a better characterization than Rank's closing statement as I can reproduce it from my notes. "Social work has been forced to change 'inside' because it did not have the outside authority of science, nor the skill and power of the professions as law or medicine. The first step in training for social work is the acceptance of difference; the second is the utilization of differentiation for growth, and the third is to permit difference, i.e., to permit the other to grow." The seriousness with which he took his new relation to the School is reflected in a note of May 20.

Thursday, May 20

Dear Jessie,

I do not know whether you and Virginia expected me to-morrow for the staff meeting or not.

But I really didn't feel well since last week and worse this week. I'll see what rest will do and what will be left (one way or the other) after having rested this coming week end.

I'll come to Philadelphia on Monday at noon and will call to see when I can see you.

My best to Virginia and you
Yours
Rank

Although his classes in Philadelphia were over by the end of May, 1937, he sends the following note on June 20.

231

Sunday, June 20

Dear Jessie,

I was glad to be able to arrange to come on Thursday to Philadelphia for the staff meeting.

I thought of having luncheon with you (and Virginia if possible) beforehand, but it seems I have to go—at last—to Swarthmore to see the Dean of Women because things are not quite straight yet. If so I may not get to Philadelphia before 1 P.M. In any case will you leave a message at the School where I may find you when I get in.

I want at least to shake hands with you for your birthday.

My best to you and Virginia.

Your

Rank

He came as promised and even managed a late lunch with me, quite unmindful of the invitation to my birthday dinner in Flourtown that I had understood him to have accepted. The disappointment was too much for my control and I failed to hold back the tears I so seldom permit, certainly not in public. It was an unhappy occasion in itself but when we reached my office, Rank's response to my hurt feelings came through with a depth of pain and self reproach that quickly turned me into the comfort-giver. I could not bear that he should condemn himself so bitterly.

Out of this emotional upset we went directly into the faculty meeting. I was apprehensive, for as I knew the faculty was having its own problems and, however polite on the surface, was in no very cordial mood. What Rank's role was to be in this meeting, no one had worked out. He could not have known anything about it in advance as it was his first appearance in this group. I have no memory of a single detail of the meeting, no idea of the problems discussed, but I still retain the sense of something strong, peaceful, and supporting that gradually took over and brought into a kind of working harmony the dissident elements in the situation; an illustration of the magic of which he was sometimes accused, for the results were not due primarily to anything he said but rather to what he was, a man somehow related to the universal.

The summer of 1937 was a hard one for Rank. Mrs. Rank came from Boston to discuss the problem of the stored furniture in Paris, but she could not bring herself to accept the permanence that having the furniture here would imply. Though she was highly successful in her Cambridge position and well protected by medical friends from Vienna, she was still not happy in America. Rank himself felt differently in his desire for greater permanency and wanting his own furniture was part of it. He had decided to move to a less expensive apartment in the same building with the same view of the Hudson but, to his regret, no terrace. Miss Robinson and I felt almost guilty that, at this moment, we were rejoicing in our newly built Vermont cottage and our first experience of actually living in it. We urged Rank to try out the guest cabin for a week end. A letter of August 14 from his attempted vacation indicates the new obstacle to restfulness.

August 14, 1937

Dear Jessie,

I don't know what is lovelier, the pictures or your description of the place and the simple life there! I like the end-of-the-porch view best but also the big windows in front. Hope I can come soon to see it!

For the time being my plans are somewhat upset. Although I was resting and relaxing in the charming section of the Finger Lakes (swimming and fishing) I didn't feel as well as I should until I found out that I have a couple of badly infected teeth that are causing trouble and have to be extracted as soon as possible. In fact my whole mouth needs a thorough clean-up for which I am returning to New York next week.

I had planned to go from here to the Adirondacks and stop on my way back at your place. But I don't feel comfortable enough with that pain and will take the rest of my vacation after the treatment during the month of September.

I have also been working somewhat on the book—more in my mind though than on paper; I found this not only more pleasant but also more helpful. So you see, I am still the old

Huck

My best to Virginia and all good wishes to your "angelic" self.

The letter of August 25 from New York gives the picture of his summer:

August 25, 1937

Dear Jessie,

I have been here a week and had three teeth pulled, two of them elephant tusks. I hope the worst is over although the whole dental treatment will take several weeks and cost me about $300.

My only distraction (beyond the extraction) was in realizing the spot you describe so vividly. I like De-Limit[10] (and not only because it is on the edge of the woods) and hope I can come there some week end in the fall although God knows I will need some rest after all this teeth trouble. But then, I have to move, too, the end of September and some rest after that won't be bad either! At any rate I'd like to go to "De-Limit."

Helen is coming back next week to New York and I don't know yet what she'll do before going back to Swarthmore. (It seems to be all settled.)

---

[10] De-Limit, evidently our proposed name for the cabin taken from a popular song of the period.

During the last few weeks the book has expanded—in my mind—and only now is really "beyond psychology" (also probably beyond the understanding of most psychologists).

Let me know when you get back and any news from the outside world.

My best to Virginia and you.

Your
Rank

In September all the getting-back-to-work annoyances are making themselves felt on both sides, as his letter of September 4 recognizes:

Saturday, September 4

Dear Jessie,

I hope it wasn't too difficult to get back into the world from your Paradise (not lost). I had a similar feeling—guess it comes with age and fulfilment of your business career, or whatever you call it:—feeling of futility in coming back to the world of work. Kind of a "what for" feeling. Hope it will pass with you, too, because otherwise it would be too hard.

Helen is here and it is good to have her—for a while at least. . . .

My teeth are getting along all right (I mean the ones that are left) only it is a nuisance to have to spend all this time and money on dentistry. I won't have any of this "removable" stuff—and this was one reason why it took me so long to get to a dentist. Those I have consulted before didn't want to make anything else (except removable) and besides had the idea of beautification. This one whom I found now is quite simple and honest and only does the necessary.

My best to you—including Virginia.
Your
Rank

By September 20 he notes that Helen is there and can't go back to Swarthmore before the 27th, adding, "but I can't have much of her nor give her much with all this moving going on. She is bored and naturally it is my fault for not providing entertainment for her." Matters are no better by September 26, when he writes from a low ebb, physically and emotionally.

Sunday, September 26

Dear Jessie,

Your letter came in the midst of moving plus a cold which I caught in some draft while working.

So I don't think I can do much this coming week (+ end). Besides I am still very low—it is for me to one of my worst periods and I am sorry to hear that you feel that bad (or felt).

Helen is leaving tomorrow and I think it will be good for both of us. It wasn't a successful time, this her last stay.

Suddenly this morning (or rather noon) while I was still resting in bed from coughing it occurred to me what really was (or is) "beyond Psychology." You know what? Stupidity! All that complicated and elaborated explanation of human behavior is nothing but an attempt to give a meaning to one of the most powerful motives of behavior, namely stupidity! I begin to think that it is even more powerful than badness, meanness—because many actions or reactions that appear mean are simply stupid and even calling them bad is a justification.

At any rate that's the last word—I realize a perfect expression of my present mood and my present philosophy of life.

But forget all about it—or if you can't then believe that this letter isn't bad—just stupid.

Yours as ever,

Rank

236

Something in this letter and my response to it brought a response from Miss Robinson, who was as concerned as I was for his health and the long time since we had seen him. He replied with his characteristic immediacy and frankness.

Wednesday, September 29

Dear Virginia,

Thanks for your sensible note! What would we do without you? God knows! May he bless you!

After the worst moving is over I can rest and take care of myself as much as possible. It seems to take its normal course and I hope will be over soon. I am afraid though I won't be able to go South because things are picking up here and I can't afford to miss a good start.

Please tell Jessie how sorry I feel that she has to make things so hard for herself and how much I'd like to make it easier.

I hope you have a good week end. I'll be with you in spirit—and before long in the flesh in Flourtown.

Cordially

Rank

The fall of 1937 was marked by a new physical ailment, overwork, and, strangely enough, a renewed sense of creativity. Early in October he writes, "I feel considerably better although not quite rid of the cold which besides left me with a rheumatic pain in my right arm (which may still be due to the teeth infection)." In a letter of October 15, he refers to a review[11] of my translations (*Will Therapy* and *Truth and Reality*) that appeared later in a social work journal. Coming from a friend of mine, a highly intelligent social worker with a Freudian background, it had evidently given me mixed reactions. His answer follows:

11 Grace Marcus, "Some Implications for Case Work of Rank's Psychology," *Family* XVIII, 272–277, December, 1937.

October 15, 1937

Dear Jessie,

Thanks for the review and letters, all of which I read. You are right—I am not grateful and I don't see why I should be for the review but I am naturally pleased because it is a good and honest piece of work.

There's only one thing I miss in it and that is a (even slight) reference to my position regarding fact and content in theory, where I think it has its place. But maybe that's not important in her review of my therapeutic concepts, although it also gives a one-sided picture of my criticism, which is not as radical in one sense and more radical in another: namely, in separating theory from therapy (or rather therapy from theory). This by the way is the real value my viewpoint has for social workers who have been studying and applying theory to their purely practical field. . . .

My arm is not better at all, hurts very much at certain movements—but I feel better just the same, coming out of a very low depth.

My best to you and Virginia

Your

Rank

The next letter, November 3, is not as low in mood as one might expect from the increasing physical symptoms.

November 3, 1937

Dear Jessie,

I have been waiting to write you until I could tell you that I am better, but I think there is not much use in waiting any longer.

My arm is not any better, indeed worse in that the pain gets more acute and more permanent. I guess I'll have to do something about it although I know not much can be done. Whether it is caused by bad circulation and causes it—the fact is that my whole circulation is bad which makes me feel—something—all over, also kind of foggy in the head. It feels like change of life and has anyway something to do with ageing—because (?) otherwise I don't feel age at all. I am kind of ageing in one spot and the rest is young. But I am afraid that is not so good!

That's all about me! and you? I have been thinking of you, of course, and like to know how you are and how things are going.

I received the announcement of the Journal, which looks very dignified and promising. Congratulations and good luck!

How is Virginia and the School and everything else?

I am kind of coming back to earth slowly.

My best to both of you
Your
Half Huck and Half Twain

My concern for his health was increased with the fear that he would not do anything about it as he had a deep aversion to putting himself under any form of medical control. As always, I could not refrain from advice, so he replies in quite a long letter regardless of the bad arm. Since Rank so rarely referred to a patient in his letters to me, in terms of his own therapeutic methods, I have decided to include the unusually specific account of someone whom I must have sent to him but have forgotten long since and who is unlikely to be identifiable after nearly twenty years. Certainly he has lost none of the confidence in his ability to help that characterized him even in that first early experience in New York with Freud's analysands.

Monday, November 9

Dear Jessie,

Thanks for your two letters and your good advice. Meanwhile I have started massage with a licensed man who works for doctors. I had three so far and feel better—at least the general condition (i.e., circulation) is greatly improved although I still have the pain in the arm where there is a local infection (about which I may have to do something else). I'll try a few more times and if there is need for more I'll see the osteopath.

Today Helen is here—just overnight on account of her naturalization. I found her much better and we had a nice evening.

I haven't been idle those last few weeks. The "Beyond" is going all over "beyond" in a big way. I have rewritten the first two chapters (which you have) on the new plan and have outlined a few more on the new basis of that bigger idea —which believe it or not works miracles in therapy too.

Your "bull-fighter" has arrived and after having spent more than one year with Adler and about three with Jung, got, in five sessions with me, more than ever before. She has a goodness and honest masochism (I mean sexual "perversion" of being beaten) that never was touched by her analysts apart from having been told to cut out those childish phantasies in favor of—one thing or another (social feeling, or anima). It really is incredible, I never would have believed it was so bad. In connecting her problem with her woman self in a positive (way) and (with) death-fear in a negative way, I produced an integration of herself that released real creative will, which the others had trampled on.

I am eager to see the Journal. I saw Arnold's new book advertised; I am not going to read it because I think he sold himself—to the Govt. or rather they bought him. (The way of all spirit).

Good luck to your individual supervision[12] and the Jews!

[12] A new form of helping with supervisory practice that I was trying experimentally for agency supervisors, many of whom came from Jewish social agencies.

It's you and them, i.e., they have to get it from a non-Jew because they are Jews.

My best to both of you
Rank

Despite the arm, he managed to write a brief note on November 18 about my introductory article on function in the new *Journal,* of which I was the first editor.

Thursday, November 18
Dear Jessie,
I read your article in the Journal—good stuff and clear but uneven. That is, where you are your real self you are philosophic (deep—too deep for them) and where you talk on their level you are not yourself.[13] I guess that can't be helped and social work lies somewhere between.

I am terribly busy now (8 hours) and too tired to do anything else. My arm is better though. I had a few electric treatments and am planning to get a lamp of my own for the winter.

Sorry to have to stop—
My best to both of you
Rank

To this letter he had attached a clipping from a New York newspaper mentioning Mayor LaGuardia's address to a Salvation Army meeting for General Evangeline Booth, which concluded with this warning, "Don't ever get too scientific, lest you lose the human touch. Christ did not know the calories in the bread he handed out."

[13] Rank was mistaken in thinking I was not myself where he says I talk "on their level." My interest in the technical, practical problems of the help-giving processes of the social agency was as great as my interest in theory, as later issues of the *Journal of Social Work Process* on family counseling, child placing, etc., bear witness.

The next letter reminds me of the *Daybook* accounts of his struggle to combine the daily job with the rush of ideas, which seems to be actually increased by the obstacles of the day.

Sunday, December 6

Dear Jessie,

The enclosed lay on my desk for several days but I really couldn't sit down for a letter. I was just as "gone" as you were, drowned in work—8 hours daily, including Saturdays so I could only rest on Sundays which I did so completely that I couldn't attend to anything.

But it is creative work, I am full of ideas and all I can do is make note of them—for future reference. I couldn't possibly tell you what they are because I dont know. . . .

I hope you didn't mind my remark about your article, it was meant to be a compliment! You are too good to write simply on Social Work. I was glad to hear that it is selling fine—it deserves it!

I read a review of Arnold's new book; it seems to be good —in my vein (he shows as I do for Psychology how economic ideologies are carried on beyond their validity in time and place). I only mind that he did it to defend the New Deal which in itself is all right, only just as full of "mythology" as was the Old Deal.

My arm is a little better but you know how it is, changeable as——(who?).

Hope to see you just the same in the near future.

My best to both of you

Your

Rank

The final letter of the year about Christmas and vacation showed an unusually philosophic acceptance of his own condition. The so-called "badness" usually refers to one of the many anticipated visits, called off at the last moment by an illness or fatigue. I wonder as I reread these letters how he could ever have contemplated the tiresome trip to Flourtown out of his overfilled days and reduced vitality.

Sunday, December 13

Dear Jessie,

I did send you and Virginia something for your new house which I hope you will like. I only mention it because I addressed it to the School where it will arrive either the 18th or 20th! Will you still be there? And when do you take your vacation anyway! Let me know please.

I hope you found Helen in good shape and spirits! She seems to be a little (more) independent—if that's possible! But maybe in a more positive way.

As to us and our occasional misunderstandings: it's good they are only occasional and kind of mutual in a way. I am not saying this to justify my last "badness"—for which I feel sorry!

My health is better, that is my arm but still I myself don't feel well and I am sure that is ageing. But I don't complain —it's all right, part of life and I had little of it. So I get my share now.

My best to you and Virginia

Your

Rank

P.S. K— phoned and wanted to know about a course in the spring. I wonder whether as a member of the faculty I am allowed to lecture elsewhere?

1938

The New Year began with an unusually cheerful, factual letter looking toward the next term of teaching.

Sunday evening, January 27

Dear Jessie,

This is a warm and hearty New Year's greeting with all my best wishes for you.

I just saw Mrs. Rank and Helen off to their respective trains. They have spent a few days here and I am glad to say that it was so much better than before.

Mrs. Rank told me what a nice letter she had from you and she really seems to get somewhere now in Boston although the work is very strenuous.

I am so glad to report that my arm has been very much better lately, although I am generally tired and run down. Didn't get any vacation to speak of.

My courses seem to have been fixed officially for Mondays 3–4:40 and evening 7–8:40.

Next week I'll see K— about my New York course and maybe can work out something more satisfactory—at least I have an idea.

Hope work doesn't start in all at once in a rush.

My best to you

Rank

After one visit to Flourtown in January to talk over the courses that were to begin on February 14, his letter of February 6 shows how far he has moved into teaching responsibility since the first lectures in Philadelphia.

Sunday, February 6

Dear Jessie,

Thank you so much for the reading list, which was quite helpful although, as you will see from my enclosed final list, I didn't think that much of it could be used in the course.

As to conditions for credit—by all means suggest them to me because on those matters I am no good at all.

I remember your suggesting to be in your office before the afternoon class! It will be good to see you there anyway (around two) whether *I* need you or not at the moment (*I* guess *I* will).

My best to Virginia and you

Your

Rank

Again a second letter, written just before the beginning of the semester, indicates the way his interest is developing, and interrelating the material of the two courses, and, in passing, throws a light on a patient of this period.

Wednesday, Feb. —

Dear Jessie,

I hope your alumni speech went off all right.

My violinist didn't do so well—I think, that is, he played well enough so that the critics said he has improved both in his technique and interpretation, but to me it seemed that he couldn't "fill" Carnegie Hall not only not with an audience but not with his personality either!

Apropos personality! I think I have an idea about the afternoon course: looking at precipitants of growth only from the environment (reality) and not psychologically, that is to say, happening vs. doing, which brings in "therapy" as a secondary factor, i.e., precipitant of growth.

This approach would somehow follow the discussion of "Symbols of Government," that is, would be an application of that approach to case work in particular.

You will see from the reading list enclosed to what extent I am planning to make that approach external, unpsychological, untherapeutic. This list is not definite or final, and I would be glad if you would make some suggestions (or criticism) regarding it.

I was glad you were and felt so much yourself and it was good to see Virginia come through so well!

My best to both of you

Rank

245

It is quite evident from a copy of the reading list before me, the roll of the forty-seven members, and a few sets of minutes prepared by different individuals in the class, that this course belonged to Rank in a new way. The reading list was his and, as he remarked in his letter, unpsychological and untherapeutic. It was at his suggestion that minutes of each session were prepared and discussants appointed in advance. The requirements for credit were severe, including reading requirement, book reviews, and term paper. Several members of the faculty took both courses for credit. Although his vast learning always came into play, he had also absorbed a new, relatively current American bibliography on economic, sociological, and political theory. This was a brilliant, fast-moving course, not primarily related to a social worker's deepest interest and yet always brought back to the underlying problem of thinking vs. doing, theory vs. practice.

At the close of the course, the papers were handled by Rank, not by me as formerly, and there were often comments on the papers on their return. He also determined the giving or withholding of credit, although in a class of this caliber there would be little possibility of failure.

With this heavy schedule of teaching and the customary program of therapy in New York, he had little time or energy left for visits to Flourtown but was planning even then on a visit to Vermont in the summer. In the late spring, practical problems brought him to Flourtown and he tried to arrange a proposed social event before the end of the course on Sunday to include other Flourtown friends, so that Monday's classes would not be involved. How it actually worked out I no longer remember. In any case it is a perfect example of his organizing facility, once he has taken hold of a problem.

Dear Jessie,   Sunday, May 29

Believe it or not I am going to tell you my plans for next week end.

I'll come on Sunday at noon (Chestnut Hill) and will stay until the next morning. Although graduation begins at 11 I like to be there sooner (between 10 and 10:30) to see Helen before (because I don't know whether I'll have time afterward, leaving for my class at 3 P.M.). If that should mean too much trouble for you—I mean to drive me to Swarthmore—I can take an early train.

Sunday afternoon if it is all right with you and them we can have a little visit to Oak Run[14] and if they want to ask a few other friends or "neighbors" for a little (I mean short) party (instead of after the lecture) I think that would be fine.

With you and Virginia I would like to discuss summer plans more definitely (once more "believe it or not").

I expect a rather quiet and restful week end today and to-morrow. Today I am going to see Mrs. Rank (who will be next week end in Swarthmore) so we can talk over things before we meet again Monday at Swarthmore.

Helen is going to be there until Monday the 6th.

> So long
> Rank

His strenuous living finally caught up with him and actually took him to a doctor for the week after Helen's graduation, he writes:

Wednesday, June 8

Dear Jessie,

I was awfully sorry that I gave you so much trouble and you were probably only too glad that there wasn't a man around all the time, to be looked after!

I saw the doctor yesterday, he examined me thoroughly (over one and a half hours) and said he was sorry he could not find anything the matter with me—except the sore throat

14 The home of friends who were members of the seminar.

(which incidentally was not due to any infection, just irritation probably due to too much smoking—this in turn to "nervousness and tension" at the end of a heavy season and at the beginning of spring). According to this verdict I should be able to have my course next Monday, if I take it easy and rest as much as possible.

I am cutting down this week and will go for the week end to Atlantic City, which he highly recommends. Unless you hear from me to the contrary (until Friday noon) I will be able to hold class on Monday.

I was sorry about the misunderstanding regarding Helen and Mrs. Rank. As usual Helen missed the train that would have brought them to town at 5 P.M. and didn't think of phoning again (after I had done it for her).[15]

My best to both of you
as always
Rank

He is still in New York in late June and still planning on Vermont as indicated in his letter of June 22.

Wednesday, June 22

Dear Jessie,

I have been back for a week now and feel better but not quite well yet. This humid heat is very bad for me anyway and the only consolation is that if I didn't have the cold already I'd surely get it in this kind of weather.

At any rate I take it easy now and only work a couple of hours in the morning and a couple of hours in the evening, resting in the middle of the day when the heat is at its height.

Was glad to hear about commencement activities and will

---

[15] Very nice notes of explanation and regret were received from Helen and her mother whose visit to my office I had given up after a long wait.

improve in my communications with the students. (*I wrote a special note apropos of Mrs.——'s paper.*)

Collecting my things, I find that I took Spooky for granted (and I hope you do too), that is, don't mind my bringing him along with me. I promise his good behavior in every respect, but can't promise that he will actually serve as a watchdog; but he certainly looks like one and that is something.

My best to both of you
Your
Rank

The two weeks Rank spent in our Vermont guest cabin, with Spooky for a companion, hold few pleasant memories for me. It is a sweet little one-room cabin with running water, electricity, and screened porch, but, as I know now, only too painfully, it was never intended for so long a stay, under weather conditions that have never been repeated in our eighteen years of experience there. The day on which Miss Buel drove him up from New York was perfect and both were enchanted by the fragrance of spruce and pine and the unexpected distant view over the Connecticut River to Mt. Monadnock in New Hampshire. That was the only good day in two weeks of intermittent rain that followed. An unsealed cabin, even with a fire, was no place for a tired man with tendencies to colds and neuritis. Daily trips up and down a wet path in rain for breakfast and lunch can make for genuine discomfort when neither sun nor view appears and only wet pine and spruce woods remain to walk in. Spooky added humor to the situation by catching the only deer mouse ever to have entered the cabin and contributed his share of anxiety by getting very sick from something he had managed to eat in the woods.

In his desire to contribute something lasting to "Deer Run" (the name of our ten-acre wood lot shared with two friends),

249

Rank conceived the idea of clearing a section of the old woods nearest to the cottage, and actually managed to engage two woodsmen with a horse. He took a childlike pleasure in carrying through this project and never lost interest in "Spooky's Forest," as it was christened. The good effects of that 1938 clearing continue to be enjoyed and never fail to remind us of the donor.

How much Rank really suffered under this rugged environment I do not know, for his mood never indicated anything but cheerfulness and he managed frequently to introduce an atmosphere that ignored the weather. Moreover, he worked steadily and, as far as one could tell from the little he said about it, was absorbed in the Bible and an analysis of Paul as the "actual propagator of the Christian movement and the real creator of the universal type of man patterned by this moral revolution." [16] I can see at this distance that the hosts suffered far more than the guest, in their failure to provide the kind of care he should have had and were far more disturbed than he over his quiet admission of cataracts then forming over both eyes.

Now it is clear that the only important factor for Rank at that time was "the book" and the necessity he felt to complete it. After the years of compelling creativity from his first effort at twenty-one to the culmination of his absorption in the artist personality twenty-five years later, the intense pressure to write had lain dormant for over six years, while the book that was to recreate his entire philosophy for him was slowly taking form (in English for the first time) and now pressed toward completion, as if some internal awareness of ending provided the necessary stimulus.

Late August finds him back in New York after several weeks spent in a writer's retreat where conditions were particularly favorable for his needs. His letter of August 22 was packed with important information tersely stated.

[16] *Beyond Psychology*, p. 155.

Monday, August 22

Dear Jessie,

It was good to hear from you—and the outside world! I have gone away, but from the whole world—and yet not so far either! I could be brought back easily and will come back before long on my own account.

This whole week since my return I have been practically confined (confining myself) to the apartment and working feverishly on the book (of which I did four chapters in Swiss Meadows). I am now at the 3rd and last part of it. My eyes seem to give out and so I am trying to get as much preliminary working done as is necessary to dictate the whole book when Miss Buel returns (the last of September). She is my "seeing eye"! (Competitor of Spooky).

I was glad to hear you enjoyed the basket and the trip besides, the thermos is still here waiting for Miss Buel to change it (I can't even bother with the telephone, let alone going to town). The Hudson is beautiful and I don't need anything else, at least not at the moment.

I saw Mrs. Rank and we decided quite amiably on a divorce. Our things are on the way over and will be divided according to need and taste. (I'll keep my books, of course).

Helen finished school all right but is still in the same fix about the next step. She attended this week the Youth Congress at Vassar and is returning tomorrow for a short stay. Then she'll go to Boston to have her tonsils out (our Vienna physician is there at the Hospital).

I myself don't pay any attention to my health and probably lost some pounds—to my advantage.

I guess that's about all the news I have to tell you.

My best to Virginia and yourself.

Spooky sends his love to the Deer Mouse!

Rank

To a note telling him of our return to Flourtown via the Hudson River Drive, he replied:

Friday, September 2

Dear Jessie,

Why didn't you stop and say Hello!? That's really too bad!
I hope you liked the Parkway and the Highway to the Hol-
land Tunnel!

I was probably writing and would have loved to be "disturbed" (if that's what stopped you).

The book is quite ready for dictation but it frightens me
as it finally crystallized—or rather decrystallized into thin air
(and hot air, too, for that matter). I have to get over the
shock before I can get near it again!

This last week I have been trying to rest, but was not so
successful! Miss Buel is due tonight!

I am sending two papers received yesterday, which I
O.K.'d. They are not so hot but the two students explained to
me their situation (finishing work at the school) and so I
think their papers will do.

My best to Virginia and you.

Your

Rank

In spite of an increasing eye problem that is becoming apparent in the handwriting, he writes cheerfully and sympathetically in relation to the School's chronic financial problem.

September 16, 1938

Dear Jessie,

This is just a word to thank you for your dear letter which
felt quite good just at a time when I needed it.

You're right, meanwhile I found—or rather had—an idea
which put so much life into the social "theory" that it
ceases to be theory and becomes life. Now, with that new
idea the book is ready to be recast and finally written.

I hope meanwhile your situation has improved and looks
somewhat brighter.

I just heard the sad news of Dr. Campbell's sudden death in England. It is too bad, he was eager and sincere and could have done in time something in England where child guidance is at least a generation behind.

How is the Clinic program proceeding and what is the news about School?

My best to Virginia and you.

Yours

Rank

P.S. I'll get a snapshot of Spooky and his master.

However, the barometer is seldom steady, with health always uncertain and family problems never settled, so by October 1 he writes:

Saturday, October 1

Dear Jessie,

This is just a line to let you know that at present I cannot write but that I am there and alive.

I haven't felt well for the last week or so and besides—partly on account of it and partly because I have a difficult time with Helen and myself—my mood was and still is quite low.

In that mood I can't dictate although if I had a little more time and could write I am sure I'd feel better because I want to finish it and I am frustrated.

So, that's that.

Please write when you feel like it. I will when I can again.

Your

Rank

There were no more letters from Rank or from me during the fall of 1938, as pneumonia took me into the hospital for six weeks in November and December and held me convalescent for many weeks more, the only severe illness I had ever experienced. It was in the days before pneumonia had been

253

conquered, and I experienced it to the full, oxygen tent and all, my first venture into the area of final ending. It was worth it for once but not to be repeated. Up to the last two weeks in the hospital I was deeply troubled by no word from Rank, although he had been told of my illness and had sent a gift to the hospital. Finally he actually got to the hospital on December 11 and spent an hour before hurrying back to New York. My relief at seeing him was so great that no shred of reproach for his silence remained even before he told of the letter I had never received. It was only much later that I learned of his own illness. He left with me a part of himself in a faded copy of Shakespeare's Sonnets from his Vienna days: the inscription on the flyleaf reads, "This book has as much of a touch of the 'other world' as anything can have in this world!"

1939

January's letters give the details of the new illness and finally his reluctance to consider any more evening courses in Philadelphia at this time.

Saturday, January 7

Dear Jessie,

I was glad to hear that you are improving although I am surprised at the slow tempo of it. You must have been really sick!

As to myself I must confess something that I withheld from you as long as you were not well yourself. I had had during this fall two severe attacks of some kind of abdominal pain that seems to be finally diagnosed as kidney stones. In the interval I was all right but what I don't like is that the attack can occur at any moment and it does so without giving notice.

As to the treatment—or possible treatment—the doctors don't agree (in general about stones). One school is of the opinion: the more you leave the stone alone the more it leaves you alone: the other is for removing, not by operation but by a much more painful and unpleasant process of picking at it from your inside with sharp instruments. I don't have to tell you what school I adhere to and for that matter tenaciously!

Yet, I am a little scared, not that there is any real danger nor of the pain (I have morphine tablets now in reserve in case) but of a general letting down of my health, which is aggravated by the "dark" prospect of having to have my cataracts removed within the next couple of years.

So, while in one sense I am taking things easier not to aggravate the kidneys, on the other hand I feel I have to hurry up with the book and other things I want to do before I become a half invalid.

I knew you'd like the animals. I was not so sure about Virginia, although the book is a first, limited edition.[17]

My best to both of you.

Your

Rank

January 17

Dear Jessie,

This is only to tell you that I am all right and working (also on the book).

I don't want you to worry about me and want you to know that my not writing (now) means that I am all right. I promise you to let you know if I shouldn't feel well.

I seem to have so much to do now—not only patients

[17] The books he had sent us were *Die Malerei der Eiszeit* with German text and beautiful illustrations of prehistoric paintings and a copy of Elinor Wylie's *The Orphan Angel* in a limited first edition, published by Knopf and signed by the author.

255

which are really fewer—but writing and the books and other things.

Hope your first steps into the world turn out all right.

My best to you and Virginia

Your

Rank

Sunday, January 30

Dear Jessie,

I hope you didn't misunderstand my letter as wanting to be left alone! I just wanted to tell you that I am all right [even] when you don't hear from me and that I am spending all my free time on writing the book [since my illness Xmas time] I did three more chapters.

From the program you reported in your last letter I gather that meanwhile you must have gotten back to normal life and enjoy the newness of it!

Since school affairs seem to have improved too you and Virginia are probably quite content and relaxed again.

I take it that your question about my course was rhetorical or, to be more polite, wishful thinking. I think it is better to take a year off in Philadelphia, although I may give again the course at the Jewish School if they can fix it into my schedule for the spring. The reason is that this school seems to be on its last leg (not legs—one is off already) and I should feel badly in deserting it at that point.

Miss Dawley has written me a rather extensive report—in personal terms though—about their enterprise not—of course —without saying that they are counting on my help in the future. So you see it is better to let the whole matter rest!

Give me news of yourself—and of goings on in your world.

With my best to you and Virginia

Your

Rank

Suddenly there comes a new burst of life and a sense of fresh self-discovery in the letter of March 9, which continued through the next letter of March 20 with the reaffirmation of his intention to move to California.

Thursday, March 9

Dear Jessie,

I was glad to hear that you are your old self again, the old self that can feel my new self! Of course you're right, I am different and I think I can tell you what it is (which incidentally also answers your question or wonder, without, of course, explaining the miracle).

It has to do with how the books came out the way they did, namely like wood-shavings in shaping the self. They are splinters, not the self. And as parts reflecting a much bigger whole they could be as whole and clear-cut as they are.

You know what I mean! With me it was always that I was bigger than the work, not, as it is usually, the other way round. And it is still so. Now, writing out this bigger plane, describing it as it were, I am still bigger and that is the difference you feel. I always seem to rise one mile or so above the plane on which I am actually operating or creating. The present book deals with the "beyond" of Psychology and yet, somehow, I am behind the "beyond." I guess otherwise I couldn't do it at all!

No vitamins of course, because there aren't any for "stratospheric" compensation.

Your
Rank

Sunday, March 20

Dear Jessie,

Yes, I have been wondering about you but didn't have time to do more than just wonder, until today when I was going to write you and find out and then your note came!

257

Poor Virginia—and poor You! But she has evidently "overdone" and needs a good rest anyhow. My best wishes for a quick recovery.

I am still in the stratosphere and hope to remain there—because it seems the only place where I can breathe now. I am thinking quite seriously now of moving to California—maybe as early as next fall. Of course, I want to keep my contact with the School provided the School will have any use for "stratospheric stuff"!

Tomorrow is my last lecture at the Jewish School (six altogether) and they tell me that it was the best course I ever gave (They don't know that it was delivered from above) and urged me to write (not write it down as previously) but a book on it. But the book I am writing now finishes all that for good!

News: An amusing episode (the bad writing is due to my eye trouble) happened the other day in my office. One of my patients who has been "Freudianized" for years brought with him Horney's last book. He asked whether I had read it; I said, No. Then he said that I don't have to because I have said all that within the last fifteen years and with those words he threw the book into my waste basket where it was left.

Another patient of mine told me that Erich Fromm in a lecture proved that my philosophy was "fascist"—whatever that means besides, "I don't like it." (He has an article announced to be published in "Psychiatry" about Rank's philosophy and its social significance which seemingly is "fascist")!

As long as I am expressing myself frankly I want to tell you that if the clinic group wants to meet me I'll be glad to come but will not give any lecture or speech or talk, except a very informal meeting over cocktails (the only compromise I am willing to make is soft drinks). The best time for it will be the latter part of April. Because over Easter I am going away and in May I am planning to leave for the coast, to look around a couple of months and then spend the summer in the Western mountains. I'll be back in the fall either to pack up my belongings and move out West or to stay maybe until next spring.

As Mahatma Gandhi said lately when interviewed and having uttered one sentence about peace to the reporter, "Isn't that enough for once!"

As always yours,
Rank

After canceling a plan to include a week end in Flourtown with his Philadelphia trip because of illness, he did manage to come to Philadelphia at the end of April for one informal three-hour visit with the staff of the Philadelphia Child Guidance Clinic and stopped to rest in my office on his way from the train. There was no satisfaction for me in seeing him, for his fatigue and the sense of some nameless physical malaise left no room for anything but anxiety and the feeling that he ought not to be adding this clinic visit to his regular work load. Yet I do not doubt that for the clinic staff he was his usual alert, responsive self.

My increasing fears for his health were not allayed by the two May letters, the first of which had a premonitory note that was far from reassuring but it was a relief to know that at least he was leaving New York with Miss Buel to take care of him.

Sunday, May 14, 1939

Dear Jessie,

It may be a long time since I saw you but I had such a hectic time of it all that I was not aware of it.

I have been feeling somewhat better but by no means well. The last diagnosis eliminated kidneys, liver and gall bladder and you may wonder what is left. The good old colon which—it is true—had been troubling me years ago but I felt different. Then it was only the colon and I knew it but now it's myself. I know I am sick, I can feel it and it must be something besides the colon!

At any rate the therapy prescribed was rest and wait and see whether, and if so, what kind of illness may develop.

I am still bound to leave the end of this month for the West although lately I have become superstitious and I am not sure whether I will be able to carry out my plans. So many things have already interfered and plenty of things still have to be attended to before I can go.

At any rate I am working toward it and hope I will succeed.

As to the prospective course I am just as uncertain as about plans in general because I don't know and they can't tell when the eyes will be ready for operation. I may be here in the fall and not in the spring (or vice versa or not at all). I am sorry to have to be so uncertain but that is the state of affairs.

All I am thinking now and hope for is to finish the book within the next few weeks.

I hope and wish that everything goes well with you and Virginia and send my best to both of you.

Your
Rank

Sunday, May 28, 1939

Dear Jessie,

Thanks for your helpful words which—although it is about two weeks now—I still remember.

I am leaving Tuesday and will go in easy stages first to Lake Tahoe on the Nevada side of which one can get the benefits of Reno.

During those six weeks I expect to finish the book and then go off to a trip to California.

I'll write you and tell you how it all is—occasionally!!

I wish and hope that you and Virginia have a good and restful summer and auf wiedersehen at the end of the summer!

Yours always,
Rank

Two cheerful notes arrived from Nevada in June which made no mention of any unpleasant aspects regarding the divorce proceedings, distasteful as they would once have been. On June 15 a postcard from Lake Tahoe says:

I am settled here in this beautiful spot for the next six weeks. The address is Zephyr Cove Beach, Lake Tahoe. I am feeling much better already but have to get used to the altitude (over 6,000 ft.). Hope you and Virginia are all right and your paper went off well. Let me hear from you and how Vermont is this year.

The cheerful mood continues but despite his new and pleasant absorption he writes with his customary relatedness and thought for the other person.

Zephyr Cove Beach
Lake Tahoe, Nevada
June 28, 1939

Dear Jessie,

I was so glad to get such a good letter from you and was happy that the Conference was so satisfactory to you. (I wonder of course what you said in the paper, not that it matters much as long as you—and others—had such a good time with it.)

I feel very well and happy here, enjoy life thoroughly with lots of exercise—not done as exercise—and good and easy writing of the book which I am sure will be done before I leave here.

It was good of you to give me so much credit for Philadelphia—but I know that it wouldn't have been possible without two people like you and Virginia.

You are right, fifty-seven is quite something—and yet it
doesn't seem a lot to my starting a new life at fifty-five
and a half!

Here's to both of our young age?! an old-fashioned "Vermont" with soda!

Greetings to Virginia and also to your neighbors. And
don't forget to greet Spooky's forest

Love
Rank

Knowing as I did the increasingly close relation to Miss
Buel, I should not have been surprised by the announcement
that reached us in Vermont sent from the very hotel that we
had recommended to him from our stay there in 1936. But
I was not prepared for the immediacy of his action following
the divorce. The note read,

THE CLIFT
San Francisco
August 13, 1939

Dear Jessie,

Here I am—or rather we are—at your Clift, married and
looking for a place to live in the future.

That's practically all I want to tell you today. It is a kind
of telegram only with the personal touch of my handwriting!

I hope you have a nice quiet summer and Virginia also
gets her well-earned rest.

Give my greetings to the friends and my best to you and
Virginia.

Your
Rank (still)

This letter plus a postcard from both is all that remains in letter form of the weeks of happy companionship with its dream of a future home in California.

The fact that my account of Rank has not included any attempt to describe or evaluate his relation to women, although I depend for whatever insight I have on his relation to me, is due in part to lack of knowledge and in part to conviction that the determining relationship of his life, apart from his attachment to his mother, was his relation to Freud, the only time in his life when he gave himself unreservedly and realistically in devotion to a living ego-ideal. So cataclysmic and prolonged was the separation that finally freed him from this relationship that it might well have resulted in the psychosis of which he has been "accused," instead of in the inner growth process that characterized the remaining years of his life. Of Rank's love life I have no knowledge, since he was incredibly reserved in regard to personal relationships. With him, each relationship was maintained within its own boundaries, not to be confused with or shared with any other. I knew from observation that his relation to his first wife, although amiable and considerate, had ceased to be essential for either. References to his daughter, Helene, were full of tenderness for her as a young child but it was apparent that her identification was with her mother, that she had little or no opportunity to know or appreciate her father in view of his many absences and his creative absorption. Yet there was no lack of a continuing responsibility on his part that could not be satisfied until his wife was well established in Cambridge, Massachusetts and his daughter put through her college course at Swarthmore.

His marriage to the second wife became possible for him only after he had completed his obligation to the first and had seen his daughter launched on her own extremely independent way. As a man driven by his own creativity, he was not and probably could never have become the devoted husband and father but within the limits of the possible for him he sustained his marital and parental responsibilities.

His relation to me is quite apparent in the letters. It was based primarily on identification—a genuine likeness in temperament, philosophy, and professional interests, that made communication between us easy and spontaneous, but always on my part with due regard for my own limitations as measured against genius.

Unlike his first marriage, which was complicated by his wife's adherence to Freud and psychoanalysis, his second was the culmination of a tested relationship; a result, not a cause of his own inner development, a true companionship that gave promise of a humanly satisfying life in the California that had always beckoned.

The weeks that followed the letter of August 13, with the news of his marriage granted but a short-lived happiness, for October finds him in New York, again beset by illness and renewed urgency to get back to the West. The last letter I received from him, dated October 16, has a note of finality that was hard for me to bear.

Monday, October 16, 1939

Dear Jessie,

Today it is two weeks since I left the hospital and it was only during the last few days that I began to feel a little better. For ten days I had a local infection and ran a temperature and didn't feel myself at all. I am still under treatment but am beginning to go about my business and take a normal interest in things.

I remember the old story of the man whose execution was set for Monday morning and who on his way to the gallows remarked: This week does not begin too well! Starting in the fall with such a "hit" doesn't seem to me a good beginning for the winter season and so I decided to move out West as soon as I can wind up my affairs here—which will be by the end of the year.

That's all I am interested in at the moment and that's all I can tell you about it now!

I was glad to hear that everything goes so much better with you this year and with the School too! It makes me feel that the School can get along without me quite well, at least for some time to come. The book, which is going to flourish under the Western skies, will furnish a substitute for my personal appearance and maybe a basis for future discussion of some world-problems—if any should be left.

With best wishes to you and Virginia—and all the other friends whom I can't see now—for a good reason,

I am as ever

Your

Rank

In response to a letter of sympathy from Miss Robinson, including a cordial invitation to him and to Mrs. Rank to visit us in Flourtown before leaving for the West, he answers with a responsible analysis of his relation to the School indicating his feeling of having completed whatever contribution he had been able to make. Final in tone though the letter is in regard to the School and to his Philadelphia connections, it manages also to express his own still developing personality that must go on.

October 22, 1939

Dear Virginia,

It was a real pleasure to receive such a good letter from you, especially at a time when I was beginning to feel a little better.

Though I was only a couple of days in the hospital—for

the removal of the stone—I was still for two weeks afterwards pretty much "hospitalized" but at least at home. The picking up is still rather slow and I am taking things easy.

It seems to me the right time to go out West, not because I am not feeling quite well but because I want and need a different kind of life. This also applies to my relation to the School. I was glad to hear that things look so much better this year and I am sure the School has a unique function to fulfil. I am naturally proud of whatever I may have contributed to its present status and future significance.

At the same time I feel that that's all I had to give, not because I don't feel so strong at the moment but because my interests are decidedly narrowing down to some problems of which there is little use in either therapy or social work. I have to come to some peace within myself and with the world at large, which is a purely personal matter. Not that others may not benefit therefrom but it is not primarily meant for that.

Yet, it is still nice to hear that the help I could give to some people has borne fruit.

I shall certainly make it a point to come to Flourtown before going West and probably wouldn't come anyway without Mrs. Rank and Spooky. I'll let you know in time.

With best wishes to both of you

Your

Rank

Nine days from the date of this writing, on October 31, 1939, Otto Rank died in Polyclinic Hospital, New York, of some kind of infection which no drug could reach. He hated hospitals and doctors. Always he feared drugs and insisted that his organism refused to accept them. An undoubtedly irrational sense of the inviolability of his body as well as his spirit may have worked against a cure; or perhaps he could no longer struggle with the insoluble problem of com-

bining the immortal self with the mortal's necessity of earning a living. In any case not even the new-found security of
marriage to a woman who was truly right for him could
reverse the trend toward ending that I had sensed with dark
foreboding for many months. There was no religious service
to mark the final gathering of friends at a funeral parlor in
New York on November 2, and only a few of those close to
him followed the body to Ferncliff Cemetery in Westchester
County for the cremation which in his youthful will he had
so ardently requested.

IV *Otto Rank, artist*

To LOOK at Rank's life in the whole, after following the detail in process, is to see that from the first his primary concern was to realize himself, to find an outlet for his tremendous urge to create, to explore to the limit the nature of art and the artist and to discover his own place in the only world he could accept as his. Whatever the external conditions, he never doubted for long that he belonged to the group he called "artist," which for him included the philosopher, the poet, the hero, the musical genius, in short all great creative personalities, whatever the medium of expression. It is not then to be wondered at that his youthful daybooks wherein he registered his response to the great men whose work and personalities he had analyzed, from Christ to Nietzsche, from Mozart to Wagner, from Hebbel to Shakespeare and Ibsen, eventuated in *Der Künstler* (*The Artist*) as his first attempt;

271

with the newly acquired tool of Freud's psychology, to trace the role of the artist in cultural development. Nor can one doubt that in *Art and Artist*,[1] completed in 1930, although not published until 1932 in an English edition, Rank attained his final comprehension, not only of the meaning and function of art on the different cultural levels, but of the nature of the modern artist, including himself, with its inevitable dualism and inner conflict. As he says in the first chapter, "Creative Urge and Personality Development,"

The religion of genius and the cult of personality thus begin, in the creative individual, with himself; he, so to say, appoints himself as an artist, though this is only possible if the society in which he lives has an ideology of genius, recognizes it, and values it. . . . The creative, artistic personality is thus the first work of the productive individual, and it remains fundamentally his chief work, since all his other works are partly the repeated expression of this primal creation, partly a justification by dynamism.[2]

Certainly this description fits the personality expressed so vividly in the daybooks, but in contrast to Freud who was finally given the collective backing for the affirmation of his genius, Rank, who attained the development he sought within himself, did not live to receive the acclaim that may one day be accorded him, whenever there develops a group with the courage to face his will psychology and its implications of individual responsibility.

Lived experience can only be understood as the expression of volitional creative impulse, and in this the two spheres of artistic production and actual experience meet and overlap. . . . For the creative impulse in the artist, springing from

[1] Otto Rank, *Art and Artist*, New York: Alfred Knopf, 1932, First Edition.
[2] *Ibid.*, pp. 27–28.

272

the tendency to immortalize himself, is so powerful that he is always seeking to protect himself against the transient experience, which eats up his ego. The artist takes refuge, with all his own experience only from the life of actuality, which for him spells mortality and decay, whereas the experience to which he has given shape imposes itself on him as a creation, which he in fact seeks to turn into a work. . . . In creation the artist tries to immortalize his mortal life. He desires to transform death into life, as it were, though actually he transforms life into death. For not only does the created work not go on living; it is, in a sense, dead; both as regards the material, which renders it almost inorganic, and also spiritually and psychologically, in that it no longer has any significance for its creator, once he has produced it. He therefore again takes refuge in life, and again forms experiences, which for their part represent only mortality—and it is precisely because they are mortal that he wishes to immortalize them in his work.[3]

Thus in his comprehension of and identification with the artist personality, Rank finds the clue to artistic development in his will psychology and the basis of his rejection of Freud's concept of sublimated sex as the root of artistic expression.

We have come to see that another factor must be reckoned with besides the original biological duality of impulse and inhibition in man; this is the psychological factor par excellence, the individual will, which manifests itself both negatively as a controlling element, and positively as the urge to create. This creator-impulse is not, therefore, sexuality, as Freud assumed, but expresses the anti-sexual tendency in human beings, which we may describe as the deliberate control of the impulsive life. To put it more precisely, I see the creator-impulse as the life impulse made to serve the in-

[3] *Ibid.*, pp. 38–39.

dividual will. When psychoanalysis speaks of a sublimated sexual impulse in creative art, meaning thereby the impulse diverted from its purely biological function and directed towards higher ends, the question as to what diverted and what directed is just being dismissed with an allusion to repression. But repression is a negative factor, which might divert, but never direct. And so the further question remains to be answered: what originally led to such repression? As we know, the answer to this question was outward deprivation: but that again suggests a merely negative check, and I, for my part, am of the opinion that (at any rate from a certain definite point of individual development) positively willed control takes the place of negative inhibition, and that it is the masterful use of the sexual impulse in the service of the individual will which produces the sublimation.

But even more important for us than these psychological distinctions is the basic problem of why this inhibition occurs at all, and what the deliberate control of the vital impulse means to the individual. Here, again, in opposition to the Freudian conception of an external threat as the cause of inhibition, I suggest that the internal threatening of the individual through the sexual impulse of the species is at the root of all conflict. Side by side with this self-imposed internal check, which is taken to be what prevents or lessens the development of fear, there stands the will as a positive factor.[4]

In his understanding of the make-up of the artist as we find him today, which undoubtedly was based not only on his psychotherapeutic practice but on his developing understanding and acceptance of himself, Rank was able to place the neurotic and neurotic symptoms as belonging at bottom to the creative personality.

[4] *Ibid.*, pp. 39–40.

Both (i.e. artist and neurotic) are distinguished fundamentally from the average type, who accepts himself as he is, by their tendency to exercise their volition in reshaping themselves.[5]

But the neurotic goes too far in his effort to dominate the impulse life, and is either checked by fear of life from productive expression or driven compulsively by will, whereas Rank sees the productive genius type as able to master fear of living by an even more powerful fear of death, and to overcome through objective creation the tendency to neurotic blocking. As Rank expresses it:

A real understanding of these neurotic illnesses could not, however, be satisfactorily obtained as long as we tried to account for them in the Freudian sense by thwarted sexuality. What was wanted in addition was a grasp of the general problem of fear and of the will psychology going therewith, which should allow for the exercise of will, both constructively and destructively, affecting the ego and the work equally. Only through the will-to-self-immortalization, which arises from the fear of life, can we understand the interdependence of production and suffering and the definite influence of this on positive experience. This does not preclude production being a creative development of a neurosis in objective form; and, on the other hand, a neurotic collapse may follow as a reaction after production, owing either to a sort of exhaustion or to a sense of guilt arising from the power of creative masterfulness as something arrogant.[6]

That Rank's knowledge of both artist and neurosis depended primarily on his own make-up, fortified as it was by

[5] *Ibid.*, p. 41.
[6] *Ibid.*, p. 43.

research and long experience as psychoanalyst for neurotic patients, seems to me to be incontrovertible. Even at nineteen and twenty the foundation of his later penetration was present. His scorn for our modern effort to explain genius, or even the neurosis, through analyzing childhood experience, is undisguised.

The mistake in all modern psychological biography lies in its attempt to 'explain' the artist's work by his experience, whereas creation can only be made understandable through the inner dynamism and its central problems. . . . In no case, however, will the individual become an artist through any one experience, least of all through the experiences of childhood (which seem pretty universal). . . . For the artistic impulse to create is a dynamic factor apart from the content of experience, a will-problem which the artist solves in a particular way.[7]

While Rank could never deny or neglect the importance of the social and the collective, any more than he would deny the tremendous effect of his meeting with Freud on his future development, nevertheless the particular way in which experience is used or transformed by the individual is determined for Rank by his own experience in combining real life with the creative impulse, or replacing "collective immortality—as it is represented biologically in sexual propagation—by the individual immortality of deliberate self-perpetuation."[8] Thus, one finds in Rank's vivid description of the internal conflict and dualism of the creative personality the picture of his own struggle with life, as "the struggle of the individual against an inherent striving after totality which forces him equally in the direction of a complete surrender to life and a complete giving of himself in production. He has to save himself from this totality by fleeing, now from the

[7] *Ibid.*, p. 49–50.
[8] *Ibid.*, p. 45.

276

Scylla of life, now from the Charybdis of creation." [9] He finds in the artist's relation to woman more of ideological than of sexual significance.

Usually, however, he needs two women, or several, for the different parts of his conflict, and accordingly he falls into psychological dilemmas, even if he evades the social difficulties. . . .

For, in the dynamism which leads him to create, the artist suffers from a struggle between his higher and his lower self which manifests itself equally in all the spheres and utterances of his life and also characterizes his attitude to woman. She can be for him at once the symbol of the highest and the lowest, of the mortal and the immortal soul, of life or of death. [10]

Rank sees in Greek "boy love" and the corresponding idealization of the boy that is found in the sonnets of Michelangelo and Shakespeare, expressions of the artist's need to "glorify it (the creative ego) by artistic idealization and at the same time to overcome its mortality by eternalizing it in art." [11] The boy because of his sex is more easily identified with while his youth carries the sense of ongoing life. The boy, also, is less a threat to his ego than the woman who represents the sexual impulse too strongly and the possibility of involving him in real life, unless he is able to keep her in the role of muse, for whom he creates but to whom he gives only through his work. However, for Rank himself, the boy offered no solution to the fundamental dualism, however well he understood its value for others and admired above all Shakespeare's comprehension of love for a youth as revealed

[9] *Ibid.*, p. 60.
[10] *Ibid.*, p. 61.
[11] *Ibid.*, p. 56.

277

in the sonnets. Rank's deepest identification in childhood was
with his mother, as his later recognition of woman and man's
inevitable relation to her shows clearly. From his own account, he found in early youth neither boy nor men friends
who satisfied him, but looked to the great in art and literature for his inspiration. His older brother, to whom one of
his early poems was dedicated in gratitude and on whom
he looked with admiration, envy, and respect, especially for
his courage in standing up to their father, seems to have
come the nearest to being his friend and adviser and later was
associated with him in his Viennese psychoanalytic enter-
prises. But for Rank, the deepest relationship of his life was
with Freud to whom, as his first ego ideal, he yielded himself with a completeness never to be risked again. The depth
of his involvement, intellectually and emotionally, is hardly
to be exaggerated, while the added complications through his
personal affection, gratitude, and guilt for deserting Freud in
his illness, made his final freeing a prolonged and painful
process. As far as Freud was concerned, Rank may well have
represented the youth who would carry on the teaching of
the master, but never with awareness on his part or any
overt expression other than the relation of master and disciple.

No one would be in a better position than Rank to utilize
the Oedipus complex in order to explain himself as well
as the modern artist, for no one has delved more deeply into
the incest motive in literature and myth. Certainly he cannot be accused of ignorance of the facts, nor of their Freudian interpretation, which he himself accepted almost completely when he began the work on his erudite book, *Das
Inzestmotiv in Dichtung und Sage*, in 1906, a book not yet
superseded in present-day speculation. Moreover, his own
childhood with the kind mother, the overbearing father, and
his unhappy introduction to sexual realities would easily have
supported the Oedipus formula. Yet, with the conviction of his
mature insight, he can now go beyond the rigid confines of his

278

early work as he discovers even in the nuclear complex of Freudian psychoanalysis further evidence of his interpretation of the artist.

That the poets struggled so intensely with the Oedipus complex was regarded at the time as a proof of its ubiquity, and so it actually was so far as concerned individual psychology. But from the standpoint of the psychology of artistic production, the poets' wrestling with the Oedipus experience seems to me to mean something essentially different: namely, that the artist reacts more strongly than, and certainly in a different way from, the normal person to this unavoidable average experience of the parental relation. This is not, however, because of the experience, but because of his peculiar reactivity, which in the case of artistic expression we call 'creative.' Now, from the comparison that I drew in my generalized formulation of 'the artist' (also in 1905) between artist and neurotic, it results that the latter also reacts differently from the average person to these and similar experiences. Only, this distinctive reaction does not, with him, lead to production, but to inhibition or to fixation. The artistic reaction is thus distinguishable from the neurotic by an overcoming of the trauma or of the potentiality of inhibition resulting therefrom, no matter whether this is achieved by a single effort or is spread over the whole life-work. This overcoming, however (so far as my researches have taken me), is only possible—or at any rate only psychologically explicable—in one way, and this, as we have learned from the therapy which helps to overcome these development-inhibitions, is through volitional affirmation of the obligatory, which in every case not only works usefully, but is also definitely creative. . . .

And with this we are back again at the fundamental process of artistic production, which consists in just this deliberate appropriation of that which happens and is given (including passive experiences) in the form of individual new

279

creation. . . . *It even seems to me as if the Oedipus myth
itself, if taken in the Greek spirit, were an experience of this
same striving for independence in human development;
namely, the deliberate affirmation of the existence forced on
us by fate.*[12]

Since I am turning to *Art and Artist* for deeper insight
into Rank's own experience as it culminates in this work, I
shall make no attempt to utilize the chapters that follow,
whose headings I list to indicate the vast amount of material
involved in the book as a whole: Art-form and Ideology, The
Play-impulse and Aesthetic Pleasure, Microcosm and Macro-
cosm (a particularly fascinating chapter), House-building and
Architecture, Myth and Metaphor, the Formation and the
Creation of Speech, The Poetic Art and its Hero, Game and
Destiny, Beauty and Truth. These chapters constitute for me
a long, detailed journey which I would bridge by holding to
the more internally based approach to the individual artist,
as it recurs in the final chapters: The Artist's Fight with
Art, Success and Fame, Deprivation and Renunciation. While
there is no doubt that Rank, like all great psychologists, utilized primarily his own inner experience as a base, it is equally
true that he never rested in the purely personal but always
sought and projected actively the universal, the underlying
significance of the particular.

In Chapter XII, The Artist's Fight with Art, he begins his
argument with an assertion that would provide a severe criterion for many who think of themselves as artists:

*Compared with the average professional man, the artist has,
so to say, a hundred-per-cent vocational psychology. . . . so
that one can say of the artist that he does not practice his
calling, but is it, himself, represents it ideologically. . . .
For the artist, therefore, his calling is not a means of liveli-*

12 *Ibid.*, pp. 63–65.

280

hood, but life itself; and this explains not only the difficulties of his existence, since his main object cannot be the earning of money, but his struggles in love and life, which in the productive type spring from the impulse to create, and not vice versa.[13]

For Rank, the urge to write and the consequent creative guilt was balanced by his therapeutic gift and its value to the other human being in need, but while this was perhaps a salvation for one so internally oriented, it also provided a secondary struggle since the two modes of creative outlet produced their own conflict, not only in terms of earning a living, a burden he had complained of from his youth, but also in terms of the burden of work imposed by the needs of too many applicants for therapy, as well as by the personal need for income. In both areas, the necessity to *be* the calling is never lessened, for as one cannot write beyond what he is at bottom, so one cannot help beyond his own personal approximation to the relation to life and living that he represents. The therapist suffers (with every patient) the fate of the artist who has become famous, as he must bow to the patient's need for a symbol, but he can accept the unreality of this symbolization as necessary for helping only if it is sustained by a greater reality within. With Rank the threefold struggle, with his genius for helping, the cumulative responsibility for others it involved, and the daylight hours it consumed, would have been enough to enable him to understand the artist's fight with art, if the urge to write had not been added to the burden, together with a drive for detail and scholarship that must have left him little time for human contacts. Happily, some of the basic research was accomplished before the time-consuming occupation of psychotherapy overtook him. For the psychotherapist who feels himself called as a helping person, there is the urge not only to

[13] *Ibid.*, p. 371.

exercise his skill, which develops continuously as one kind of creating, but also the necessity to form developing theories of the nature of the process itself as well as the nature of the human beings involved. Add to this the obligation to restrain his own creativity in favor of the patient, who needs above all to experience his own capacity to create, and one has a picture of the complex forces that the practicing artist-therapist must bring into some kind of balance. There is no such freedom to create within the helping medium as would seem to obtain in the ideological realm where there is no patient to be considered. And yet, as one reads Rank's description of the growth of an artist in ideological terms, one can be sure that he has also described in projection his own painful experience with Freud, for ideology too is only another way to externalize the inmost self and its beliefs.

The first stage in the growth of an artist is that which we have described as his "nomination" and which marks the subordination of the individual to one of the prevailing art-ideologies, this usually showing itself in the choice of some recognized master as the ideal pattern. In doing so, he becomes the representative of an ideology, and at first his individuality vanishes, until, later, at the height of his achievement, he strives once more to liberate his personality, now a mature personality, from the bonds of an ideology which he has himself accepted and helped to form. This whole process of liberation from a personal or ideal identification is so particularly intense and therefore difficult in the artist (and the productive type generally), not only because he has a stronger personality, but because this needs stronger identification for its artistic ideologizing; the process of liberation being thus particularly complex, and exposing the artist to those dangerous crises which threaten his artistic development and his whole life. . . . In this creative conflict it is not only the positive tendency to individual self-liberation

282

from ideologies once accepted and now being overcome that plays a great part. There is also the creative guilt feeling, and this opposes their abandonment and seeks to tie down the individual in loyalty to his past. This loyalty again is itself opposed by a demand for loyalty to his own self-development, which drives him onward, even to strive beyond his own ego and artistic personality. So the struggle of the artist against art is really only an ideologized continuation of the individual struggle against the collective; and yet it is this very fact of the ideologization between the productive and the unproductive types, the artist and the neurotic: for the neurotic's creative power, like the most primitive artist's, is always tied to his own self and exhausts itself in it, whereas the productive type succeeds in changing this purely subjective creative process into an objective one, which means that through ideologizing it he transfers it from his own self to his work.[14]

This describes Rank's fundamental pattern so exactly that it provides at once his refutation of the accusation made against him by the group around Freud, that he suffered from a neurosis.[15] Suffer he certainly did, for each step in his ideological development away from Freudian psychology and practice, but every shred of personal suffering was utilized ultimately for new creation, first objectively in his publications, finally in personal development. He pursues this developmental process still further in even more general terms:

In the ceaseless struggle for liberation of self from the moral, social, aesthetic ideologies and the people who represent them, the individual goes through a disjunctive process of which I have regarded the process of birth as the prototype. But the

[14] *Ibid.*, pp. 371–372.
[15] Finally, as his departure became fact, the diagnosis "manic-depressive psychosis" was imposed for life by the inner circle.

process, though similar in principle to, is not a simple repetition of, the trauma of birth; it is, broadly, the attempt of the individual to gain a freedom from dependence of any sort upon a state from which it has grown. According to the stage of development, this separation will take the most varied forms and symbols, whereas the basic conflict is always the same: the overcoming of previous supporting egos and ideologies from which the individual has to free himself according to the measure and speed of his own growth, a separation which is so hard, not only because the victory is always, at bottom and in some form, won over a part of one's own ego. We may remark here that every production of a significant artist, in whatever form and of whatever content, always reflects more or less clearly this process of self-liberation and reveals the battle of the artist against the art which expresses a now surmounted phase of the development of his ego.[16]

The speed of this developmental process in Rank was such that at every turn he left would-be followers so far behind that they could only feel alienation or even desertion. I recall my own sense of hurt and loneliness when my still-consuming interest in psychotherapy met no answering interest in Rank. True, he could not afford to give up the reality of his therapeutic practice, but it had become a burden that no longer held challenge for him. For him the problem was solved and he would willingly have parted with the psychotherapeutic ego that had been in process of development since 1920. Yet no one with his genius for meeting the other person's need could cut off such a skill without a pang. In teaching he found a brief substitute but it offered no permanent solution. Ideologically he had completed his contribution to and his understanding of the neurotic and the artist: whether in everyday living he could have accepted the loss of his only

[16] Ibid., pp. 374–375.

remaining professional milieu, plus withdrawal from work that provided social justification, no one can say. The threat of a possible blindness, enforcing dependence upon another, seemed to me at the time to provide for a man of Rank's temperament an impasse too great even for his capacity for creative overcoming. It is significant that, at this crisis, he turned to real life in his marriage and for his ego-identification, to Mark Twain who provided the necessary object on which to project the new self. It is interesting to find among his papers a large envelope with numerous clippings and references to books on humor, together with outlines for a book of his own based on his feeling of kinship, twinship rather, with Mark Twain. This final period of Rank's development seems to me to express an effort to break up the totality tendency of the artist, by a new acceptance of life experiences in their partiality and a relinquishment of the illusory creation of the artist as a substitute for reality.

. . . the artist type, with his tendency to totality of experience, has an instinct to flee from life into creation, since there to a certain extent he can be sure of matters remaining under his own control; but this totality tendency itself, which is characteristic of the really productive type, in the end takes hold of his creation also, and this totality of creation then threatens to master the creative artist as effectually as the totality of experience.[17]

If ever anyone inclined to give himself totally to creative work Rank did and yet his capacity for practical detail and effective administration of complicated secretarial and editorial tasks is not to be doubted. The same paradox appears in his writing and thinking. Always he leaps to the universal application of an idea, but no one includes a greater complexity of detail, no one utilizes scholarship and the results of

[17] *Ibid.,* p. 385.

285

painstaking research more thoroughly. Rank tries to answer the question as to how the artist escapes the struggle "against his own creation, against the vehement dynamism of this totality-tendency which forces him to complete self-surrender in his work." [18]

He mentions the dividing of attention by beginning another work when threatened by complete absorption. Rank himself seems to have done this quite consistently in the years of his greatest productivity. A new book would be planned, outlined, or even written simultaneously with another, as he reports having done in the case of *Truth and Reality*, which accompanied his work on *Will Therapy* as the philosophic basis of the practical exposition. And again he turns to humor and Mark Twain as an antidote to *Beyond Psychology*, his last book, over which he spent many years of thought and revision.

The restraint which holds the totality-tendency in check is basically fear, fear of life and of death, for it is precisely this that determines the urge to eternalize oneself in one's work. Not only, however, has the completed work the value of an eternity symbol, but the particular creative process, if it involves an exhaustive output, is by the same token a symbol of death, so that the artist is both driven on by the impulse to eternalization and checked by the fear of death.[19]

Rank notes in the modern artist:

. . . the diversion of creation into knowledge, of the shaping of art into science, and above all, psychology. Naturally, spiritual self-representation in the work is always one essential element in artistic creativity and in art, but it is only in modern artists that it becomes a conscious, introspective, psychological self-analysis.[20]

18 *Ibid.*, p. 385.
19 *Ibid.*, p. 386.
20 *Ibid.*, p. 387.

He is not referring to the artists who use their work for pure psychological confession but to what he calls a far more interesting halfway type:

> . . . which, whether in the course of an ensemble of creation or even within the compass of a single work, passes suddenly from the formative artist into the scientist, who wishes— really he cannot help himself—to establish, or, rather, cannot help trying to establish, psychological laws of creation or aesthetic effect. This diversion of artistic creation from a formative into a cognitive process seems to me to be another of the artist's protections against his complete exhaustion in the creative process. . . . In this sense, in the need, that is forced on him by that dynamism, for putting order, meaning, and control into the psychic chaos into which his totality-urge drives him, the artist, even if he is never conscious of the fact, is always a bit of a scientist.[21]

Certainly no one could have known this form of protection more convincingly than Rank, who was so driven by the search for creative expression in his youth; finding neither in poetry, drama, nor fiction a suitable outlet for the intense introspective bias and seizing avidly upon the legitimate expression offered by Freudian psychology, enriched as it was by the direct firsthand contact with the realistic data of psychoanalytic experience. Here, for a time, the creative necessity could be objectified by the requirements of literary research and consequent new theory formation and socially justified by the needs of the psychoanalytic movement itself as well as by the human demands of the neurotic patient. In the first ten or fifteen years of his participation in the efforts of psychoanalysis to become an international project, Rank must have enjoyed to some extent the sense of collective support that all art demands.

[21] *Ibid.*, pp. 387–388.

287

For unless it has some collective or social basis—for instance, in religion or, later, the "genius-religion"—artistic creation is impossible, and the last hopeless effort to base it on a psychological ideology not only leads away from art into science, but, even so, fails on points of principle. Education or art can no more be supported on psychological ideologies than religion can be replaced by psychology. For psychology is the individual ideology par excellence and cannot become collective, even if it is generally accepted or recognized.[22]

Through his own increasing experience of isolation, and deprivation of all but the most limited form of group understanding and support, Rank was led to a realization of the illusory nature of creative expression that has lost its relation to the past, to tradition, and even to a collective present. From this final and apparently hopelessly pessimistic outlook, Rank saw a potential solution in a new structure of personality:

This will be able to use in a constructive form the psychological insight which is so destructive when it exists as introspection, and the individual impulse to creation will turn positively towards the formation of its own personality, as indeed it did, and actively, in the earliest phases of primitive art. . . .[23]

This new formation of personality must be a:

. . . constructive process of acceptance and development of one's individual personality as a new type of humanity, and in order to create the new it will have to give up much that has been received from tradition and become dear to it. This new must first of all be a new personality-type, which may thereafter perhaps find a new art-form suited to it, but

[22] *Ibid.*, p. 389.
[23] *Ibid.*, p. 391.

in any case will not feel any compulsion to justify its personal impulse to create by starting from the ideology of long-surmounted art-forms.[24]

After a discussion of the meaning of success and fame to the artist and to society, Rank returns, in the last chapter, to the solution of the problem posed in Chapter XII, of what can be hoped for beyond the neurotic attempt to resolve the conflict which is so prevalent today.

For we have seen that the basic conflict of the creative personality is that between his desire to live a natural life in an ordinary sense and the need to produce ideologically—which corresponds socially to that between individuality and collectivity and biologically to that between the ego and the genus. . . . But since the artist must live as a human being and yet feels compelled to make this transitory life eternal in an intransient work, a compromise is set up between ideologized life and an individualized creativity—a balance which is difficult, impermanent, and in all circumstances painful, since creation tends to experience, and experience again cries out for artistic form.

In this sense the general problem of the artist—not only in its psychological, but in its human aspect—is contained in the two notions of deprivation and renunciation. . . . The great artist and great work are only born from the reconciliation of the two—the victory of a philosophy of renunciation over an ideology of deprivation.[25]

By this Rank means to accept willingly and affirmatively "the limitations that appear in the form of moral conventions and artistic standards, not merely as such, but as pro-

24 *Ibid.*, pp. 391–392.
25 *Ibid.*, pp. 416–417.

tective measures against a premature and complete exhaustion of the individual." [26]

There is, perhaps, in Rank's attempt to go beyond the seemingly insoluble problem of the modern artist, his own lack of the necessary experience at that point on which to base it. He himself was caught in the very dilemma he has here expressed as he became increasingly aware of a failure to live really in the present.

It is certainly not, however, merely the outward deprivation (that is, the pressure of a mechanical age) that obstructs the artistic development of modern individuals, but the strong impulse towards life which goes hand in hand with personality-development and makes the creative will of the individual feel that artistic creation is an unsatisfactory substitute for real life.[27]

The conclusion he reaches is:

. . . that we are at one of those crises in human history in which once again we must sacrifice one thing if we want the full enjoyment of another. . . . Only a full renunciation, such as a few great artists have achieved despite their natural inclinations, can overcome this feeling of sacrifice, so that surrender means, not an imposed necessity, but a freely chosen decision.[28]

Whether he himself believed in these final paragraphs of *Art and Artist* except as an affirmation of his own belief in life, even out of the depths of a depression so soon to overtake him when he came face to face with the living reality of

26 *Ibid.*, p. 417.
27 *Ibid.*, p. 428.
28 *Ibid.*, pp. 428–429.

problems he had verbalized in general terms, there is no way to determine; but however subjective the source, Rank was so much a repository for the universal that his generalizations have a way of becoming reliable predictions. At any rate, in coming to the end of twenty years of tireless productivity, he can affirm his faith in a new era yet to be realized.

The new type of humanity will only become possible when we have passed beyond this psycho-therapeutic transitional stage, and must grow out of those artists themselves who have achieved a renunciant attitude towards artistic production. A man with creative power who can give up artistic expression in favour of the formation of personality—since he can no longer use art as an expression of an already developed personality—will remould the self-creative type and will be able to put his creative impulse directly in the service of his own personality. In him the wheel will have turned full circle, from primitive art, which sought to raise the physical ego out of nature, to the voluntaristic art of life, which can accept the psychical ego as part of the universe. But the condition of this is the conquest of the fear of life, for that fear has led to the substitution of artistic production for life, and to the eternalization of the all-too-mortal ego in a work of art. For the artistic individual has lived in art-creation instead of actual life, letting his work live or die on its own account, and has never wholly surrendered himself to life. In place of his own self the artist puts his objectified ego into his work, but though he does not save his subjective mortal ego from death, he yet withdraws himself from real life. And the creative type who can renounce this protection by art and can devote his whole creative force to life and the formation of life will be the first representative of the new human type, and in return for this renunciation will enjoy, in personality-creation and expression, a greater happiness.[29]

[29] *Ibid.,* pp. 430–431.

It was just at the time when *Art and Artist* was being published by Knopf (1932), when Rank had returned to New York, partly to be able to work on problems of editing this difficult book with its many illustrations and references, that he reached the climax of his struggle to relate to life and at the same time reach a deeper self-possession that should not deny either the human or the creative urge. He has described in his letters to me following that crisis something of his experience in attaining to a more natural self, free to realize the possibility of greater spontaneity in living.

It was inevitable that what he thought of as the rescue of the natural, human self should be followed by a period of externalization in activity and what he called a "sabbatical leave" from writing. The one persistent urge toward a final organization of his thought had taken nebulous form, even before he was through with *Art and Artist*, as a continuation of *Seelenglaube*, which he seems to have valued beyond any of the technical volumes derived from psychotherapy. During the six years in which he allowed his writing to lie fallow, the plan for a book on social psychology that should lead beyond individual psychology was never absent from his thinking, as is evident from the frequent references to it in his letters. Moreover, his tempo in relation to it was entirely different from the almost frantic speed with which his former work had been produced. *Beyond Psychology*, as it finally emerged almost completed just before his death in 1939, is obviously the result of a slow internal growth process, the maturing of a creative personality that has finally arrived at an acceptance, or rather at a new appreciation, of the irrational forces that obtain without as well as within the human being. Facing the loss of eyesight and perhaps sensing within himself the approach of the final limitation, he feels great urgency to combine in one work a last effort to portray the sweep of the irrational forces that underlie the development of civilization and society, together with his complete personal renunciation of ideologies as a substitute for spiritual values or as an expression of absolute truth.

In the preface to *Beyond Psychology*, his first book written in English, and dedicated to his wife, whose devoted help as secretary had made its completion possible, Rank is now able to express the solution that escaped him in *Art and Artist*, although touched too much, perhaps, by his sense of ultimate withdrawal from life.

When I first realized that people, though they may think and talk rationally—and even behave so—yet live irrationally, I thought that "beyond" individual psychology simply meant social or collective psychology until I discovered that this too is generally conceived of in the same rational terms. Hence my recognition of the ideologies—including those determining our psychological theories—were not sufficient to complement our understanding of individual behavior because they too were stated in terms of the rational aspect of human life. In fact these ideologies more than anything else seem to carry the whole rationalization which man needs in order to live irrationally. . . .

In this sense the "beyond" individual psychology meant not, as I first thought, a resorting to collective ideologies as the subject of social psychology; it actually meant the irrational basis of human nature which lies beyond any psychology, individual or collective.[30]

He deplores his inability to find words to express this experience, not because of any problem with English but because language is itself the rationalization of thought and action.

In fact this linguistic inability to express the irrational verbally only reflects the deepest human problem, the clash be-

---

[30] Otto Rank, *Beyond Psychology*, published privately by friends and students of the author, 1941, pp. 11–12. Paper edition, New York: Dover, 1958.

tween *the two worlds in which man attempts to live simultaneously, the natural world and the man-made world. Man
in his development of civilization has practically made over
the universe, or at least the earth, in terms of his self only to
fail, finally, in making this self over in terms of the world
he has created.*[31]

He continues with the declaration that a new kind of artistic
creation will be required to express the irrational directly,
as is evidenced by the failure of modern artists in their "extremely conscious effort to reproduce what they call the 'unconscious.' " [32]

*As we become increasingly aware that we have already gone
"beyond psychology," I have realized more and more that,
because of the inherent nature of the human being, man
has always lived beyond psychology, in other words, irrationally. If we can grasp this paradoxical fact and accept it as the
basis of our living, then we shall be able to discover new
values in place of the old ones which seem to be crumbling
before our very eyes—vital human values, not mere psychological interpretations predetermined by our preferred ideologies.*[33]

In the first chapter, entitled "Psychology and Social Change,"
after years of rethinking and rewriting an article with this
title that he wrote first for the opening of the Psychological
Center in Paris in 1934, Rank develops at length his conception of the relativity of all psychological theories, including
his own, as based on the needs and rationalizations of a
particular era or civilization. Following this chapter, he traces

[31] *Ibid.*, p. 13.
[32] *Ibid.*, p. 13.
[33] *Ibid.*, p. 14.

294

his basic concept of duality, as expressed first on the most abstract level of rational versus irrational, from the primitive's acceptance of the supernatural to our own search for spiritual values in a mechanistic world. The chapter headings indicate the depth and scope of his analysis: The Double as Immortal Self, The Emergence of the Social Self, The Creation of Personality, Two Kinds of Love, The Creation of the Sexual Self, Feminine Psychology and Masculine Ideology, and finally, Psychology Beyond the Self.

In his concluding chapter, Rank reaffirms the necessity to go beyond the hyperrationalized, mechanistic psychology of our present culture.

The only remedy is an acceptance of the fundamental irrationality of the human being and life in general, an acceptance which means not merely a recognition or even admittance of our basic "primitivity," in the sophisticated vein of our typical intellectuals, but a real allowance for its dynamic functioning in human behavior, which would not be lifelike without it. When such a constructive and dynamic expression of the irrational together with the rational life is not permitted, it breaks through in violent distortions which manifest themselves individually as neurosis and culturally as various forms of revolutionary movements which succeed because they are irrational and not in spite of it.[34]

The ultimate duality he expresses without evasion of its negative implications.

The ego needs the Thou in order to become a Self, be it on the individual plane of human relationship or on the social plane of a foreign group-ideology, or on the broadest basis of one civilization needing another one for its development and

[34] *Ibid.*, p. 289.

maintenance. The tragic element in this process is that the ego needs a Thou to build up an assertive self with and against this Thou. . . .

The psychology of the Self is to be found in the Other, be that Other the individual Thou, or the inspirational ideology of the leader, or the symbiotic diffusion of another civilization.[35]

Thus, in the most general terms, Rank has presented not only his own process of self-development with its abandoned "Thous" but the inevitability of the process for all development, whether or not one can admit it.

For his own affirmation, one must go to the concluding paragraph of the Preface, with its note of fulfilment and farewell:

This book is an attempt to picture human life, not only as I have studied it in many forms for more than a generation, but as I have achieved it for myself, in experience, beyond the compulsion to change it in accordance with any man-made ideology. Man is born beyond psychology and he dies beyond it, but he can live beyond it only through vital experience of his own—in religious terms, through revelation, conversion, or re-birth. My own life work is completed, the subjects of my former interest, the hero, the artist, the neurotic appear once more upon the stage, not only as participants in the eternal drama of life but after the curtain has gone down, unmasked, undressed, unpretentious, not as punctured illusions, but as human beings who require no interpreter.[36]

[35] *Ibid.*, p. 290.
[36] *Ibid.*, p. 16.

296

PUBLISHED WORKS OF
OTTO RANK

Der Künstler, 1907. Revised editions, 1918, 1925.

Der Mythus der Geburt des Heldens, 1909.

The Myth of the Birth of the Hero, 1914. English translation, *Nervous and Mental Disease Monograph Series* No. 18; Italian translation 1921; Republished with *The Trauma of Birth* by Robert Brunner. Taken over by Basic Books, 1952.

"Ein Traum der Selbst Deutet." *Jahrbuch für Psychoanalyze* II, 1910; English translation, *Psychoanalytic Review*, Vol. V, 1918.

"Die Lohengrin Sage," 1911. (Used as dissertation for his Ph.D. degree at the University of Vienna.)

Das Inzest-Motiv in Dichtung und Sage, 1912. Franz Deuticke, Leipzig and Vienna; Revised, enlarged edition 1926; French translation, revised, 1934.

"Die Nacktheit in Sage und Dichtung," *Imago* II, 1913.

Die Bedeutung der Psychoanalyse für die Geisteswissenschaften (with H. Sachs), 1913.

The Significance of Psychoanalysis for the Mental Sciences. English translation, *Nervous and Mental Disease Monograph Series*, No. 23, 1915.

Psychoanalytische Beiträge zur Mythenforschung, 1919. (Gesammelte Studien aus den Jahren 1912–1914); Revised edition, 1922.

"Der Doppelgänger," 1914. *Imago* III. Pamphlet, 1925. Internat. Psycho. Verlag., Leipzig and Vienna; Abstract, Psychoanalytic Review, Vol. VI, 1919.

"Homer: Psychologische Beiträge zur Entstehungsgeschichte des Volksepos," 1917. *Imago* V.

"Das Volksepos: Die Dichterische Phantasiebildung," 1917. *Imago* V.

"Die Don-Juan Gestalt," 1922. *Imago* VIII; In book form, 1924; English translation, Psychoanalytic Review, 1926, Vol. XIII; French translation, 1932.

"Eine Neurosenanalyse in Träumen," 1924. Int. Psycho. Verlag. Leipzig, Vienna, Zurich.

Sexualität und Schuldgefühl, 1926. *Psychoanalytische Studien* 1912-1923; Translation of two articles, "Perversion and Neurosis," "International Journal of Psychoanalysis, 1923; "Contribution to the Study of Narcissism," Psychoanalytic Review, 1920, Vol. VII.

Entwicklungsziele der Psychoanalyse (with Sandor Ferenczi), 1924.

The Development of Psychoanalysis, 1925. English translation by Carolina Newton, Nervous and Mental Disease Pub. Co., 1925.

Das Trauma der Geburt, 1924. Inter. Psycho. Verlag. Leipzig, Vienna, Zurich. French translation, 1928; *The Trauma of Birth*, English translation 1929, Routledge & Kegan Paul, London. Harcourt, Brace, N.Y.; with *The Myth of the Birth of the Hero*, Basic Books, N.Y., 1952.

The Practical Bearing of Psychoanalysis, 1927. Four lectures given in New York in 1924. Published 1927, National Committee for Mental Hygiene.

Technik der Psychoanalyse: Vol. I. *Die Analytische Situation,* 1926; Vol. II. *Die Analytische Reaktion,* 1929; Vol. III. *Die Analyse des Analytikers.* 1931; Franz Deuticke, Leipzig and Vienna.

Will Therapy. Authorized English translation of Vols. II and III of *Technik der Psychoanalyse* by Jessie Taft, with summary of Vol. I. Alfred A. Knopf, 1936.

Grundzüge einer Genetischen Psychologie auf Grund der Psychoanalyse der Ich- Struktur. In 3 volumes: Vol. I. *Genetische Psychologie.* 1927; Vol. II. *Gestaltung und Ausdruck der Persönlichkeit.* 1928; Vol. III. *Wahrheit und Wirklichkeit.* 1929, Franz Deuticke. Leipzig and Vienna.

Truth and Reality. Authorized English translation of *Wahrheit und Wirklichkeit* by Jessie Taft. Alfred A. Knopf, 1936. Reprinted in one volume with *Will Therapy,* Knopf, 1945.

English translations of chapters from Genetic Psychology published as follows:—"Genesis of Genitality," Psychoanalytic Review XIII, 1926; "Psychoanalytic Problems," Psychoanalytic Review XIV, 1927; "Beyond Psychoanalysis," Psychoanalytic Review, XVI, 1929; "Character Formation and the Task of Education," Pamphlet, N.Y., Commission for Mental Hygiene, 1928.

Seelenglaube und Psychologie, 1930. Franz Deuticke, Leipzig and Vienna.

Psychology and the Soul, English translation by William D. Turner, 1954; University of Pennsylvania Press, Philadelphia, 1954.

Modern Education. Authorized English translation by Mabel E. Moxon, 1932: Alfred A. Knopf, 1932.

Art and Artist. English translation by Charles Francis Atkinson, 1932: Alfred A. Knopf, 1932.

Beyond Psychology. Posthumously and privately printed by friends of the author, 1941. Printed by the Haddon Craftsmen, New Jersey. Paper edition, Dover, New York, 1958.